This book is dedicated to Barbara.

—Roberto Brunetti

This book is dedicated to my parents. Thanks!

—Paolo Pialorsi

This book is dedicated to my mother, Vanna, the strongest woman I have ever known.

—Luca Regnicoli

Build Windows® 8 Apps with Microsoft® Visual C#® and Visual Basic® Step by Step

Luca Regnicoli
Paolo Pialorsi
Roberto Brunetti

005.446
REG

Published with the authorization of Microsoft Corporation by:
O'Reilly Media, Inc.
1005 Gravenstein Highway North
Sebastopol, California 95472

ISBN: 978-0-7356-6695-5

1 2 3 4 5 6 7 8 9 QG 8 7 6 5 4 3

Printed and bound in the United States of America.

Microsoft Press books are available through booksellers and distributors worldwide. If you need support related to this book, email Microsoft Press Book Support at mspinput@microsoft.com. Please tell us what you think of this book at *http://www.microsoft.com/learning/booksurvey*.

Microsoft and the trademarks listed at *http://www.microsoft.com/about/legal/en/us/IntellectualProperty/ Trademarks/EN-US.aspx* are trademarks of the Microsoft group of companies. All other marks are property of their respective owners.

The example companies, organizations, products, domain names, email addresses, logos, people, places, and events depicted herein are fictitious. No association with any real company, organization, product, domain name, email address, logo, person, place, or event is intended or should be inferred.

Acquisitions and Developmental Editor: Russell Jones

Production Editor: Melanie Yarbrough

Editorial Production: S4Carlisle Publishing Services

Technical Reviewer: John Mueller

Indexer: WordCo Indexing Services

Cover Design: Twist Creative • Seattle

Cover Composition: Zyg Group, LLC

Illustrator: Rebecca Demarest

Contents at a Glance

Contents

Introduction

Windows 8 is Microsoft's newest operating system, intended to let developers fluent in various programming languages—such as C#, VB, C++, or JavaScript—leverage its powerful infrastructure with a brand new library, called the Windows Runtime API, to build successful applications.

This book provides an organized walkthrough of the Windows 8 features, APIs, and user experience. The text is definitely introductory; it discusses each component from a theoretical viewpoint interspersed with basic but effective code samples, which you can follow to get a jump start in developing for the Windows 8 platform.

The book provides coverage of almost all the main Windows 8 aspects and features, and it offers essential guidance for learning them using the classic Step-by-Step approach.

In addition to its coverage of core Windows 8 features using C# and XAML, the book discusses some related topics such as WCF Data Services, OData, ADO.NET Entity Framework, and applications architecture. Beyond the explanatory content, each chapter includes a rich set of step-by-step examples, as well as downloadable sample projects that you can explore by yourself.

Who should read this book

This book's goal is to provide developers conversant with .NET programming the experience they need to begin working with the main components of the Windows 8 operating system and Windows Runtime. Starting with the Windows Runtime APIs, the book drives the reader into a comprehensive discussion on the new user experience—including how to design for keyboard, mouse, and touch screen interfaces. A solid knowledge of the .NET Framework is helpful to understand the code presented in the book fully, and to follow along, perform the exercises using Microsoft Visual Studio 2012. This book is also useful for software architects who need an overview of the components they would plan to include in the overall architecture of a real-world Windows 8 solution.

Who should not read this book

If you have worked with Windows 8 already, this book is probably not for you; this is an introductory guide to developing applications that leverage the platform.

Assumptions

To get the most out of this book, you should have at least a minimal understanding of .NET development and object-oriented programming concepts. Although you can develop for Windows 8 using all .NET languages—as well as C++ and JavaScript—this book includes examples in C# only in the text, but includes Visual Basic samples in the downloadable companion code.

If you have not yet picked up C# or Visual Basic, you might consider reading John Sharp's *Microsoft Visual C# 2012 Step by Step* (Microsoft Press, 2012).

In addition to a .NET language, the examples on application architecture chapter assume you have a basic understanding of ASP.NET and Windows Communication Foundation (WCF), although the presented code doesn't use any advanced features of either of those two technologies.

Organization of this book

This book is divided into 10 chapters, each of which focuses on a different aspect or technology within the Windows 8 operating system and the Windows Runtime APIs.

Finding your best starting point in this book

We suggest that you start reading the book from the beginning. By following this path, you will discover all the aspects of the new look and feel, the new user experience, and new user interface for touch-based devices that are required for building successful Windows 8 applications. Chapter 2 is particularly important because you need to understand the design concepts underlying the Windows 8 UI style. Chapter 3 is the fundamental starting point for building your first Windows 8 application. Use the following table to determine how best to proceed through the book.

If you are	Follow these steps
New to Windows 8 development	Start with Chapter 1
New to Windows 8 UI style	Start with Chapter 2
Not new to Windows 8 development using the provided templates	Start with Chapter 4
XAML developer	Start with Chapter 3 and then skip to Chapter 9 to gain a solid understanding of the controls that are specific to Windows 8 apps and how to design flexible layouts.

Most of the book's chapters include hands-on procedures and examples that let you try out the concepts discussed in each chapter. No matter which sections you choose to focus on, be sure to download the companion code from the publisher's site (see the "Code samples" section of this Introduction), and install them on your system.

Conventions and features in this book

This book presents information using conventions designed to make the information readable and easy to follow.

- Each exercise consists of a series of tasks, presented as numbered steps (1, 2, and so on) listing each action you must take to complete the exercise.

- Boxed elements with labels such as "Note" provide additional information or alternative methods for completing a step successfully.

- Text that you type (apart from code blocks) appears in bold.

- A plus sign (+) between two key names means that you must press those keys at the same time. For example, "Press Alt+Tab" means that you hold down the Alt key while you press the Tab key.

- A vertical bar between two or more menu items (for example, File | Close), means that you should select the first menu or menu item, then the next, and so on.

System requirements

You will need the following hardware and software to complete the practice exercises in this book:

- Windows 8, installed

- Visual Studio 2012—any edition tailored for Windows 8 (the Express edition for Windows 8 is free)

- A computer with a 1.6 GHz or faster processor

- 1 GB of RAM (1.5 GB if running on a virtual machine)

- 10 GB (NTFS) of available hard disk space

- 5400 RPM (or faster) hard disk drive

- DirectX 9-capable video card running at 1024 x 768 or higher display resolution

Depending on your Windows configuration, you might require Local Administrator rights to install or configure Visual Studio 2012.

Code samples

Most of the chapters in this book include exercises that let you interactively try out new material learned in the main text. All the sample projects are available for download from the book's page on the website for Microsoft's publishing partner, O'Reilly Media:

http://go.microsoft.com/FWLink/?Linkid=275453

Click the Examples link on that page. When a list of files appears, locate and download the 9780735666955_files.zip file.

 Note In addition to the code samples, your system must have Microsoft Visual Studio 2012 installed.

Installing the code samples

Follow these steps to install the code samples on your computer so that you can use them with the exercises in this book.

1. Unzip the 9780735666955_files.zip file that you downloaded from the book's website (name a specific directory along with directions to create it, if necessary).

2. If prompted, review the displayed end user license agreement. If you accept the terms, select the accept option, and then click Next.

 Note If the license agreement doesn't appear, you can access it from the same webpage from which you downloaded the 9780735666955_files.zip file.

Acknowledgments

We'd like to thank all the people who have supported us in writing this book.

Marco Russo has shared with all of us in the most important phases of writing this book and its twin, *Building Windows 8 Apps with Microsoft Visual C++ Step by Step*.

Vanni Boncinelli tested all the code samples we wrote in C# and adapted each sample to Visual Basic.

Errata and book support

We've made every effort to ensure the accuracy of this book and its companion content. If you do find an error, please report it on our Microsoft Press site at oreilly.com:

1. Go to *http://microsoftpress.oreilly.com*.

2. In the Search box, enter the book's ISBN or title.

3. Select your book from the search results.

4. On your book's catalog page, under the cover image, you'll see a list of links.

5. Click View/Submit Errata.

You'll find additional information and services for your book on its catalog page. If you need additional support, please e-mail Microsoft Press Book Support at *mspinput@ microsoft.com*.

Please note that product support for Microsoft software is not offered through the addresses above.

We want to hear from you

At Microsoft Press, your satisfaction is our top priority, and your feedback our most valuable asset. Please tell us what you think of this book at:

http://www.microsoft.com/learning/booksurvey

The survey is short, and we read every one of your comments and ideas. Thanks in advance for your input!

Stay in touch

Let's keep the conversation going! We're on Twitter: *http://twitter.com/Microsoft-Press*

CHAPTER 1

Introduction to Windows Store apps

After completing this chapter, you will be able to

- Understand the main features of a Windows Store app.

- Evaluate the key benefits of creating an app for Microsoft Windows 8.

- Recognize the main capabilities and features of the new Windows 8 operating system.

This chapter provides an overall introduction to Windows 8 and the new world of the Windows Store apps from a developer perspective. In this chapter you will learn the basics of the Windows 8 user interface (UI), as well as gain an overview of the new features and capabilities that this new platform provides. The chapter targets any developer—even those who have not yet seen Windows 8. You will also learn how to set up a development environment for building your own Windows 8 apps.

The Windows 8 experience

Windows 8 is one of the most innovative and revolutionary operating systems investments made by Microsoft in the last decade. Before Windows 8, the operating systems market was divided into at least three main families: server operating systems, client/desktop operating systems, and mobile/tablet-oriented operating systems.

Windows 8, together with its sibling on the server side, Windows Server 2012, introduces a new paradigm where the client/desktop OS and the mobile/tablet-oriented OS can be exactly the same, sharing features, capabilities, user interfaces, and behaviors. In the last few years, there has been an explosion of tablet devices, and the number of people working at home and in their offices using the same small tablet devices is increasing. Nevertheless, until the release of Windows 8, it was not so simple to combine the preferences and needs of users with the infrastructure constraints of corporate networks. For example, employees would like to be able to install software on their own tablets, taken from a more-or-less checked and trustable marketplace available on the Internet, regardless of the corporate policies of their companies. Moreover, these employees would like the ability to check their corporate email accounts, as well as any private email accounts, using a unique device and unique email client software. Furthermore, the emerging social-oriented consumption of devices leads to the sharing of private contacts, agendas, tasks, pictures, and instant messages through business contacts, meetings, and corporate network instant communication and video-conferencing.

However, technology without governance could become a nightmare both for users and IT professionals. With Windows 8, employees can leverage a corporate-provided tablet device that allows them to install their choice of software from a safe and secure marketplace, either publicly or corporately constrained. Using this single device, they can check multiple email accounts or socialize with friends, colleagues, and business contacts—all while remaining compliant with their employer's security policies within a safe and sandboxed environment.

Moreover, for the sake of backward compatibility, most of the software targeting Windows 7 desktops will still continue to work on Windows 8, using the old-style desktop-oriented approach.

So, let's explore the new Windows 8 UI and the key features of this new operating system. Figure 1-1 shows the new Start screen, which is one of the most apparent changes introduced with Windows 8.

FIGURE 1-1 The new Windows Start screen.

As shown in Figure 1-1, the new Start screen is composed of a set of squares and rectangles, called *Tiles*, each of which represents a link to a software application, and can provide animated feedback to users. Tiles can be either square or wide tiles. Many apps provide both sizes so users can choose the one that best suits their needs. For example, in the upper-left corner of Figure 1-1, just under the Main title, there's a wide tile for the Mail App, which indicates that there are 15 email messages in the inbox. The tile also provides a brief preview of the messages.

To reduce the size of the tile you can right-click it, or swipe down on the tile, which selects it and activates a command bar, called the App Bar, which will be discussed later. Figure 1-2 shows how the Mail App tile looks after it has been selected.

FIGURE 1-2 The Mail App tile is selected, and the App Bar is visible.

Several commands are available in the App Bar. For example, you can select the Smaller command to reduce the tile's size from wide to square. You can also turn off the dynamic update feature of the tile, by clicking Turn Live Tile Off, or you can click Uninstall to remove the app from your device. If you click the Smaller command, the tile becomes square and the preview of unread email disappears (see Figure 1-3).

FIGURE 1-3 The Mail App tile after clicking the Smaller command on the App Bar.

A user with a tablet device can tap (that is, touch using a single finger) a tile to start an application instance or to resume an already running instance. A user with a desktop PC and a mouse can click the tile to get the same result. The Start screen is based on the idea of the panorama view, which has been available in the Windows Phone since version 7.0. You can scroll horizontally, using either touch gestures on a touch-enabled device or the mouse wheel, or if you are working on a desktop, the keyboard. You can also use the traditional scrollbar that appears at the bottom of the screen.

As soon as you tap an app tile, that app will become the foreground application. If you are starting that app for the first time in a given session, Windows will create and load the app instance in memory. Subsequently, when the app is already running, tapping the app tile switches that app to the foreground application. In both cases, the previous application is sent into the background and may eventually be suspended by the operating system. Suspension means freezing; a suspended app uses no CPU threads and no I/O functionality is provided to the application, leaving all the computer resources to the main (foreground) application. When you return to a suspended application, the operating system resumes it in its previous state. In Chapter 4, "Application lifecycle management," you will learn more about the application lifecycle for Windows Store apps. Figure 1-4 shows the Bing Weather App running in the foreground.

FIGURE 1-4 The Bing Weather App running in the foreground.

By default, an app uses the entire screen, in order to satisfy one of the main concepts of the user experience design of Windows Store apps: "content, not chrome." In Chapter 2, "Windows 8 UI style," you will discover more about exactly what user experience design means.

Not all apps that run under Windows 8 are Windows Store apps. If you start an old-style desktop application, you will see the classic and familiar Windows Desktop UI, just as if you were running a previous version of Windows. Figure 1-5 shows an old-style application, in this case SQL Server Management Studio, running in desktop mode. Notice the absence of the classic "Start" button.

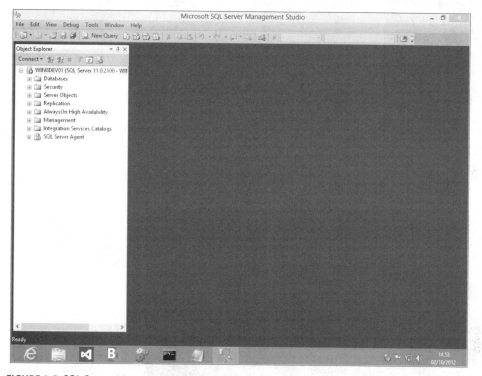

FIGURE 1-5 SQL Server Management Studio running in the classic desktop mode.

You aren't always limited to a single full-screen application, however. If you have a device with a 1366 × 768 or higher resolution, you can leverage the Windows 8 capability to "snap" two applications into the display area. Figure 1-6 shows the Bing Weather App snapped together with the new Microsoft Internet Explorer 10 for Windows 8.

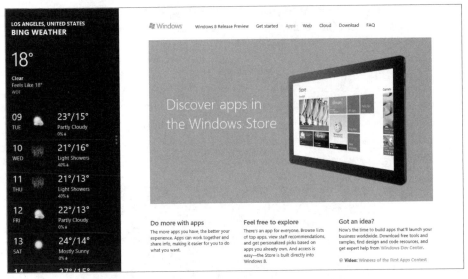

FIGURE 1-6 The Bing Weather App snapped together with Internet Explorer 10.

Of course you can also switch the relative sizes of two snapped apps, as shown in Figure 1-7.

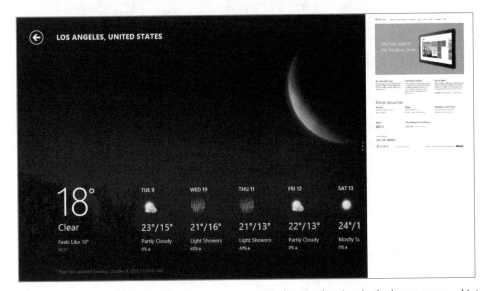

FIGURE 1-7 An example of switching two app panes, with the Weather App in the larger pane and Internet Explorer 10 in the smaller pane.

From a developer perspective, the important thing to understand and master is that every Windows Store app must support snapping; otherwise, it won't be certified by the Windows Store. The Bing Weather App, as shown in the previous figures, supports the snapped view. When snapped, it adapts its page layout to present information in a small horizontal portion of the screen. If your apps are unable to present information in a snapped view, you must fill the snapped pane where your application would be with a clear message for the user. You should never use the "full-screen" view for a snapped view because the user would not be able to interact properly with the application.

In fact, whenever you want to develop and publish a Windows Store app you have to submit it to the Windows Store, or eventually to a corporate catalog. From the official and public Windows Store viewpoint, an app must adhere to a clear set of requirements to be certified. Any application that does not adhere to these requirements will be rejected. You can find more details about the requirements in the Windows 8 developer section of MSDN (Microsoft Developer Network): *http://msdn.microsoft.com/library/windows/apps/hh694083.aspx*. For example, one rule states that you have to provide a privacy information page if your app connects to the Internet for any purpose. Thus, if your app invokes a remote web service, which is a common situation, you must provide a privacy page illustrating how you manage users' data. In Chapter 4, you will learn how to submit an app to the Windows Store.

Turning the focus back to the Start screen, another useful feature is that you can collect tiles into groups to organize them better in the menu. To move a tile from one group to another you just drag it, using touch gestures or the mouse. To create a new group you need to move a tile into the middle region between two existing groups. A gray bar will appear that represents the frame of the new group, and dragging the tile onto this gray bar will create the new group. By using a specific gesture (pinch) that will be explained in Chapter 2, or rolling the mouse wheel backward while pressing the Ctrl key, the Start screen zooms out so you can see more groups. By clicking a group, or swiping your finger down on a group to select it, you can give that group a name using a command in the App Bar. In Figure 1-8, you can see the UI of the Start screen while zoomed out, with a group of tiles selected and the App Bar showing the available commands.

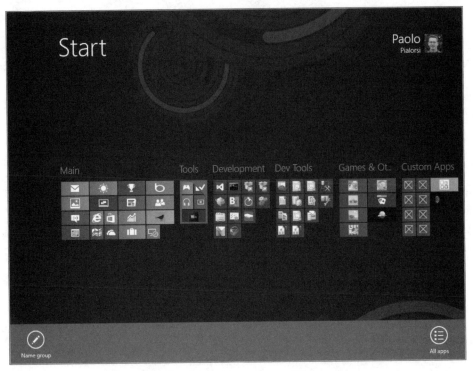

FIGURE 1-8 The Start screen zoomed out with the App Bar available.

Charms and App Bars

Other new and key features of Windows 8 are the App Bars and Charms. In Chapter 2, you will see more information about these features and the philosophy behind them. For now, simply consider that the need to support new devices, such as tablet and mobile devices, and the need to make the apps usable with just your hands, introduced new tools through the new touch-oriented perspective and solutions. In Windows 8 you have two kinds of App Bars: the bottom App Bar and the top App Bar. As their names indicate, these two kinds of App Bars are shown, respectively, in the lower and upper regions of the screen. Using the bottom App Bar, you manage tasks and actions related to the current context or item. Figure 1-9 shows an example with Internet Explorer 10, where you use the bottom App Bar to edit the current URL or enter a new URL, refresh the page, pin the page to the new Start screen, or change browser settings.

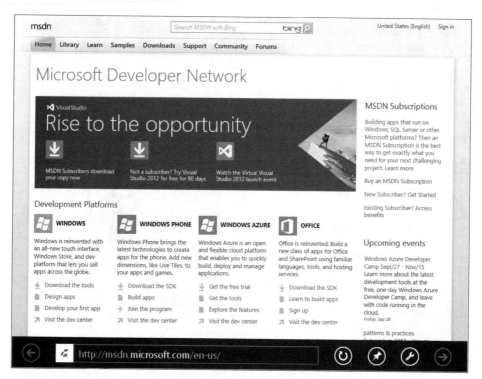

FIGURE 1-9 Internet Explorer with the bottom App Bar showing the URL.

In contrast, the top App Bar is used to provide navigation aids. For example, you can use it to show such things as a top-level menu or a list of main sections available in the current app. Figure 1-10 shows the top App Bar of the Windows Store app, which is an app you can use to search, download, buy, and install other apps.

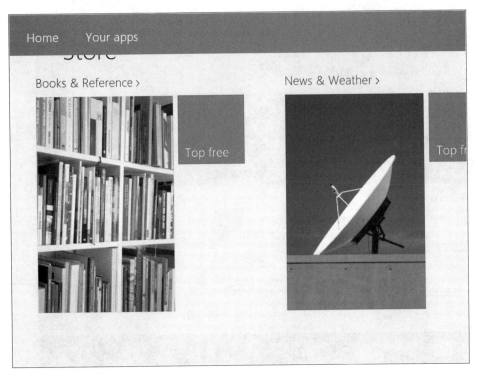

FIGURE 1-10 The Windows Store app with the top App Bar showing.

To show the App Bars, you can swipe your finger from the top or bottom border of the screen to the center of the screen. Alternatively, you can press Windows+Z on the keyboard, or right-click.

Charms allow you to access the most useful features and actions provided by the operating system. For example, you can use Charms to access system settings, the local search engine, the sharing features, and so on. Figure 1-11 shows Charms in action.

FIGURE 1-11 Charms are on the right side of the screen.

To display Charms, you can swipe your finger from the right border of the screen to the center of the screen, or you can press Windows+C. You can also move the cursor to either of two invisible "hot spots" in the lower-right or upper-right corner of the screen. Finally, you can directly activate specific Charms using keyboard shortcuts. For example, pressing Windows+Q activates a search for the installed applications (Q stands for query), whereas pressing Windows+F
(F stands for Find Files) activates the search for files function. To activate the sharing feature, press Windows+H.

Through Charms you can also activate specific panels, such as the Settings Panel, which can be activated by pressing Windows+I. In Figure 1-12, you can see the Settings Panel in action.

FIGURE 1-12 The Settings Panel is visible on the right side of the screen.

One key feature of Charms is that you can also host custom commands and custom panels in it. For example, if you are developing a Windows Store app and you want to provide some custom settings for users, you can add a custom Charm. By selecting the custom command while the app is in the foreground, you can activate a *fly-out panel*, which is a custom control that renders within the Charms. Figure 1-13 shows the fly-out panel.

FIGURE 1-13 A custom fly-out panel rendered within Charms.

The Charms shown in Figure 1-13 provides Support Request and Privacy Policy commands, which are custom and specific to the app currently in the foreground. The latter command leads users to the privacy page required for any Windows Store app that consumes a remote service over the Internet, as you learned earlier in this chapter.

The Windows Runtime

A Windows Store app is a software solution that adheres to the UI and technical specifications of the Windows Store. You can create a Windows Store app using any language that supports the Windows Runtime (WinRT). The WinRT is a rich set of application programming interfaces (APIs) built upon the Windows 8 operating system, providing direct and easy access to all the main primitives, devices, and capabilities for any language available to develop Windows 8 apps. The WinRT is available only for Windows 8 apps and its main goal is to unify the development experience of building a Windows 8 app, regardless of the programming language you use.

Saying that you can use any language supporting the Windows Runtime means that, currently, you can choose from C++, .NET (C# or VB), and JavaScript. Nevertheless, there are no technical limitations to support the Windows Runtime from any other language, as long as it adheres to the Windows Runtime specifications.

In Chapter 5, "Introduction to the Windows Runtime," you will learn more about this topic and the architecture of the Windows Runtime. For now, you can imagine the Windows Runtime as an infra-structural framework of libraries that allows easy development of Windows Store apps, hiding all the inner details of the operating system from the common and everyday developer perspective. For instance, you can ask the Windows Runtime to open the webcam standard UI to capture photos or videos without knowing anything about the underlying driver or Win32 API.

For example, in the following code excerpt you can see how simple it is to capture a picture from the camera of your PC, using the C# language.

```csharp
private async void TakePhoto_Click(object sender, RoutedEventArgs e) {

    var camera = new CameraCaptureUI();
    var img = await camera.CaptureFileAsync(CameraCaptureUIMode.Photo);
    if (img != null) {
        var stream = await img.OpenAsync(FileAccessMode.Read);
        var bitmap = new BitmapImage();
        bitmap.SetSource(stream);
        image.Source = bitmap;
    }
}
```

You can perform the same action using JavaScript, with the following code excerpt:

```javascript
var dialog = new Windows.Media.Capture.CameraCaptureUI();
dialog.captureFileAsync(Windows.Media.Capture.CameraCaptureUIMode.photo).done(function (file) {
        if (file) {
            var photoBlobUrl = URL.createObjectURL(file, { oneTimeOnly: true });
            document.getElementById("capturedPhoto").src = photoBlobUrl;
        }
    };
```

Moreover, you can achieve the same result using C++, as shown in the following code excerpt:

```cpp
void CaptureWin8::MainPage::TakePhoto_Click(Platform::Object^ sender,
        Windows::UI::Xaml::RoutedEventArgs^ e) {


    CameraCaptureUI^ dialog = ref new CameraCaptureUI();
    concurrency::task<StorageFile^> (
        dialog->CaptureFileAsync(CameraCaptureUIMode::Photo)).then([this]
        (StorageFile^ file) {
        if (nullptr != file) {
            concurrency::task<Streams::IRandomAccessStream^> (
            file->OpenAsync(FileAccessMode::Read)).then([this] (
            Streams::IRandomAccessStream^ stream) {
                BitmapImage^ bitmapImage = ref new BitmapImage();
                bitmapImage->SetSource(stream);
                image->Source = bitmapImage;
            });
        }
    });
}
```

Badges, Live Tiles, Toasts, and Lock Screen

Another set of new features found in Windows Store apps includes Badges, Live Tiles, Toasts, and the Lock Screen. Badges and live tiles show dynamic information to users even while they are not directly using the app providing the information—the tiles display such information directly on the Start screen. You can use a badge and/or a live tile to provide information about news, new items to check, new tasks to execute, or whatever else is meaningful for the user to best experience your app from the Start screen, without opening the application. For example, the out-of-the-box Mail App uses the badge to show the number of unread emails in the inbox, and a live tile to show a rotating list of excerpts from all the unread messages. Moreover, the Windows Store App notifies you through a badge about the number of updates available for apps you have installed. In Figure 1-14, you can see these badges and live tiles in action.

FIGURE 1-14 The Start screen with badges and live tiles in action.

Notice the number 4 in the bottom-right corner of the Windows Store app; this badge indicates that there are four pending updates. You can also see the badge with 15 in the bottom-right corner of the Mail app, indicating 15 new emails in the inbox. Furthermore, the Mail app uses a live tile to show an excerpt of the most recent unread emails, but a live tile can do even more. For example, a live tile can completely change its content in order to be dynamic and fresh and to trigger curiosity in the mind of the user. Figure 1-15 shows four different states that the tile of a single app can assume (the Bing Travel app that ships with Windows 8).

FIGURE 1-15 The Bing Travel App tile assuming four different states.

The official guidelines for Windows Store apps (see *http://msdn.microsoft.com/en-us/library/windows/apps/hh465403.aspx*) suggest using a wide tile only when your app has live tiles to show. Otherwise, you should use square tiles when your tiles contain static content, and simply use a badge for small and lightweight notifications. In Chapter 9, "Rethinking the UI for Windows 8 apps," you will learn how to create a live tile.

Toasts are another technique for providing asynchronous alerts to the user. For example, an alert or alarm application can ask the operating system to send to the user a toast at a preset time; the Windows Runtime will send the toast even if the application is not running at that time. Moreover, when users are working on an app in the foreground, background apps will not be able to interact with them unless the app uses a toast.

In fact, as you will see in Chapter 4, due to the architecture of Windows 8 and because of the application lifecycle management of Windows Store apps, only the foreground app has the focus and is running; all the other background apps can be suspended (or even terminated) by the Windows Runtime. A suspended app cannot execute or consume any CPU cycle. However, you can define a background task (more on this topic later in this chapter) that will work in the background, even in a separate process from the owner app, and you can define background actions. When these actions need to alert users about their outcomes, they can use a toast.

A *toast* can be plain text, an image, or any combination of the two. In the upper-right corner of Figure 1-16, you can see a toast provided by the Windows Store app informing the user that an app installation task has completed in the background.

FIGURE 1-16 An example toast message shown in the upper-right corner of the screen.

In Chapter 9, you will learn how to create a toast for your own Windows 8 apps.

One other option you possess while developing a Windows Store app is to provide lightweight information to the user through the Lock screen. The Lock screen is the screen that is shown when a Windows 8 user session is locked out, for example after a period of inactivity or when a user presses Windows+L to lock the session.

Figure 1-17 shows the Lock screen providing some information about the current date and time, the next appointment in the user's agenda, and a set of small icons, in the lower part of the screen.

FIGURE 1-17 Lock screen showing status information.

Those icons provide information about the network connection status, battery status (for a device running on battery power), number of unread emails in the inbox, and some other lightweight information. A user can choose what information appears in the Lock screen by using the proper panel in the system configuration. However, you are limited to no more than seven Lock screen items simultaneously providing detailed information. All seven apps will be able to show badges and toasts in the Start screen, but only one of those apps will be allowed to show the text of its latest tile notification in the Lock screen. Figure 1-18 shows the configuration panel for the Lock screen. To reach it, you need to display the Charms; for example, press Windows+C, and then select the Settings command. Finally, click the Change PC Settings command. Under the Personalize section in the Lock screen tab, you will find the Lock screen configuration.

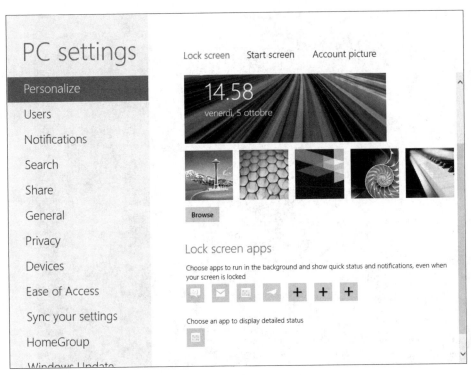

FIGURE 1-18 The Lock screen configuration panel in the PC Settings.

The Lock screen configuration allows you to choose a background image, select which seven apps will execute in the background to provide information through the Lock screen icons, and—last but not least—choose the app that will be allowed to display detailed text status. The last one, by default, is configured to be the Calendar app. For your apps to be available as Lock screen apps, your software must declare that capability within an *app manifest file*, which will be explained later in this book, starting with Chapter 3, "My first Windows 8 app."

The information shown by a Lock screen–enabled app is the same as the information provided by the app's tile on the Start screen. In fact, the text shown beside the Lock screen icon is taken from the badge of the app, whereas the detailed text status is taken from the tile text of the app.

Background tasks

As stated earlier in this chapter (and as will be explored more in Chapter 4), a Windows Store app executes code only when it is the foreground app. However, there are situations where you want to execute some code when your app is in the background. A background task can execute code even when the corresponding app is suspended, but it runs in an environment that is restricted and resource-managed. Moreover, background tasks receive only a limited amount of system resources. You should use a background task to execute small pieces of code that require no user interaction. You should *not* use a background task to execute complex business logic or calculations because the amount of system resources available to background apps is both tight and limited. In addition, complex background workloads consume battery power, reducing the overall efficiency and responsiveness of the system.

To create a background task, you have to define a class and register it with the operating system. A background task is just a class that implements a specific interface (*IBackgroundTask* in C#, for example) defined by WinRT and that is registered by using a *BackgroundTaskBuilder* class instance. There are many types of background tasks available, and these respond to different kind of *triggers*, such as the following:

- **ControlChannelTrigger**   Raised when there are incoming messages on the control channel.

- **MaintenanceTrigger**   Raised when it is time to execute system maintenance tasks.

- **PushNotificationTrigger**   Raised when a notification arrives on the Windows Notifications Service channel.

- **SystemEventTrigger**   Raised when a specific system event occurs.

- **TimeTrigger**   Raised when a time event occurs.

In particular, a *SystemTrigger* can occur in response to any of the following system events:

- **InternetAvailable**   An Internet connection becomes available.

- **LockScreenapplicationAdded**   An app tile is added to the Lock screen.

- **LockScreenapplicationRemoved**   An app tile is removed from the Lock screen.

- **ControlChannelReset**   A network channel is reset.

- **NetworkStateChange**   A network change, such as a change in cost or connectivity, occurs.

- **OnlineIdConnectedStateChange**   An online ID associated with the account changes.

- **ServicingComplete**   The system has finished updating an application.

- **SessionConnected**   The session is connected.

- **SessionDisconnected**   The session is disconnected.

- **SmsReceived**   A new SMS message is received by an installed mobile broadband device.

- **TimeZoneChange**   The time zone changes on the device (for example, when the system adjusts the clock for daylight saving time).

- **UserAway**   The user becomes absent.

- **UserPresent**   The user becomes present.

Whenever such an event occurs, you can check a set of conditions to determine whether your background task should execute. The conditions you can check include the following:

- **InternetAvailable**   An Internet connection must be available.

- **InternetNotAvailable**   An Internet connection must be unavailable.

- **SessionConnected**   The session must be connected.

- **SessionDisconnected**   The session must be disconnected.

- **UserNotPresent**   The user must be away.

- **UserPresent**   The user must be present.

To optimize resource consumption, some trigger notifications are provided only to apps that have been included in the Lock screen. For example, a *TimeTrigger* can be leveraged only by an app in the Lock screen. The same requirement holds true for *PushNotificationTrigger* and *ControlChannelTrigger*. Even some of the *SystemTrigger* events are reserved for apps in the Lock screen, including events such as *SessionConnected*, *UserPresent*, *UserAway*, or *ControlChannelReset*. Because you should register for these events and triggers only if your application is in the Lock screen, you use the *SystemTrigger* events *LockScreenApplicationAdded* and *LockScreenApplicationRemoved* so that your app can register and unregister such triggers accordingly.

Generally speaking, in common language runtime (CLR) and C++ apps, you can execute a background task in the app itself or in a system-provided host (*BackgroundTaskHost.exe*). Additionally, you can also execute tasks for triggers of the type *PushNotificationTrigger* or *ControlChannelTrigger* in the app process.

One last topic to properly complete the introduction of background tasks is *resource management*. Every background task must execute its code using a constrained amount of CPU and network bandwidth. For example, each app on the Lock screen receives two seconds of CPU time every 15 minutes, plus two more seconds allotted to background task execution just after the previous two seconds. In contrast, apps that are not on the Lock screen receive one second of CPU time every two hours.

From a network bandwidth perspective, these constraints are a function of the amount of energy consumed by the network interface. For example, with a throughput of 10 Mbps, an app on the Lock screen can consume about 450 MB per day, whereas an app that is not on the Lock screen can consume about 75 MB per day.

These constraints are defined to reduce battery and resource consumption. It's worth noting that these rules do not apply to apps that rely on critical background tasks, such as *ControlChannelTrigger* and *PushNotificationTrigger*. Instead, these kinds of tasks receive guaranteed resources. Finally, there is a global pool of resources (CPU and network) that is shared across apps and can be used to provide some extra resources to those apps that need them. Of course, an app should not rely on such resources being available because they are shared between *all* background tasks for any app—in other words, another app could have already consumed all the global pool resources. The global pool is refilled every 15 minutes, with a refill quota related to the power source of the device (AC adapter or battery).

Contracts and extensions

Another powerful set of features available for developing Windows Store apps are *WinRT Contracts*. The Windows Runtime and Windows Store apps can share data, information, features, and behaviors through shared *communication contracts*. A contract is an agreement between an app and the Windows 8 operating system that allows an app to talk to and exchange data with any other app, without directly knowing anything about the other app, using the operating system and WinRT as a proxy.

For example, launch the Bing Travel app from the Start screen and navigate to a target travel location, such as Rome in Italy. Then show the Charms (Windows+C) and select the Share command. You will see a fly-out panel within the Charms that lets you select how you want to share that location: by email, to friends using the People app, or via any other Windows Store app configured as a sharing target for the current content. Figure 1-19 shows an example of this process.

FIGURE 1-19 Sharing a location by taking advantage of a communications contract baked into the Bing Travel app.

As soon as you have made a choice, for example by selecting Mail, Windows will take you into the sharing target app, and you can handle the shared content there. For example, Figure 1-20 shows how you can send the Rome information to someone via email in Windows Mail.

FIGURE 1-20 Sharing Rome information by email via the Windows Mail app.

It's worth reiterating that neither of the apps involved in this sharing transaction (Bing Travel or Windows Mail) is aware of the other. The Windows Runtime, sitting in the middle, joins them through a contract called a Share contract.

Similarly, when you are using an app such as the Windows Store app, and you activate the search feature (Windows+Q), the operating system uses a Search contract to query the Windows Store app for apps that satisfy the search criteria provided.

The Windows Runtime exposes a rich set of contracts, as shown in the following list:

- **Cached File Updater contract**   You can leverage this contract to keep track of file changes and cache them. For example, an app like SkyDrive uses this contract to monitor file changes.

- **File Picker contract**   You can register your app as a target for the File Picker UI.

- **Play To contract**   This allows your app to be enlisted in the list of apps available in the Play To section of the Connect command in the Charms.

- **Search contract**   This provides search capabilities to your app.

- **Settings contract**   This contract provides a panel for custom settings of your app.

- **Share contract**   This contract shares content between apps.

There are also extensions that allow an app to adhere to an agreement with the operating system instead of with a third-party app. You can use these extensions to extend standard Windows features. For the sake of simplicity, consider what happens when you connect a new device or insert a disk into the CD/DVD reader. An operating system message appears that informs users that they can play the new device or media, providing a list of available actions and players. For example, you can register your app as supporting the *AutoPlay* extension, and subsequently your app will be listed in the list of available autoplay targets.

You can see an enumeration in the following list:

- **Account picture provider**   When a user changes his or her account picture, you can register an app as an account picture provider.

- **AutoPlay**   The app will be listed as an autoplay target.

- **Background tasks**   The app can run background tasks.

- **Camera settings**   The app provides custom UI for camera settings.

- **Contact picker**   The app is registered as a contact picker provider.

- **File activation**   The app is registered as being associated with a specific file type based on the file extension.

- **Game Explorer**   You can register the app as a game, providing a Game Definition File (GDF), and your app will be available as a game only if compliant with the target machine's family safety rules.

- **Print task settings**   This declares that your app has a custom printer UI and can print by talking directly to a printer device.

- **Protocol activation**   You can register a protocol moniker associated with your app. For example, Windows Mail can be activated with a *mailto:* protocol moniker. Internet Explorer 10 can be activated with an *http:* protocol moniker. You can register your own moniker and use it to activate your app.

- **SSL/certificates**   Enable your app to install a digital certificate onto the target device.

As you will see in Chapter 3, registering or consuming a contract through WinRT is very straightforward.

Visual Studio 2012 and Windows 8 Simulator

To develop a Windows Store app, you will need to install a development environment such as Microsoft Visual Studio 2012. To accomplish this task, you can buy and install a regular license of Microsoft Visual Studio 2012 directly from Microsoft or from an authorized reseller. However, you can also get started by downloading and installing a free edition of Visual Studio 2012, called Visual Studio 2012 Express edition. In particular, the Express family contains one product named Visual Studio 2012 Express for

Windows 8. Using this development tool, you can create Windows Store apps by starting from scratch or starting with a set of prebuilt application templates and models. You can download Visual Studio 2012 Express for Windows 8 from the Microsoft website at *http://www.microsoft.com/visualstudio/*, or you can find it in the Windows Store app, under the "Tools" app category. Figure 1-21 shows the page dedicated to Visual Studio 2012 Express for Windows 8 in the Windows Store app.

FIGURE 1-21 The Visual Studio Express 2012 for Windows 8 page in the Windows Store app.

After installing Visual Studio Express 2012 for Windows 8, you will be able to create custom apps and publish them to the Windows Store—a process discussed in much more detail in Chapters 3 and 4.

Note that you can download and install a retail version of Microsoft Visual Studio 2012 (that is, Professional, Premium, or Ultimate) even on previous editions of Windows. For example, suppose you don't have a Windows 8 PC; instead, you have a machine running Windows 7. You can still install Visual Studio 2012 and develop your software solutions on Windows 7, but you will not be able to develop Windows Store apps on it.

Note You cannot download and install the free Microsoft Visual Studio 2012 Express for Windows 8 edition on a computer without Windows 8; that edition *requires* you running Windows 8 or later.

One useful option for testing and executing your apps is to use the Windows 8 Simulator, which is part of the Windows 8 SDK included in Visual Studio 2012.

Figure 1-22 shows the Windows 8 Simulator in action.

FIGURE 1-22 The Windows 8 Simulator.

As you can see, the simulator looks like a small tablet PC running Windows 8. On the right side there is a set of commands to simulate various scenarios. These commands are, from top to bottom:

- **Always on top**   Puts the simulator always on top.

- **Mouse mode**   When you move and click your mouse, the simulator will react to mouse interactions as well.

- **Basic touch mode**   Your mouse pointer will become like a finger and when you click the simulator it will be handled as a finger touch.

- **Pinch/zoom touch mode**   Similar to the previous option, but used to simulate zoom in and zoom out via touch gestures.

- **Rotation touch mode**   Similar to the previous option, but used to simulate touch rotation gestures.

- **Rotate clockwise (90 degrees)**   Rotates the device clockwise 90 degrees.

- **Rotate counterclockwise (90 degrees)**   Rotates the device counterclockwise 90 degrees.

- **Change resolution** Changes the screen resolution of the simulator device. The available resolutions are:

  - 10.6" 1024 × 768

  - 10.6" 1366 × 768

  - 10.6" 1920 × 1080

  - 10.6" 2560 × 1440

  - 12" 1280 × 800

  - 23" 1920 × 1080

  - 27" 2560 × 1440

- **Set location** Allows simulating a GPS location for testing location-based apps.

- **Copy screenshot** Creates a screenshot of the simulator screen. This is useful for creating promotional pictures of your apps and the required images to publish an app on the Windows Store.

- **Screenshot settings** Configures copy screenshot behavior, such as the destination directory of the image files.

- **Help** Provides a link to the simulator's Help.

Using the Windows 8 Simulator, you can test your apps fully, even without a real tablet device or a Windows 8 environment.

One of the most important features of the simulator is the ability to change the resolution, orientation, and form factor of the screen to test the application behavior for many different "devices" without the need to buy real ones.

Also, remember that you cannot develop a Windows Store app using Microsoft Visual Studio 2010 or any other earlier edition of the product. The only edition of Microsoft Visual Studio suitable for developing Windows Store apps is Visual Studio 2012 or later.

Summary

In this chapter, you have been introduced to some basic information about Windows 8 and Windows Store apps. You learned the key new features of the Windows 8 UI, as well as the main goals behind the development of a Windows Store app. You saw several apps and features, including the Windows Store, badges, live tiles, toasts, background tasks, the new Lock screen, the new Start screen, and more. You also learned about the development environment required to develop Windows Store apps.

Quick reference

To	Do this
Notify a user of an action happening in the background	Use a toast, a badge, or a live tile. You can also use the Lock screen, in case it is suitable for your context.
Execute some code while the app is suspended	Use a background task.
Make the contents managed by your app searchable by the user	Support the Search contract.
Develop a Windows Store app	Install Microsoft Visual Studio 2012 Express edition for Windows 8 or Microsoft Visual Studio 2012 on a Windows 8 device.
Simulate the execution of a Windows 8 app in different resolutions, orientations, and form factors	Run the Windows 8 Simulator available within Visual Studio 2012.

CHAPTER 2

Windows 8 UI style

After completing this chapter, you will be able to

- Understand the design concepts underlying the Windows 8 UI style.

- Understand the user experience of a Windows 8 app.

Why devote a chapter of this book to design concepts? If you are reading this book, you probably want to create great applications for the Windows Store—and great apps must be graphically in sync with the Microsoft Windows 8 ecosystem—which means they must be designed according to the Windows 8 design and usability guidelines. Therefore, it is worthwhile to dedicate a full chapter to exploring the details of the new design language for Windows 8: the Windows 8 UI style.

From the beginning, it is important to understand that a design language is not like a programming language. A design language does not have strict, enforced rules; instead, it is a set of ideas and philosophies related to graphics and—specifically for applications—to the user experience. A design language doesn't have a "compiler" that lets you know what is right and what is wrong. To discover whether your results are in line with a particular design language, you have to rely not only on your experience and graphic sense, but also, and even more importantly, on the study of the basic ideas behind that design language.

Influences

To fully understand the concepts underlying Windows 8, which represents the (for now) culminating point of a long journey, you need to understand where that journey began. This section touches on the historical artistic movements that inspired the ideas behind the user experience of Windows 8.

The primary source of influence is the School of Architecture, Art, and Design called *Bauhaus* (its full name was actually Staatliches Bauhaus). Figure 2-1 shows the school's logo.

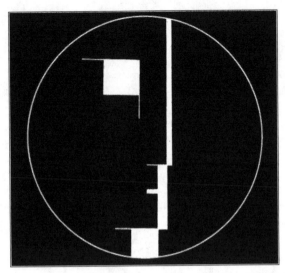

FIGURE 2-1 The logo of the School of Architecture, Art, and Design called Bauhaus.

You could describe this logo in technical terms by specifying the element colors, the thickness of the lines, and so on, but the first thing you notice about this logo is its modernity—even without any knowledge of art history, you have probably assumed that the image is contemporary. Yet the Bauhaus school operated in Germany from 1919 to around 1933! The fundamental principle of the Bauhaus philosophy is the concept of "fair reduction," that is, removing all the adornments and reducing everything to its essence. It's this very idea—which results in simplicity—that makes the works of this movement, including the previous logo, so modern.

Bauhaus represented not only a school for learning the art of design, but also a point of reference for the artistic movements generated by rationalism and functionalism, which were part of the modern movement or modern design. Rationalism and functionalism were not confined to architecture and design; they included all forms of art and communication.

Functionalism was originally an architectural movement that held the belief that any building should be functional for its purpose: a school of thought where what is "useful" is opposed to what is "beautiful." The rules dictated by functionalism are simple but clear:

- Function comes first.

- Function determines shape and characteristics of an object.

- Function makes an object beautiful.

- In essence, the function is the object.

Those concepts can be easily adapted to the computer world. In fact, saying that "function makes an object beautiful" is the analogue of such common ideas as "an app is beautiful simply because it is useful and because it offers interesting content and important functionality, not because it has nice graphics."

At the time of the Bauhaus school, the design works were produced only by skilled craftsmen who made unique pieces for their customers. Bauhaus revolutionized the market by claiming that the design could be industrialized without sacrificing quality. To demonstrate that point, it produced some works realized with easy-to-assemble industrial elements. In creating these design elements (chairs, tables, bookcases, and so on), the designers' attention focused on planning and product design, not on the production itself, as was the case with handcrafted design.

Going into further detail about the works of the Bauhaus school is beyond the scope of this chapter, but the Wikipedia page at *http://en.wikipedia.org/wiki/Bauhaus* has good general information. You can find more detailed information on the Bauhaus website at *http://bauhaus-online.de/en/atlas/das-bauhaus*. The influence of the school is apparent; if you just type "Bauhaus furniture" into any search engine you'll find some products that are still on the market today.

In the world of software development, the concept of industrialization introduced by the Bauhaus school of design morphs into the idea of software industrialization. Actually, you have been industrializing software for many years already using object-oriented techniques. For example, creating a base class with all the shared functionality needed by subclasses avoids wasting time rewriting the same functionality in different final products. Basically, you invest your time in creating projects, not products. These concepts also apply to the user interface. According to this principle, indeed, you should invest your time in creating templates for your graphics, not in drawing each graphic object from scratch every time you need it.

The other source of inspiration for the Windows 8 UI style is the International Typographic Style, or Swiss Design, an artistic movement developed in Switzerland in the 1950s whose style was based on clear typography, symmetry, and the use of few and contrasting colors.

This style has a predilection for photography instead of drawings, and places particular emphasis on typography. In fact, Swiss Design gave rise to fonts that are still largely popular such as Univers and Helvetica, both based on the Akzidenz Grotesk font, shown in Figure 2-2.

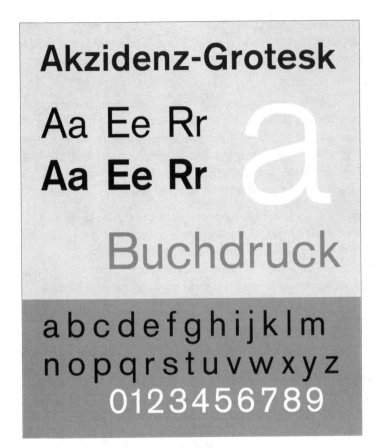

FIGURE 2-2 The Akzidenz Grotesk font.

Swiss Design devised a framework for organizing the information included on a page in a consistent way. This artistic approach acquired the name "grid system." The core ideas of the grid system were presented in the book Grid Systems in Graphic Design, by Josef Müller-Brockmann, whose book was seminal in spreading the knowledge of the grid layout. The success of such a layout system is attested to by daily experience: the newspaper you read every morning and many of the websites you consult. Moreover, signs in airports, railway stations, and throughout cities use grids to separate the various graphic elements and organize information semantically, as shown in Figure 2-3.

FIGURE 2-3 A real-world example of the Swiss Design.

In Figure 2-3, you can see a real-world application of some of the ideas of Swiss Design: the grid layout, the simple, straightforward, and clear typography, the wise use of element symmetry, and essential iconography—and if you can see the colors in this picture, you should note that it contains only three major color variations.

One important principle of the International Typographic Style is related to the use of an "international language," which means that it tried to avoid conventions or styles that could be traced back to specific countries, groups, or companies. Instead, it adopted a style that could be understood anywhere in the world. Figure 2-4 shows an example of such a principle. Even though the first line of the sign is in Italian, the meaning of the iconography is so clear that the underlying text is almost superfluous.

FIGURE 2-4 A real-world example of the "international language."

The use of an international language becomes, in the case of Windows 8 applications, absolutely critical. If you want to increase the revenue of your apps, you need to forego concentrating only on what might appeal to your friends, your local customers, or your fellow citizens and instead try to imagine how to communicate your ideas, features, and your messages to an international audience.

Another suggestion from Swiss Design is to reduce the iconography, leaving only the distinctive features of a graphic message. Figure 2-5 is a clear example.

FIGURE 2-5 A real-world example of a simple iconography.

In Figure 2-5, the directions to get to the departures area are unmistakable. Once you start looking, you'll notice the hundreds of road signs, television spots, advertisement signs, and so on that are based on an essential iconography.

To sum up the different ideas and philosophies underlying the Windows 8 UI style, the principles are as follows:

- Enhance the functionality and the content, not the container.

- Industrialize the software and user interface; create projects and not products.

- Use clear typography.

- Take advantage of the grid system.

- Prefer photos over drawings.

- Select few and contrasting colors.

- Strive for international language.

- Employ essential iconography.

Seeing the Bauhaus style in the Windows 8 UI

Keeping the principles you saw in the previous section in mind, try to find the implementation of those principles in Figure 2-6 of the Windows 8 Start screen.

FIGURE 2-6 The Windows 8 Start screen.

Enhance the functionality and the content, not the container

Without a doubt, the star of the Windows 8 Start screen is the content. There is no longer an empty desktop with a few colorful icons; the old icons have been replaced with new Tiles. Tiles are personal—they contain important information for the user. Users can customize the appearance of the Start screen to make it unique. The focus of customization lies in the content, which is not impersonal but applies directly to the user—such as contacts from social networks, personal photos, weather forecast based on the user's current GPS position, interesting news based on user topic selections, and so on. It is clear that the PC customization rises to a new level compared to simply arranging icons or choosing wallpaper, as in previous versions of Windows and other operating systems on the market.

As a developer, you can customize the content that your app's tiles display, giving you a way to improve the overall quality of your software (see Chapter 9, "Rethinking the UI for Windows 8 apps," for further details). Remember that a tile is not just an icon, it's an extension of your app.

Industrialize the software and user interface, create projects, not products

Tiles are also a good example of the concept of industrialization of the user interface. The old icons are a case in point: graphic designers used to spend several hours to complete each single icon. Now, with tiles, the efforts of Microsoft's graphic designers have been focused on the creation of "tile projects," or tile templates, if you prefer. As a developer, you need only provide the content for a tile (text and/or images) and the Windows 8 framework takes care of the rest.

Use clear typography

Focusing on typography, Windows 8 uses a brand new version of the Segoe UI font that has a number of redesigned default characters, new Microsoft OpenType alternates, new weights, and expanded language support. Just open any app in Windows 8 to appreciate the quality of the typography in the new operating system. Notice how the use of fonts with a pronounced difference in size provides a natural semantic organization of information on the Start screen. At first glance you intuitively understand what represents the title of a tile and what represents the content.

Take advantage of the grid system

The grid system has been used extensively in conceiving the new Windows 8 user experience. The Start screen provides a clear example of a layout grid, but a grid-based layout is also clearly distinguishable in various apps. For example, look at the native Weather App in Windows 8 shown in Figure 2-7.

FIGURE 2-7 The grid system used in the Weather App.

Prefer photos over drawings

With regard to the principle of "prefer photos to drawings" mentioned previously, the Start screen (like many other apps in the Windows Store) is full of examples: the People application uses a collage of your friends' pictures, Bing shows the photo of the day, the news reader shows the picture of the most important news of a user selected category, and so on.

Select few and contrasting colors

If you take a look at the Windows 8 Start screen, or even at the Weather App, you notice that the foreground color is just one and it stands out clearly against the tile background color. For your information, you can customize the foreground of the tile in a Windows 8 app. In fact, you can choose between a "dark" and a "light" template to achieve a better contrast, and therefore a greater legibility, between the background and foreground.

Strive for international language and employ essential iconography

The last two principles, those relating to international language and the reduction of the iconography, can be described together; one of the ways to make a message more "international" is to use the technique of simplifying the graphics. Look at the Windows Store tile. Its icon is universally recognized and contains the concept of shopping, but it is not an icon with a complex three-dimensional shape or colorful gradient effects; just a simple stroke is sufficient to convey the message. The human mind does not need more information to understand and process the visual input.

> **Note** One piece of advice to improve the international language of your app is to use widely accepted conventions. For example, you do not need to invent a new way to represent navigating to the home page of your app; the classic home-shaped icon is already widely used and accepted. One trick that can help you evaluate whether your app is headed in the right direction for internationalization is to translate all the text in the app into a language unfamiliar to your testers, and then conduct usability tests. If the testers are actually able to perform some or most of the app's required tasks without depending (too much) on the text, you have achieved a real international language.

Characteristics of a Windows 8 app

The previous section discussed the basics of the design language called Windows 8 UI style; this section defines the characteristic features of a Windows 8 app.

Silhouette

The most important aspect of an operating system is the ability to create a harmonious, homogeneous user experience—switching between applications should not be "traumatic" for the user, instead, apps should seem linked by a common theme in terms of user experience. To achieve this goal, it is essential for Windows 8 apps to have the same "silhouette," where silhouette means the look of the app at a glance, without focusing on specific functionality or context. Therefore, having the same silhouette means that the basic elements are always positioned in the same location and with the same characteristics (Figure 2-8).

FIGURE 2-8 A composition of different apps for Windows 8.

Figure 2-8 isn't a single app; it's a composition of several different apps for Windows 8 (Bing Sports, Bing Finance, Bing Daily, and Bing Travel). Each app has different features, a different purpose, and a different context, but they all share the same silhouette—the title is in the same position, the back button has the same shape and position, the font is identical, and so on. In addition, the texts are aligned: indeed, if you were to "zoom in" to the first two apps of the composition, you would see that the texts are perfectly in line, as shown in Figure 2-9.

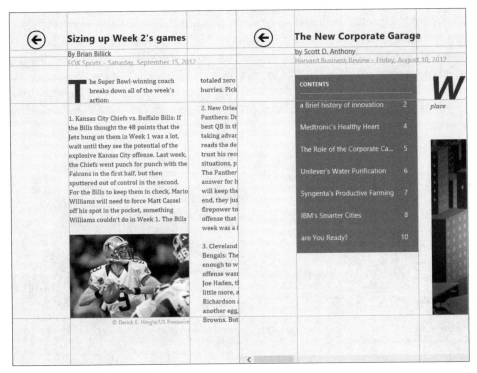

FIGURE 2-9 The text of two different apps is perfectly in line.

It is precisely this attention to detail that is the key to creating a harmonic system.

The Microsoft website has many documents that relate to various specific techniques for improving the silhouette of your app, but the simplest and most straightforward way is to use the project templates provided by Visual Studio 2012. Figure 2-10 shows some of the project templates for Visual Studio 2012.

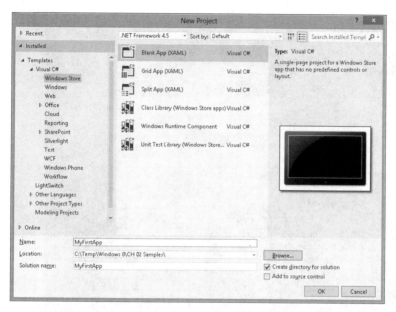

FIGURE 2-10 The project templates provided by Visual Studio 2012.

The Grid App (XAML) template provides a multipage project for navigating multiple layers of content. Users reach details for an item by tapping or clicking on the item itself. The details are then displayed on a dedicated page. The Split App (XAML) template is a good starting point for creating a master/details list, where items appear in a list on the left side of the page and the details for a selected item appear on the right side of the same page.

Note The next chapter provides a more complete description of the various templates.

Selecting the Grid App (XAML) or the Split App (XAML) template results in an app that obviously still needs to be customized and filled with content and functionality, but that already has a silhouette in line with the specifications. Figure 2-11 shows the home page of an app created with the default Grid App (XAML) template.

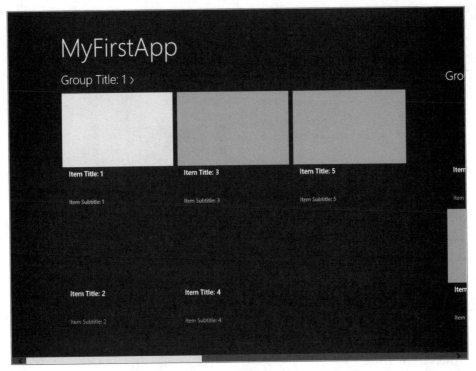

FIGURE 2-11 The default layout of a home page created by the Visual Studio 2012 project templates.

If you compare Figure 2-11 with Figure 2-12, which shows a custom photo application, you can see how the project templates provided by Visual Studio 2012 can simplify the development of an app. By starting with these projects, all you have to do to create an app consistent with the operating system is add your own content.

FIGURE 2-12 The home page of a custom application created using Visual Studio 2012 project templates.

The various templates also include the display of the item details. Figure 2-13 shows the layout of the Grid App (XAML) template.

FIGURE 2-13 The default layout of an item details page created by the Visual Studio 2012 project templates.

In Figure 2-14, you can see one of the news items from the Bing Daily App. It uses the same layout as the previous figure, but this time is filled with real content.

FIGURE 2-14 The Bing Daily App.

Full screen

The fundamental purpose of Windows 8 app design is to emphasize the content, not the container. The motto "content not chrome" has become a symbol of the Windows 8 UI style philosophy, but—in addition to what has already been explained in the previous section—it's important to add another key concept. In earlier versions of Windows, not only was an application relegated to a window, but a good portion of that window was filled with bars, widgets, panes, gadgets, and so on. In contrast, in a Windows 8 app the entire surface of the screen is dedicated to content. Figure 2-15 shows a classic screenshot of Microsoft Internet Explorer running on the desktop. In comparison to the clean Windows 8 design, the application (the website in this case) seems "smothered" by the other onscreen elements.

FIGURE 2-15 Internet Explorer 10 running on the desktop.

The user experience in Internet Explorer 10, specifically designed for Windows 8, assumes a decidedly new connotation. Figure 2-16 shows the same website in Internet Explorer 10. Notice how the entire screen of the app is now available for content, creating a more immersive user environment.

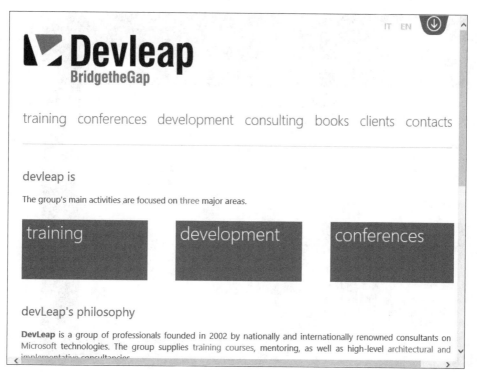

FIGURE 2-16 Every Windows Store app runs in full screen mode.

Edges

In Windows 8, the edges of the screen assume a very important role. As a matter of fact, the left side of the screen is entirely dedicated to the "back" functionality—by swiping from left to right (performed on the left side of the screen) Windows will cycle through all the open applications. You can think of this as the new implementation of the classic Alt+Tab functionality, but now based on a gesture. Swiping from the right side of the screen activates the Charms, which are five icons representing operating system functions that provide the following features: Search, Share, Start, Devices, and Settings. Figure 2-17 shows the Charms after activation by a right-to-left swipe.

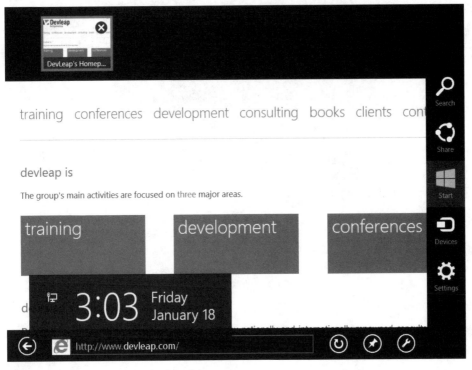

FIGURE 2-17 Charms on the right side of the screen.

Because both the left and right side swipe operations are reserved for the operating system, to prevent user frustration you should avoid placing common user interface controls such as buttons in those areas. However, your application can leverage both the top and the bottom edge of the screen to place your own menus and toolbars. A swipe from bottom to top, performed on the bottom side of the screen, or a swipe from top to bottom, performed in the top edge of the screen, activates a custom App Bar control where you can place required buttons and custom controls. These features are available to all Windows 8 applications, including most system applications such as Internet Explorer or Microsoft Office. Figure 2-18 shows the App Bar for Internet Explorer 10.

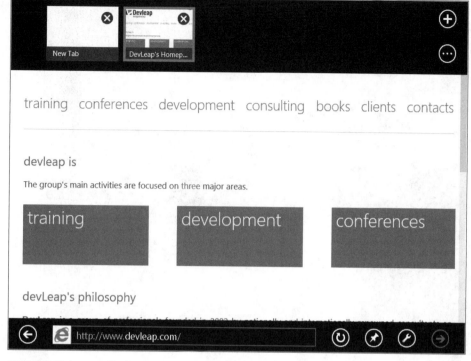

FIGURE 2-18 Internet Explorer 10 with the App Bars open.

It's important to include only the most vital and frequently used controls in the main canvas, leaving the less important commands visible only through edge gestures (typically in the App Bar). A Windows 8 user should be able to discover your application commands in a natural way because nearly all apps on Windows 8 work in exactly the same way.

Comfort and touch

Windows 8 and the innovations concerning the user experience have been developed to satisfy the growing demand for a more touch-friendly operating system. Designing a user interface for tablets, for example, is not just a question of adjusting size and displaying objects in a canvas, but is mainly a rediscovery of the interaction between man and machine. The main input mechanism is represented by touches and gestures, which required a great deal of studies about usability. Microsoft has performed a lot of usability testing with Windows 8 installed on tablet devices to understand how to improve the usability in these contexts. From various experiments, some interesting facts have emerged. One of the first findings is that most users hold the tablet with both hands, but leave their thumbs free to move on the screen. Thanks to this information, Microsoft engineers have developed a sort of map that identifies which areas of the screen are easiest to reach with thumbs, and which are more difficult. The result is shown in Figure 2-19.

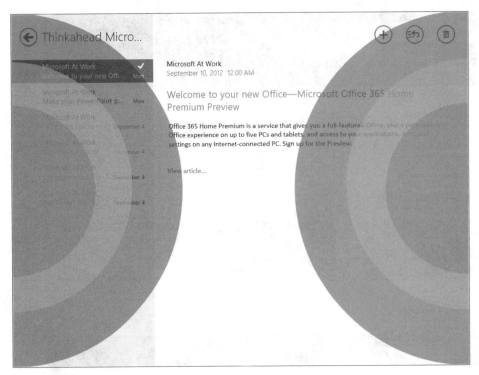

FIGURE 2-19 The map of the easiest areas to reach.

This map makes it easy to see that the inner green areas are the easiest to reach, while the middle yellow ones are less comfortable to reach, and the outer red areas require an even greater effort.

This valuable image is important to you as developer or designer because it reveals that you should put the most common controls in the user interface in the green (inner) area of the image, thus increasing the usability of your application—but remember to avoid areas managed by the operating system. The map can also help you see when to place controls in the App Bar. In fact, according to this scheme you should place the most frequently used commands in the left or right side of the App Bar and less frequently used controls towards the center of the App Bar. Figure 2-20 illustrates some examples.

FIGURE 2-20 A composition of different App Bars.

Even the Windows 8 touch keyboard presents a nice feature that allows users to split the keyboard into segments so that the most used parts are within the green (inner) area of the scheme. Figure 2-21 illustrates this feature.

FIGURE 2-21 The software keyboard in the split mode.

It thus becomes crucial to design applications so that they become fully usable with various input modes (it is important to think about touch and gestures, but don't forget the classic mouse and keyboard). One recommendation is to design your user interface by considering touch input first, and if you use the framework standard controls (which you will become acquainted with in later chapters), you will get support for mouse and keyboard "out of the box," that is, without the need to write code to specifically enable those input devices. To clarify these concepts, try the following procedure.

Touch, mouse, and keyboard support

1. Start Windows 8.

2. From the Start screen, click or touch the Weather App tile. The Weather App will launch.

3. If you have a touch screen, swipe your finger from bottom to top, starting at the lower edge of the screen. The App Bars will appear.

4. Take a look at the two App Bar controls in the top and bottom of the screen.

5. Close the App Bar by touching the middle of the screen.

   If you're using a mouse, place your mouse cursor anywhere on the screen and right-click. The App Bars will appear. Take a look at the App Bar controls.

6. Close the App Bars by clicking in the middle of the screen.

   If you have a touch screen, perform a swipe from right to left in the right-hand side of the screen. The Charms will appear. Take a look at the Charms.

7. Touch the screen inside the app to make the Charms disappear.

   If you're using a keyboard, press Windows+C. Take another look at the Charms.

As you can see, all the native objects of the framework fully support all input modes: touch, mouse, keyboard, and digital stylus. This is definitely a great convenience for developers.

Design the user experience of your apps for touch-first, following the same approach that even the designers of complex applications such as Microsoft Office for Windows 8 have followed. Avoid designing different user interfaces for touch, mouse, and keyboard; use a single layout for all the input modes. If you have a traditional mouse and keyboard setup, you will be able to create and test applications for the touch environment using the Windows 8 Simulator that is included with Visual Studio 2012. In fact, the tool has a command called Basic Touch Mode. In this mode, your mouse pointer becomes like a finger; when you click the simulator it will be handled as a finger touch. It thus becomes vital to understand the new touch language introduced with Windows 8, how to use it in your app, and to avoid inventing new fancy or special gestures that would result only in confusion for the user. Fortunately for all developers, Microsoft designers have performed a sublime job of simplifying the various modes and minimizing the number and the types of gestures supported. The ultimate goal of the new Windows is simplicity of use, and having a large number of complex gestures would certainly decrease the usability of the entire system. Figure 2-22, taken from Microsoft documentation, summarizes the touch gestures supported by the system and explains their meaning.

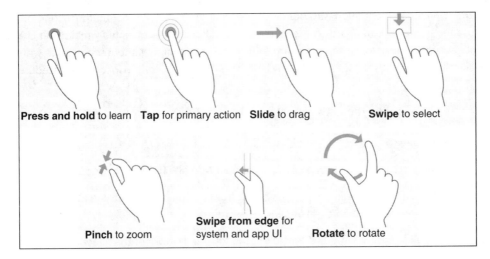

FIGURE 2-22 Touch gestures supported by Windows 8.

Gestures such as tap, slide, pinch (and stretch), and rotate are so frequent in any touch system that there is not much to add here to describe them. However, a few of the others deserve some further explanation. The first gesture illustrated in Figure 2-22, "press and hold," is associated with the action of "learn," so it should be used to show a tooltip, a help screen, or something that can provide further information and explanation. You should avoid using such a gesture to show a contextual submenu or enable some editing mode. As you can see from the image, there is no double-tap gesture because that was considered to be too difficult to use.

The swipe gesture, typically performed on an element of a collection, allows you to select or deselect an item. If you have a device with touch support, try the following procedure.

Swipe gesture

1. Start Windows 8.

2. In the Start screen, move your finger from the top toward the bottom of a tile.

   It now shows a selected checkbox in the top-right corner.

3. Perform a swipe gesture on another tile.

   Notice that a selected checkbox appears on that tile.

4. Perform a swipe on the tile you selected at the beginning of this procedure.

   Notice how the current element is now deselected.

5. Swipe again on the second tile.

   Notice how the second tile is now deselected.

6. Perform another swipe on any tile, but this time keep dragging the tile towards the bottom. You will notice that the tile becomes "detached" from the rest of the Start screen.

7. Drag the tile where you prefer and then release it.

The previous procedure, very trivial and at first glance obvious, has brought some interesting considerations about the touch gesture to light. First, the various gestures are reversible, that is, no matter which state you are in you can always go back to the previous state. Another important consideration is based on the absence (or, at least, the strong reduction) of the "modes." In the previous procedure, you did not have to choose some other element, such as a menu item, to enter the element selection mode; a gesture was the only thing you needed. Similarly, you did not have to take multiple actions to get to tile positioning mode; a natural gesture (drag and move) was sufficient to complete the step.

Semantic Zoom

Another very important feature of the new Windows 8 touch language is represented by the innovative Semantic Zoom. The pinch and stretch gestures are usually associated with an optical zoom feature, and Windows 8 fully respects this principle, though the Semantic Zoom extends the concept to allow simple navigation among larger data sets. The next procedure illustrates this feature.

Semantic Zoom

1. Start Windows 8.

2. If you have a touch screen, perform a swipe from right to left starting from the right-hand side of the screen and then touch the Search charm.

   If you don't have a touch screen, press Windows+F. Windows 8 will open the search page.

3. Click or tap "Apps" in the list on the righthand side of the screen. The list of applications installed on your PC will appear.

4. If you have a touch screen, perform the pinch gesture in the middle of the screen.

If you don't have a touch screen, scroll down the mouse wheel while holding the Ctrl button.

Notice the new visualization—a set of letters representing the initials of the applications presented in the previous list.

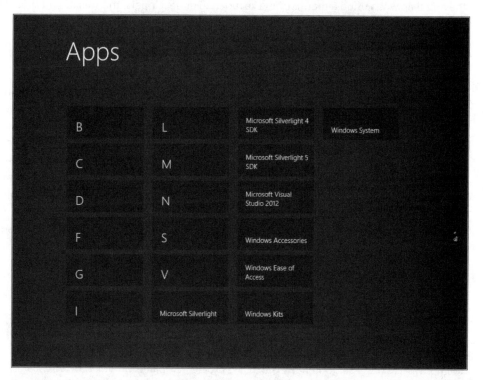

As you can see, the pinch operation isn't just an optical zoom (in this case, it would have rendered the same list shown in the previous screenshot, just with different dimensions). Instead, it's a higher-level semantic visualization of the data.

5. Touch or click a letter. You will go back to the default visualization, but the focus is now on the applications grouped under the letter you selected; in fact, the Semantic Zoom's purpose is to simplify navigation through long lists of data on a touch device.

As you saw, Semantic Zoom offers two different views of the data: a "zoomed-in" view (the default view), where the list of data is presented expanded, and a "zoomed-out" view that typically represents the grouping keys of the underlying data. For a complete example of these concepts and the use of the *SemanticZoom* control, see Chapter 9.

Discussing touches and gestures also raises some questions about performance. Mouse and keyboard input is "indirect" input to a device, and people are usually inclined to tolerate slight lags in interface response better using this type of input. In contrast, touch, which is by definition a "direct" input, amplifies any problems associated with an app's performance. In other words, if you select a user interface element through a gesture, people tend to expect a more immediate response from the app than when using a mouse or the keyboard. For developers, this means you should test your apps fully for performance, especially on low-end devices.

Animations

To increase the perception of fluidity within the entire system, Windows 8 uses lots of animations. If you pay attention, you will notice that the Microsoft designers have inserted animations in most operations: opening an application, removing an element from a list, tapping a user interface control, navigating from one page to another, closing an application, and so on. These animations are light, non-invasive, and non-tiring in the long run. They give a sense of fluidity to the entire system. So you can take advantage of animations easily, Microsoft has developed the Animation Library, a collection of fluid and natural animations that you can use in your applications. Interestingly, the standard framework controls already use the features offered by this library. For example, the *GridView* control uses animations when you select an element (using the same look and feel as the selection of a tile in the Start screen).

Different form factors

Windows 8 is not just for tablet devices; it can be installed on traditional notebooks, desktops, and ultrabooks. Each device may have its own screen size, resolution, and definition. As a developer or designer, it is your job to make sure that your application can be used on any of these form factors to improve its sales. The good news is that the project templates provided by Visual Studio 2012 and the standard controls of the framework provide excellent scaling support, even though not all that support comes pre-defined "out of the box." You will always need to use the various controls in the most appropriate way and test your code often to ensure that the user interface adapts appropriately to whatever device is in use. In Chapter 7, "Enhance the user experience," you will work with the Windows 8 Simulator installed with Visual Studio 2012. This tool lets you test your Windows 8 app with varying resolutions.

Figure 2-23 shows a screenshot of an app running on a device with a resolution of 1366 × 768 pixels (a tablet device with an 10.6' screen). Notice how the list of elements exceeds the screen dimensions on the right side.

FIGURE 2-23 The Bing Travel App running on an 10.6 inch screen.

Figure 2-24 shows the same application running at a resolution of 2560 × 1440 pixels (on a 27-inch screen), where the available space has been used to display more content.

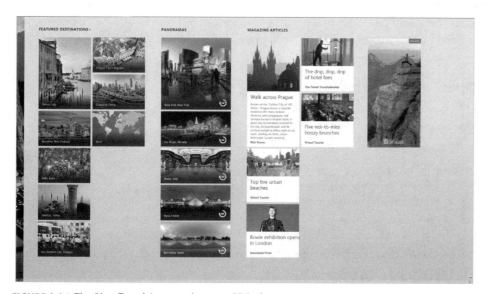

FIGURE 2-24 The Bing Travel App running on a 27-inch screen.

More specifically, this app is based on the Grid App (XAML) project template and uses a unique *GridView* control to display the data, so that you don't need to use different forms for different resolutions—a single layout is sufficient.

As far as the graphic assets are concerned, you have two different options. The first option involves vector art and thus uses Path objects from the XAML framework. The second option consists of rasterized assets (such as .jpg and .png files). For vector art, scaling support is completely transparent and guaranteed, while for raster assets, you can address scaling sufficiently by including three distinct versions of the same image in your Visual Studio 2012 project with a scaling of, respectively, 100 percent, 140 percent, and 180 percent. At runtime, the platform will analyze the device in use and load the most appropriate asset. Figure 2-25 is a rasterized graphic asset from a real app with the three different scales.

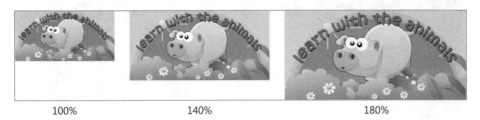

| 100% | 140% | 180% |

FIGURE 2-25 Different scales of the same graphic asset.

Don't forget that you must take into account not only the landscape display (the default visualization) but also the portrait display. It's your job to discover which mode is enabled and what changes to the user interface your app must implement to respond to a change in orientation (for example, the back button might be smaller in the portrait version, the left margin of the application might be different, and so on). Chapter 9 contains an example of these concepts.

Snapped and fill view

The last feature of a Windows 8 app to take into account is related to the "snapped" state of an app. The following procedure is useful to explain the idea.

Snap state

1. Start Windows 8.

2. From the Start screen, launch the Weather App.

3. Press the Window button on the keyboard to go back to the Start screen. If you have a touch device, you can touch the Windows charm.

4. From the Start screen, launch Internet Explorer.

5. Place your mouse cursor in the top-left corner of the screen to open a thumbnail of the previous active application—in this case, that should be the Weather App.

6. Drag the thumbnail to the center of the screen. You'll see a snapped area outlined on the left. At that point, release the mouse.

The Weather App is running and is in the snapped state, a state that offers a "reduced" visualization of its content (the snap view is 320 pixels wide).

7. Move the delimiter of the snapped area to the right and release the mouse button at around two-thirds of the overall screen size.

Now the Weather App is currently in the filled state, while Internet Explorer has been reduced to the snapped state.

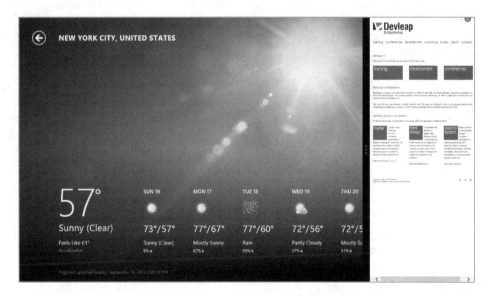

From this procedure, you have learned that an app may be in one of three different states: full screen (default), filled, or snapped. It is a good idea, as a developer or designer, to provide a special display for the snapped status because it allows users to run your app even while performing other activities with other applications. Chapter 9 contains an example on how you can customize your user interface when a change in app state occurs.

Many native Windows 8 applications can inspire you as to how you might want to handle the snapped application state for your apps. Figures 2-26 and 2-27 show side-by-side screenshots of snapped (on the left) and full screen (on the right) applications (the full screen views have been cropped so they'll fit in this book). Figure 2-26 is taken from the Bing Daily App; Figure 2-27 is taken from the Bing Finance App.

FIGURE 2-26 The Bing Daily App running in snapped state (on the left) and in full screen state (on the right).

FIGURE 2-27 The Bing Finance App running in snapped state (on the left) and in full screen state (on the right).

Summary

In this chapter, you have explored the basics of Windows 8 UI style—a little history, the influences, and the philosophy underlying the user experience upon which the entire operating system is based. You've seen how Windows 8 values contents over the container ("content not chrome"), a crystal clear typography, the grid system, and the simplification of iconography. You have also seen the basics of how you can design the user experience for your own applications so that they are consistent with the operating system principles. These basics include using the Visual Studio 2012 templates to create a proper "silhouette"; designing the interface for "touch-first," using common conventions, creating custom tiles, employing App Bars and Charms correctly, and making your application aware of snapped and filled states and orientation changes. Also remember that an app in harmony with the ecosystem of Windows 8 is, most likely, an app that is pleasant to look at and comfortable to use.

Quick reference

To	Do this
Design a great Windows 8 UI style app	Respect the following principles: • Enhance the functionality and the content, not the container • Industrialize the software and user interface, create projects and not products • Use clear typography • Take advantage of the grid system • Prefer photos over drawings • Select few and contrasting colors • Strive for international language • Employ essential iconography
Improve the "silhouette" of your app	Use the project templates provided by Visual Studio 2012.
Enhance the integration with the operating system	• Customize the application's tile • Use the App Bar controls • Implement the snapped state
Design the user experience for different input devices	Design for "touch-first," and use the standard framework controls.
Define the positions of the controls	Position the most important controls in the areas that are the easiest to reach and make less common commands reachable through the edge gestures (typically in the App Bar).

CHAPTER 3

My first Windows 8 app

After completing this chapter, you will be able to

- Install and use the Microsoft Visual Studio 2012 tools to develop a Windows 8 app.

- Understand and use the Project template.

- Create a simple application using C# and Visual Basic (VB).

- Test the application.

- Use the Windows 8 Runtime (WinRT) APIs from a Windows 8 application.

The preceding chapters showed you how Microsoft Windows 8 provides a new user interface, a completely new user experience, and exposes a new set of application programming interfaces (APIs) called Windows Runtime APIs (WinRT). The new user interface and experience is based around the Windows 8 UI style you just learned about in Chapter 2, "Windows 8 UI style."

This chapter translates what you saw into practice. You will start by creating a simple Windows 8 app from scratch using one of the templates provided by Visual Studio 2012. Then you will deploy it to the local machine. Finally, you will implement a simple call to some WinRT APIs.

Software installation

To start developing Windows 8 applications, you need Visual Studio 2012. This new version of Visual Studio can be installed to run side by side with an existing Visual Studio 2010 installation and contains the .NET Framework version 4.5. The .NET Framework 4.5 is not a major release but it does contain some important features that enable the use of WinRT APIs. Even though you can develop applications using other versions of Windows and deploy them to a Windows 8 box or test it in the provided emulator, we suggest you install the development environment directly on a machine with Windows 8. This will speed up the development and testing processes on hardware-related components: for instance, if your apps use the accelerometer, the inclinometer, the camera, or any other sensor, the testing and debugging phase will be more accurate and quicker.

To download Windows 8, go to *http://msdn.microsoft.com/windows/apps*—the home page for the Windows 8 app development. From this page, it is easy to reach all the downloads for Windows 8. In the Getting Started section, you can find useful information for the download and installation process.

Note Because URLs and component packaging may vary over time, start looking for Windows 8 and Visual Studio 2012 on the Windows 8 home page (*http://msdn.microsoft .com/windows/apps*) or search for it on Bing (*http://www.bing.com*).

As you saw in Chapter 1, "Introduction to Windows Store apps," Visual Studio 2012 Express for Windows 8 is a free version of Visual Studio tailored to contain just what you need to develop a Windows 8 app. You can also use the full version of Visual Studio 2012 by installing it on top of the Express edition or you can keep it as a separate installation.

To summarize, the components you need to start developing a Windows 8 app are the following:

- **Visual Studio 2012 Express edition for Windows 8**   On top of this version, you can install a more advanced edition of Visual Studio 2012 (for instance the Ultimate edition).

- **The Windows 8 SDK**   To obtain the templates and the integration with the Windows 8 environment, this component is packaged together with Visual Studio 2012 Express for Windows 8.

- **Windows 8**   You'll need this to test the application in the real environment.

- **A developer license**   The integrated development environment (IDE) handles this requirement automatically and all you need to do is select Yes when the dialog box pops up.

Windows Store project templates

The easiest way to start developing a Windows 8 application is to use one of the out-of-the-box project templates that are available. Visual Studio 2012 provides a group of templates called "Windows Store" templates to develop an application for the Windows Store. These templates create all the files you need in the project to start developing, testing, and deploying the application on your local machine and the emulator, and they include a procedure to create an application package suitable for the Windows Store.

Each supplied template provides a solid starting point so that you can begin developing different kinds of Windows Store applications. The following list summarizes the characteristics of the various templates:

- **Blank App (XAML)**   This template provides a minimal skeleton using Windows Store frameworks.

- **Grid App (XAML)**   This template provides a multipage project for navigating multiple layers of content. The item details can be reached by tapping or clicking on the item itself and are displayed on a dedicated page.

- **Split App (XAML)**   This template is a good starting point to create a master details list of items using a list on the left of the page and the details directly shown in the right of the same page.

- **Class Library (Windows Store apps)** The resulting project is the classic class library that can be used to centralize the code for Windows Store applications. This template can also be used to create a Windows Runtime component.

- **Windows Runtime Component** This allows the development of a component that can be used by Windows Store applications, regardless of the programming languages in which the app is written.

- **Unit Test Library (Windows Store apps)** The goal for this template is to create a project that contains unit tests to be used with Windows Store apps, Windows Runtime components, or class libraries for Windows Store apps.

In the following procedure, you'll create a project.

Create the project

As you may remember from Chapter 1, the SDK setup process installed some new templates and wizards to facilitate the creation of a Windows Store project. In the graphic that follows step 3, under the C# or VB project types, you can see a new section, named Windows Store, which represents the entry point for this new kind of project. This section exposes all the templates that are tailored to Windows 8.

1. Create a new Application project. To do that, open Visual Studio 2012, and from the File menu, select New Project (the sequence can be File | New | Project for full-featured versions of Visual Studio). Choose Visual C# in the Templates tree and Windows Store from the list of installed templates. Then choose Blank App (XAML) from the list of available projects.

2. Select version 4.5 as the target .NET Framework version for your new project (this step is not necessary in Visual Studio Express edition).

3. Name the new project **MyFirstApp**. Then choose a location on your file system as well as a solution name. When you're finished, click OK.

   If you use a source control system, you can select the Add To Source Control check box.

   The following graphic shows the first step of the New Project wizard: both the project and the solution will be assigned the name MyFirstApp.

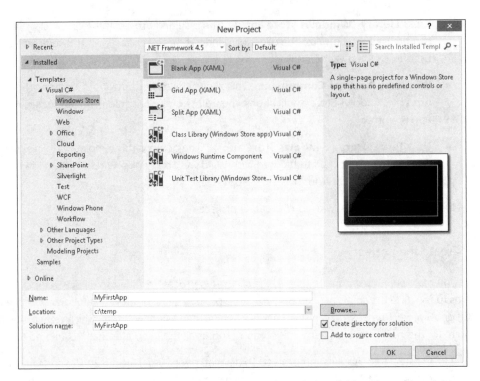

At this stage, Visual Studio 2012 normally creates the solution folder, the project folder, and a project related to the chosen template.

Because you selected the Blank App project template, Visual Studio uses the simplest project structure to create your new application. Figure 3-1 shows the result of the procedure you just completed.

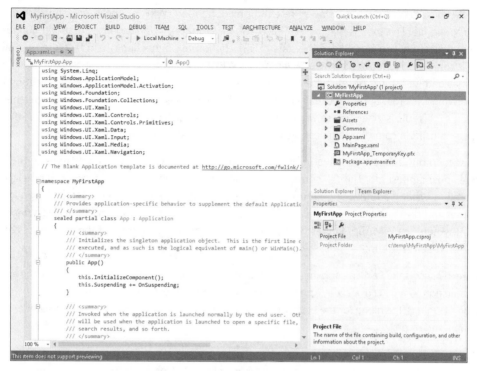

FIGURE 3-1 A blank Windows Store app in Solution Explorer.

In fact, you can easily find a file called App.xaml and one named MainPage.xaml, as well as a folder named Properties, that contains the classic AssemblyInfo.cs file. The file list is similar to the one you would get if you had created a Windows Presentation Foundation Browser application (or even a Windows Presentation Foundation application); however, there are some differences.

The first difference from a Windows Presentation Foundation (WPF) application is the absence of the app.config file. This means that, as in a Microsoft Silverlight or Windows Presentation Foundation Browser application, you cannot use the classic .NET configuration mechanism. In fact, the runtime system is somewhat sandboxed as in a Silverlight or WPF Browser application: specifically, the users cannot navigate to the file system where the application will be installed and change application files because Windows Store apps are usually downloaded and installed from the Windows Store. The exception to this rule is when you're working in the development environment, where Visual Studio 2012 (or you using a command-line tool) can install the application for testing purposes.

The second difference from Silverlight and WPF Browser applications is the presence of the Package.appxmanifest file. This file contains a description of the application (its icon and synergy with the operating system) and the operating system features that the application uses, called "application capabilities and declarations." From this perspective, the project is similar to one targeting Windows Phone 7.x, where the WMAppManifest.xml file informs the operating system of the capabilities the application requires to run.

Figure 3-2 shows the Package.appxmanifest designer that Visual Studio provides to simplify the application definition. As you can see, the Application UI tab lets you choose the Display Name of the application—that is, the name for the Start screen—the application description, three logos for the application, and so on.

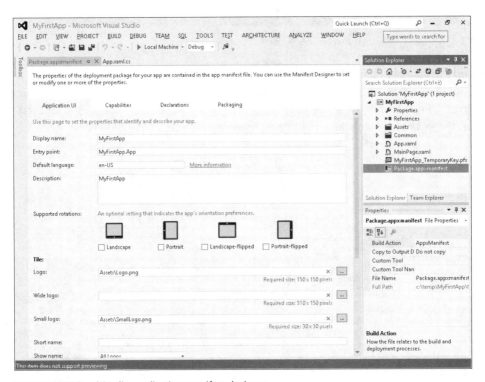

FIGURE 3-2 Visual Studio application manifest designer.

Another similarity with a Windows Phone project is the presence of some default images in the project. These images are available in the Assets folder and are referenced from the Package.appxmanifest file. The default template uses an application logo image for the default application tile (Logo.png), an image for the initial splash screen (SplashScreen.png), a small logo image displayed in the application's tile—used if the application changes the tile size from code (SmallLogo.png)—and last but not least, the image used by the Windows Store to represent the application (StoreLogo.png). As you can see from Figure 3-2, there is no default wide logo, nor is this image referenced by the Package.appxmanifest.

If you run the application now, leaving all the default files and manifest settings intact, you will experience a short delay while Visual Studio deploys the application to the developer system, and then you will see the splash screen, followed by a completely blank screen that represents the application. This may seem strange—because Visual Studio has traditionally added some sample text to all its templates—but as you will discover in the following procedure, many things happened during application deployment.

Explore the deployed app on the system

First, note the absence of the classic window frame with the "X," minimize, and maximize buttons. In fact, this is the first version of Windows without windows.

Follow these steps to explore what Visual Studio has asked Windows 8 to do during the deployment of the application.

1. Click the Start button of your tablet or keyboard, or go to the left-bottom corner of the screen using your mouse and click Start to return to the Start screen.

2. Scroll to the right using your finger, the mouse wheel, or the bottom scroll bar until you reach the rightmost end of the application Tiles on the Start screen.

    At the very end of the application tiles, you'll see your first deployed Windows 8 app, which has a tile with the name "MyFirstApp."

3. Click on the app's tile to reopen the application.

4. Return to Visual Studio and stop the debugging session by clicking Stop Debugging or pressing Shift+F5.

5. Repeat steps 1 and 2 and now tap and hold your finger (or right-click). The command bar will ask if you want to uninstall or simply unpin the application; "unpin" means deleting the application tile from the start menu, while leaving the application on the system.

6. Unpin the application by clicking Unpin.

7. Move your mouse to the bottom-right corner of the screen to view the Charms, and then choose Search, or press Windows+Q on the keyboard. The Search pane will appear at the right of the screen.

8. Type the first few letters of the name of the application and choose Apps from the list of places where Windows should search. Your application will appear in the left pane.

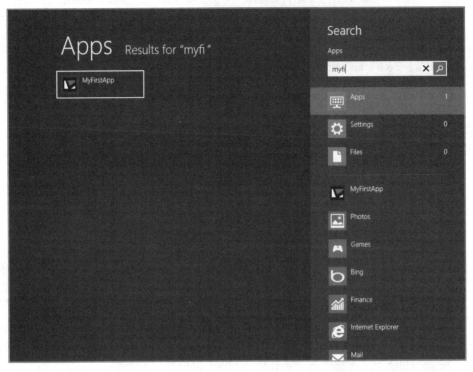

9. You can launch the application by either tapping or clicking the application's name—but don't do that now. Instead, tap and hold (or right-click) the application to open the command bar.

10. Pin the application using the Pin button. The application is now listed in the Start screen using the default tile. You can verify the tile's presence by repeating steps 1 and 2 of this procedure.

Note that you can search for files or settings within the same Search pane, as well as perform a search inside the listed applications. These applications have declared the Search capability in their Package.appxmanifest. Next, you'll add the Search capability declaration to the simple application you are developing in this chapter.

Before proceeding, if you launched the application from the Search pane or the Start screen—that is, if you launched the application from outside of Visual Studio—you need to close it before you can deploy it again. If you use Visual Studio to launch an application, the first operation that the IDE requests from the operating system is package deployment. When deployment is complete, Visual Studio starts the application and attaches the debugger to it. If you stop the debugging session from Visual Studio, the Windows process is terminated; the same termination occurs if the application crashes. If the application is launched outside of Visual Studio using the default template, you do not have any close button—as you saw in the previous examples. The application occupies the entire screen and you will need to manually stop (*kill* is a better word) the process from running indefinitely. You can do this through the Windows Task Manager, or by pressing Alt-F4, or using the application close gesture to close the application in a more graceful way. (The application close gesture closes an application when you quickly swipe your finger from the top-center of the screen to the bottom-center.)

You will learn the details of the application lifecycle in Chapter 4, "Application lifecycle management," but for now it is important to understand that Windows 8 has a completely new way of managing the lifecycle of applications. An application is in the running state when the user uses it (the user has chosen the application as the foreground application); when the user leaves the application in any manner—by clicking Start, going back to the previous application, or starting a new search, and so on—the system may suspend the application or terminate it if the system needs more memory. This behavior is in some ways similar to the application lifecycle management in Windows Phone 7.x, as well as other modern operating systems.

As mentioned, Task Manager provides another way to stop a running application. Task Manager has been modified in Windows 8 so you can also see an application's status under the advanced options of the View menu. If you cannot see the View menu, click More Details in Task Manager. Figure 3-3 shows MyFirstApp in the suspended state within Task Manager. Save the Planet, a real application ported from Windows Phone 7 to Windows 8, is not in the suspended state—meaning that it is still running.

Name	Status	9% CPU	37% Memory	0% Disk	0% Network
Apps (7)					
Calendar	Suspended	0%	37.0 MB	0 MB/s	0 Mbps
Games	Suspended	0%	52.6 MB	0 MB/s	0 Mbps
▷ Microsoft Visual Studio 2012 (32...		0%	91.7 MB	0 MB/s	0 Mbps
MyFirstApp (32 bit)	Suspended	0%	7.5 MB	0 MB/s	0 Mbps
Save The Planet		1.1%	26.6 MB	0 MB/s	0 Mbps
Photos	Suspended	0%	38.5 MB	0 MB/s	0 Mbps
▷ Task Manager		0.9%	7.9 MB	0 MB/s	0 Mbps
Background processes (15)					
COM Surrogate		0%	0.9 MB	0 MB/s	0 Mbps
Communications Service	Suspended	0%	5.2 MB	0 MB/s	0 Mbps
Communications Service	Suspended	0%	7.8 MB	0 MB/s	0 Mbps
Device Association Framework ...		0.9%	3.5 MB	0 MB/s	0 Mbps
Host Process for Windows Tasks		0%	2.9 MB	0 MB/s	0 Mbps

FIGURE 3-3 Task Manager showing the suspended/running state for a Windows Store app.

This mechanism applies only to Windows Store applications and not to classic .NET or Win32 applications. In fact, the two instances of Visual Studio, Paint (used to take the screenshots for this book) and many other Win32 applications are in the running state.

Adding the Search Declaration to the application manifest

In this procedure, you will add the Search Declaration to the application manifest to let the user search for text "inside" this sample application. Follow these simple steps inside the Visual Studio 2012 project you are building.

1. Double-click the Package.appxmanifest file inside the MyFirstApp application to open the designer.

2. Click the Declarations tab to manage the declarations for this application.

3. Choose Search from the Available Declaration listbox, and then click Add. As stated in the Description section, the Search declaration "...registers the application as providing search functionality. Users will be able to search the application from anywhere in the system." The phrase "search the application" means passing the search text entered by the user to the application so it can search inside the application.

4. Before testing the application, click the Application UI tab and make sure that All Logos is selected in the Show Name drop-down list.

5. To change the default logo, copy the .png files you can find in the Chapter 03 Demo Files in the Logos folder to the Assets folder of the project. The files have the default names so you do not need to modify the Package.appxmanifest.

6. Right-click the project item in the solution (MyFirstApp) and choose Deploy. This operation deploys the application to Windows 8 without launching a debugging session.

7. Open the Start screen by using the Start button and scroll to the right to verify that the name and the new logo appear on the application tile.

8. Press Windows+F or Windows+Q to activate one of the Windows Search interfaces (the first opens the search page to search for files; the second to search for applications), and type some text in the textbox. Scroll the resulting list of applications to verify that your application is shown in the list. You can click an application to open it (the sample application does nothing right now); you will add the code to implement the search in the last part of this chapter.

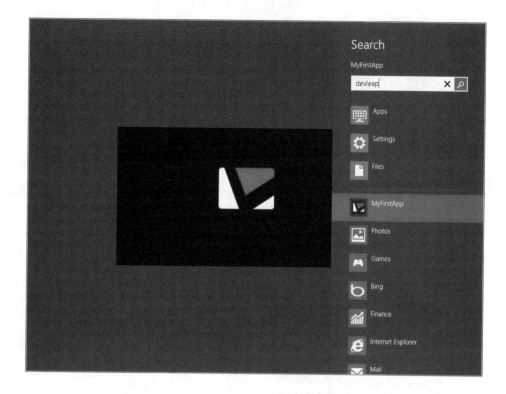

Adding UI elements

In this section, you will analyze the remaining project items that the template created and add some code to build a list of people and bind it to the user interface.

> **Note** It is beyond the scope of this chapter to analyze the various binding techniques, as well as the user interface patterns such as MVVM (Model View ViewModel) or MVC (Model View Controller).

Let's start by analyzing the code proposed by the Visual Studio 2012 template. You have explored the meaning and functionality of the application manifest and the image folder. Listing 3-1 shows the XAML source code for the main page, which has been modified to contain a *ListView* standard user control that will display the *FullName* property of a list of bound elements.

LISTING 3-1 Modified MainPage.xaml page

```
<Page
    x:Class="MyFirstApp.MainPage"
    xmlns="http://schemas.microsoft.com/winfx/2006/xaml/presentation"
    xmlns:x="http://schemas.microsoft.com/winfx/2006/xaml"
    xmlns:local="using:MyFirstApp"
    xmlns:d="http://schemas.microsoft.com/expression/blend/2008"
```

```
    xmlns:mc="http://schemas.openxmlformats.org/markup-compatibility/2006"
    mc:Ignorable="d">

    <Grid Background="{StaticResource ApplicationPageBackgroundThemeBrush}">
        <ListView x:Name="list" DisplayMemberPath="FullName" />
    </Grid>
</Page>
```

The page includes the classic XAML definition for a page control represented by the *MyFirstApp.MainPage* class. The user control references four XML namespaces—just like a Silverlight project, a WPF app, or a Windows Phone 7.x application.

By default, the template uses a *Grid* for the layout, but you will change this in a later procedure, where you will add some styling to change the look and feel of this simple application.

You will also modify the code behind for the MainPage.xaml page, as shown in Listing 3-2, so that it calls a fake "business layer" that returns a list of people represented by the *Person* class you will also implement shortly.

LISTING 3-2 Modified MainPage.xaml.cs code

```csharp
using System;
using System.Collections.Generic;
using System.IO;
using System.Linq;
using Windows.Foundation;
using Windows.Foundation.Collections;
using Windows.UI.Xaml;
using Windows.UI.Xaml.Controls;
using Windows.UI.Xaml.Controls.Primitives;
using Windows.UI.Xaml.Data;
using Windows.UI.Xaml.Input;
using Windows.UI.Xaml.Media;
using Windows.UI.Xaml.Navigation;

// The Blank Page item template is documented at http://go.microsoft.com/fwlink/?LinkId=234238

namespace MyFirstApp
{
    /// <summary>
    /// An empty page that can be used on its own or navigated to within a Frame.
    /// </summary>
    public sealed partial class MainPage : Page
    {
        public MainPage()
        {
            this.InitializeComponent();

            // Fill the ListView
            var biz = new Biz();
            list.ItemsSource = biz.GetPeople();

        }
```

```
/// <summary>
/// Invoked when this page is about to be displayed in a Frame.
/// </summary>
/// <param name="e">Event data that describes how this page was reached.  The Parameter
/// property is typically used to configure the page.</param>
protected override void OnNavigatedTo(NavigationEventArgs e)
{
}
    }
}
```

Modify and test the application

1. Modify the MainPage.xaml file so that its contents are identical to Listing 3-1.

2. Open the code-behind file (MainPage.xaml.cs) and insert the bold lines in Listing 3-2.

3. Add a new class file to the project to implement the *Biz* class by right-clicking the term *Biz* in the code behind. Then choose Generate | Class.

4. Generate a method stub for the *GetPeople* method by using the same technique: right-click the *GetPeople* method, choose Generate | Method Stub. Use the following code to replace the code of the Biz.cs file.

```
using System;
using System.Collections.Generic;
using System.Linq;
using System.Text;

namespace MyFirstApp
{
    public class Biz
    {
        public List<Person> GetPeople()
        {
            return new List<Person>()
            {
                new Person() { FullName = "Roberto Brunetti" },
                new Person() { FullName = "Paolo Pialorsi" },
                new Person() { FullName = "Marco Russo" },
                new Person() { FullName = "Luca Regnicoli" },
                new Person() { FullName = "Vanni Boncinelli" },
                new Person() { FullName = "Guido Zambarda" },
                new Person() { FullName = "Jessica Faustinelli" },
                new Person() { FullName = "Katia Egiziano" }
            };
        }
    }

    public class Person
    {
        public string FullName { get; set; }
    }
}
```

5. Run the application.

The code in the *Biz* class simply returns a list of people represented by the *Person* class. For the sake of simplicity, this class has just one property, *FullName*.

When you run the app, the result will look similar to Figure 3-4. You should be able to select a person from the list.

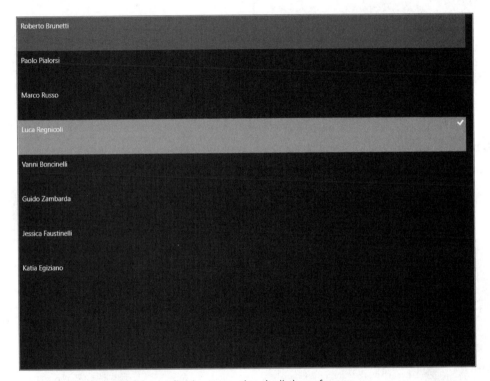

FIGURE 3-4 Main page of the application presenting the listbox of names.

It is time to forget the developer inside you and put on your designer hat to transform the plain vanilla list into something more appealing. Stop the debugging session and return to Visual Studio 2012.

Before refining the appearance of the list, you need to add some more user interface elements to the page—such as a TextBlock control to display the application's title—and make your first app appear more integrated with the Windows 8 environment.

To add a title, you need to modify the XAML source in the MainPage.xaml file, as shown in Listing 3-3:

LISTING 3-3 MainPage.xaml with a *GridView* control

```
<Page
    x:Class="MyFirstApp.MainPage"
    xmlns="http://schemas.microsoft.com/winfx/2006/xaml/presentation"
    xmlns:x="http://schemas.microsoft.com/winfx/2006/xaml"
    xmlns:local="using:MyFirstApp"
    xmlns:d="http://schemas.m icrosoft.com/expression/blend/2008"
```

```
xmlns:mc="http://schemas.openxmlformats.org/markup-compatibility/2006"
mc:Ignorable="d">

<Grid Background="{StaticResource ApplicationPageBackgroundThemeBrush}">
    <Grid.RowDefinitions>
        <RowDefinition Height="140"/>
        <RowDefinition Height="*"/>
    </Grid.RowDefinitions>

    <!-- page title -->
    <Grid Grid.Row="0" Grid.Column="0">
        <Grid.ColumnDefinitions>
            <ColumnDefinition Width="120"/>
            <ColumnDefinition Width="*"/>
        </Grid.ColumnDefinitions>
        <TextBlock x:Name="pageTitle" Grid.Column="1" Text="My First Windows 8 App"
            Style="{StaticResource PageHeaderTextStyle}"/>
    </Grid>

    <ListView x:Name="list" DisplayMemberPath="FullName" Grid.Row="1" Grid.Column="0"
        Margin="116,0,0,46"/>
    </Grid>
</Page>
```

Now, if you press F5 in Visual Studio, your page should look similar to the one shown in Figure 3-5.

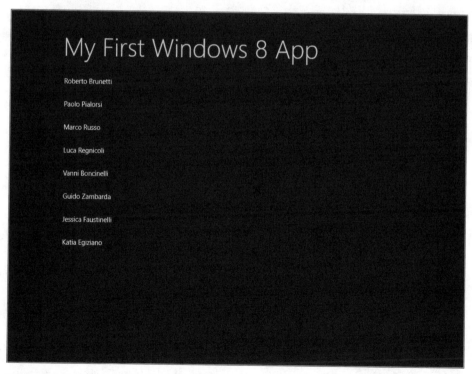

FIGURE 3-5 The main page with the title.

Listing 3-3 used a Grid element as the root element of the page. In XAML, the *Grid* panel allows you to place child elements in rows and columns, as well as define in advance the number and the properties of each row and column by leveraging the *RowDefinitions* and *ColumnDefinitions* properties of the Grid control.

In the example, the main grid was split into two rows. But now it is time to return to the code for a deeper explanation. The first four lines of the *Grid* control definition are as follows.

```
<Grid Background="{StaticResource ApplicationPageBackgroundThemeBrush}">
    <Grid.RowDefinitions>
        <RowDefinition Height="140"/>
        <RowDefinition Height="*"/>
    </Grid.RowDefinitions>
```

To define rows and columns of the main Grid control, we used the *Grid.RowDefinitions* property. This syntax (in the form *classtype.propertyname*, also known as extended property syntax) represents a standard way to set complex properties using the XAML markup language. Within the *RowDefinitions* property you'll find two instances of *RowDefinition*: the first sets the height equal to 140 pixels, whereas the second uses the "*" (star) character to define an unknown-at-design-time value that can fill the remaining space on the screen. Keep in mind that it is very important to design a user interface that can adapt to the user's screen resolution; tablets and devices are available with widely varying screen resolutions and orientations. Using relative rather than absolute sizing helps a great deal in achieving the goal of an adaptive interface.

Assigning each graphic element to a cell of the grid suffices to set the *Grid.Row* and *Grid.Column* properties of the element itself. These properties are also called *attached properties* because they don't belong to the object model of the target element, but are instead "attached" to the control itself. This scenario includes two child elements in the main grid.

- First, a secondary *Grid* control that will contain the title page elements. This *Grid* control has two attached properties: *Grid.Row*, with a value of *0*, and *Grid.Column*, also with a value of *0*. This will place it in the first row and first column of the main grid.

- Next, there is a *ListView* control, with the properties *Grid.Row = "1"* and *Grid.Column = "0,"* that place it in the second row of the first column.

Here are some other useful tidbits of information about how to use the *Grid* control.

- You can omit the *Grid.Row* and/or *Grid.Column* properties if their value is 0.

- If a *Grid* control does not explicitly set the *RowDefinitions* property, it is treated as having a single *RowDefinition* definition whose *Height* property is set to "*".

- If a *Grid* control does not explicitly set the *ColumnDefinitions* property, it is treated as having a single *ColumnDefinition* definition whose *Width* property is set to "*".

- You can set the RowDefinition's *Height* property to "Auto," in which case its size is defined at runtime by the height of the controls it contains.

- You can set the ColumnDefinition's *Width* property to "Auto," in which case its size is defined at runtime by the width of the controls it contains.

Continuing the analysis of the XAML code, you'll find a secondary *Grid* control, further divided into two columns, whose only child is a *TextBlock* control.

```
<TextBlock x:Name="pageTitle" Grid.Column="1" Text="My First Windows 8 App"
    Style="{StaticResource PageHeaderTextStyle}"/>
```

The property setting *Grid.Column = "1"* means that the *TextBlock* control will be positioned in the second column of the parent *Grid* control, whereas the *Style* property references a style called PageHeaderTextStyle using the special *{StaticResource}* syntax (you will explore the basic concepts underlying such styles in later chapters). For now, just remember that a style is simply a container for property settings—a shared object that can be reused in different scenarios.

The property *Grid.Row = "1"* has been added to the *ListView* control so that it will occupy the entire second row of the main grid, and the property *Margin = "116,0,0,46"* places the *ListView* control a few pixels away from the edges of the cell. The *Margin* property is set using four numbers separated by commas. The first number identifies the distance from the left edge and then continuing clockwise; in our example, the *ListView* control is placed 116 pixels away from the left edge, 0 from the top and right edges, and 46 pixels from the bottom edge.

Now try to add some photos to the project. To do that, simply drag the folder called Photos (included in the Demo Files for this chapter) into Visual Studio, and drop it when your cursor is on the project root called MyFirstApp. As a result of this operation, Visual Studio will create a directory called Photos in the project's root (at the same level as the Assets and Common folders) containing some .jpg files.

The next step is to modify the *Person* class to add a custom property called *Photo*, and define the business component to set that property.

Listing 3-4 shows the code for the modified Biz.cs file. Copy Listing 3-4 into the Biz.cs file.

LISTING 3-4 Modified Biz.cs code.

```
using System;
using System.Collections.Generic;
using System.Linq;
using System.Text;

namespace MyFirstApp
{
    public class Biz
    {
        public List<Person> GetPeople()
        {
            return new List<Person>()
            {
```

```
                new Person() { FullName = "Roberto Brunetti", Photo = "Photos/01.jpg" },
                new Person() { FullName = "Paolo Pialorsi", Photo = "Photos/02.jpg" },
                new Person() { FullName = "Marco Russo", Photo = "Photos/03.jpg" },
                new Person() { FullName = "Luca Regnicoli", Photo = "Photos/04.jpg" },
                new Person() { FullName = "Vanni Boncinelli", Photo = "Photos/05.jpg" },
                new Person() { FullName = "Guido Zambarda", Photo = "Photos/06.jpg" },
                new Person() { FullName = "Jessica Faustinelli", Photo = "Photos/07.jpg" },
                new Person() { FullName = "Katia Egiziano", Photo = "Photos/08.jpg" }
        };

        }
    }

    public class Person
    {
        public string FullName { get; set; }
        public string Photo { get; set; }
    }
}
```

To make the view of the people contained in the *ListView* control more appealing, you must modify the control's *ItemTemplate* property. It is important to understand that in XAML, a template object is equivalent to the concept of "structure," and the *ItemTemplate* property represents the structure of the individual items in the *ListView* control.

You start by editing the XAML source code of the MainPage.xaml page to make some tweaks to the *ListView* control.

Replace the ListView definition in the MainPage.xaml:

```
<ListView x:Name="list" DisplayMemberPath="FullName" Grid.Row="1"
    Grid.Column="0" Margin="116,0,0,46"/>
```

with this markup code:

```
<ListView Grid.Row="1" Grid.Column="0" x:Name="list" Margin="116,0,0,46">
    <ListView.ItemTemplate>
        <DataTemplate>
            <TextBlock Text="{Binding FullName}" FontSize="10" />
        </DataTemplate>
    </ListView.ItemTemplate>
</ListView>
```

The second example removes the *DisplayMemberPath* property, which displayed only simple strings connected to the *FullName* property of the bound objects, and replaces it with the *ItemTemplate* property that accepts objects of type *DataTemplate*. In this scenario, the *DataTemplate* consists of a simple label (a TextBlock) with its *Text* property connected to the *FullName* property of the bound object; if you now run the application, you will see the list of people displayed in a smaller font. This is not a huge graphical improvement over the previous version, but these steps function as the basis for subsequent activities you will perform.

In the next step, you will try to change the *DataTemplate* of each item to display both the name and the photo. Replace the DataTemplate definition of the *ListView*.

```
<DataTemplate>
        <TextBlock Text="{Binding FullName}" FontSize="10" />
</DataTemplate>
```

with this code:

```
<DataTemplate>
        <StackPanel Width="200" Height="200">
                <TextBlock Text="{Binding FullName}" />
                <Image Source="{Binding Photo}" />
        </StackPanel>
</DataTemplate>
```

Compared to the previous step, this uses a new panel called *StackPanel*, which places child items arranged vertically, one under the other, or—if the *Orientation* property is set to *Horizontal*—side by side. In this scenario, each item in the *ListView* will be displayed using a *StackPanel* that will render the person's name and photo by binding, respectively, the *FullName* property with the *Text* property of a *TextBlock* and the *Photo* property with the *Source* property of an *Image* control.

Until now we have used the *ListView* control, which can display a series of vertical elements; now, let's try to replace the previous *ListView* definition:

```
<ListView Grid.Row="1" Grid.Column="0" x:Name="list" Margin="116,0,0,46">
        <ListView.ItemTemplate>
                <DataTemplate>
                    <StackPanel Width="200" Height="200">
                        <TextBlock Text="{Binding FullName}" />
                        <Image Source="{Binding Photo}" />
                    </StackPanel>
                </DataTemplate>
        </ListView.ItemTemplate>
</ListView>
```

with this new markup code that uses a *GridView* control:

```
<GridView Grid.Row="1" Grid.Column="0" x:Name="list" Margin="116,0,0,46">
        <GridView.ItemTemplate>
                <DataTemplate>
                    <StackPanel Width="200" Height="200">
                        <TextBlock Text="{Binding FullName}" />
                        <Image Source="{Binding Photo}" />
                    </StackPanel>
                </DataTemplate>
        </GridView.ItemTemplate>
</GridView>
```

The *GridView* control, as the name suggests, is able to display its items in a tabular form, or grid.

If you press F5 in Visual Studio, you will see the result shown in Figure 3-6.

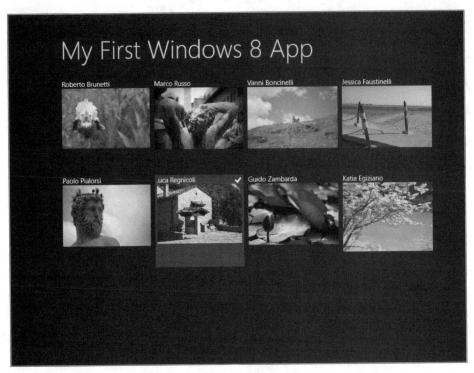

FIGURE 3-6 Element selected in the customized *GridView* control.

This outcome is acceptable, but you can do even better using just a bit of creativity and a few lines of XAML code within the *DataTemplate*. The next listing shows the entire MainPage.xaml page with the code changed in the previous step highlighted in bold.

Replace the entire code of the MainPage.xaml with the following.

```
<Page
    x:Class="MyFirstApp.MainPage"
    xmlns="http://schemas.microsoft.com/winfx/2006/xaml/presentation"
    xmlns:x="http://schemas.microsoft.com/winfx/2006/xaml"
    xmlns:local="using:MyFirstApp"
    xmlns:d="http://schemas.microsoft.com/expression/blend/2008"
    xmlns:mc="http://schemas.openxmlformats.org/markup-compatibility/2006"
    mc:Ignorable="d">

    <Grid Background="{StaticResource ApplicationPageBackgroundThemeBrush}">
        <Grid.RowDefinitions>
            <RowDefinition Height="140"/>
            <RowDefinition Height="*"/>
        </Grid.RowDefinitions>
```

```xml
<!-- Back button and page title -->
<Grid Grid.Row="0" Grid.Column="0">
    <Grid.ColumnDefinitions>
        <ColumnDefinition Width="120"/>
        <ColumnDefinition Width="*"/>
    </Grid.ColumnDefinitions>
    <TextBlock x:Name="pageTitle"  Grid.Column="1"
        Text="My First Windows 8 App" Style="{StaticResource PageHeaderTextStyle}"/>
</Grid>

<GridView Grid.Row="1" Grid.Column="0" x:Name="list" Margin="116,0,0,46">
    <GridView.ItemTemplate>
        <DataTemplate>
            <Grid>
                <Image Source="{Binding Photo}" Width="200" Height="130"
                    Stretch="UniformToFill" />
                <Border Background="#A5000000" Height="45" VerticalAlignment="Bottom">
                    <StackPanel Margin="10,-2,-2,-2">
                        <TextBlock Text="{Binding FullName}" Margin="0,20,0,0"
                            Foreground="#7CFFFFFF" HorizontalAlignment="Left"  />
                    </StackPanel>
                </Border>
            </Grid>
        </DataTemplate>
    </GridView.ItemTemplate>
</GridView>
    </Grid>
</Page>
```

The new *DataTemplate* uses a *Grid* as the root element, with two elements nested within it: an *Image* and a *Border*. Because the *Grid* has neither *RowDefinitions* nor *ColumnDefinitions*, it will render as a single cell containing the two child elements, following the order defined in the markup—that is, the first child element rendered by the runtime will be the *Image* control, then the *Border* control (with all its children) will be rendered in overlay. Beyond those changes, the XAML markup adds only one new thing: the *Background* property of the *Border* control that contains the following string "#A5000000." It is worth noting the first two characters after the #: they represent the alpha channel, or transparency, of the color defined by the subsequent six characters (black, in this case). In fact, in this example, the *Border* does not have a full and "opaque" color as background, but rather uses a semi-transparent black for graphical purposes.

The result is quite in line with the Windows 8 ecosystem and visually pleasing, as you can see in Figure 3-7.

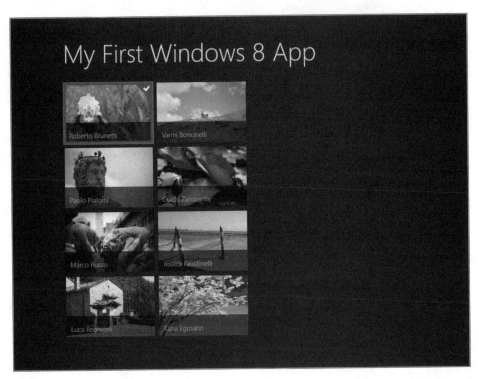

FIGURE 3-7 A different customization of the *GridView* control.

It is worth noting that the controls provided by the framework support all types of input, such as mouse, keyboard, touch screen, and pen for free—in other words, you don't have to write code to make the controls respond to normal input.

Adding search functionality

In this section, you will add the code that enables the searching capability inside the application.

One thing you may notice in a Windows Store application project is the absence of direct references; if you open the *References* element in the project tree you will not find the classic *System. Something* assembly. Instead, there is just a .NET for Windows Store apps reference and a Windows reference. These contain all the Windows Runtime classes you need to develop Windows Store apps.

You can add the complete implementation of the search feature inside the application without adding any references; you need only to add a reference if you create your own class library, for which you would need to add a reference to the corresponding assembly. You can find more information about developing custom class libraries in Chapter 5, "Introduction to the Windows Runtime."

In a previous procedure, you added the Search Declaration to the application, letting the operating system include the application in the Search pane. The declaration in the manifest tells the Windows 8 runtime: "I'm a searchable application." In other words, the system will present the application as a possible target for a search inside the application itself. A search target is the scope for the user's search, which may be a file in the file system, an installed application, a setting in the control panel, or some text inside a searchable application.

When the user selects the application as the target for his or her search, the application is activated for the search and the search string typed by the user is passed to the application. The idea is simple: the application is the only component that can correctly show the search result; no other component, nor the operating system itself, knows about the data inside the application. The way the application presents the data is tailored to the specific application data. In Chapter 6, "Windows Runtime APIs," you will learn more about search integration as well as about other WinRT APIs, such as Share, Webcam, FilePicker, and so on.

The search feature is implemented by a contract, called a *search contract*, that regulates the search interaction between an application and the operating system. The search contract states the following:

- The application needs a registration. This registration is based on the manifest declaration.

- The declaration can include the executable name, that is, the application .exe file name—the entry point for the application that the system will call when the user chooses the application as the search target.

- The application will present the data in the appropriate format using a page.

- The application will receive the search text entered by the user in the entry point. It is the responsibility of the application to present the page with some feedback to the user; the feedback can be the list of items found or a message (in case of search failure). The failure can be a "Not Found" text or graphics, or "Data not available, try again later." Be as specific as you can with the message.

- Windows manages the Search History for the user.

- The application can provide suggestions for the text entered by the user.

Add the search contract

There is a Visual Studio template that provides a simple implementation of a contract that covers all the search points in the preceding list—except for the last one. The first step you will perform in this procedure is to remove the Search Declaration you added in a preceding procedure to explore the default implementation. Then follow the remaining steps to add the search functionality.

1. Remove the Search Declaration from the manifest opening the Package.appxmanifest. Go to the Declarations tab, look for "Search" in the Supported Declaration list, select it, and click Remove. Save the manifest.

2. Add a new Search Contract item by right-clicking the project in the Solution Explorer and choosing Add | New Item.

3. In the Add New Item dialog, select Search Contract and name it **SearchPeople.xaml**.

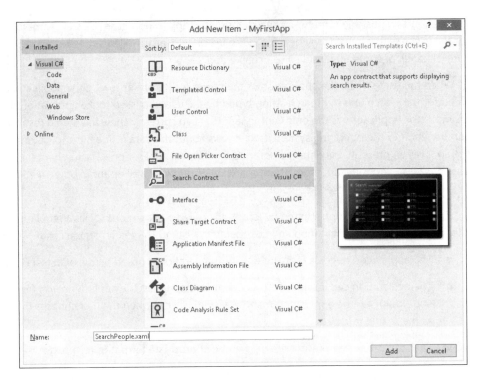

Click OK.

4. In the dialog that asks you to add all the files you need to implement the contract, click Yes.

Test the default search component

Before doing anything else, you can test the application immediately to fully understand the complete flow. You will implement the people search in the procedure after this one.

1. Deploy the application from Visual Studio by right-clicking the project element in the Solution Explorer and choosing Deploy.

2. Press Windows+Q to activate the Search pane.

3. Type the text you want in the search box and choose MyFirstApp from the application list. The operating system will launch the application (which was not running yet because you just deployed it), and activate the search inside the application using a call to the search contract entry point. The application shows the SearchPeople.xaml page that, obviously, presents no results yet.

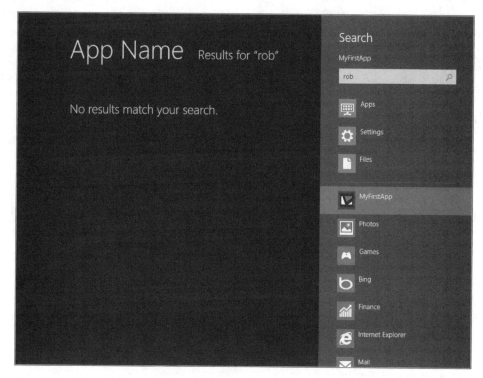

4. Close the application using Alt+F4 or Task Manager.

5. Start the application from the Start screen.

6. Press Windows+Q again to start a new search.

7. Type some text in the search box and choose MyFirstApp in the application list. The result page is identical to the previous one, but the Back button is now enabled because the search target (your application) was already running when you activated the search.

8. Click the Back button and note that the application is in the same state.

9. Go to the Start screen and open another application (Mail works fine). Repeat steps 6 through 8. The result will be always a blank page. However, if you click the Back button, you can see the page that shows the previous search; this demonstrates that the application was put into the suspended state and resumed when the search target was activated.

10. Press Alt+Tab (yes, that key combination still works in Windows 8) to select another application for the foreground.

11. Go to the Start screen and launch your application. The application presents the search result because Windows 8 suspends the application and restores it if the user comes back.

Now that you have explored the search flow, it's time to implement the Search Contract template. The template adds the Search Declaration to the Package.appxmanifest, as you can verify by double-clicking the file and selecting the Declarations tab.

This template also modifies the project—among other things, it adds a new page to display the search results (SearchPeople.xaml or whatever name you used in the Add New Item dialog) that you saw in the previous procedure when you chose MyFirstApp as the search target.

This new page is shown when a search is activated. The contract defines the entry point for the "search call" that, by default, is the *App* class.

The Search Contract Visual Studio Template also modified the App.xaml.cs file to override the *OnSearchActivated* method of the base class so that it shows the search result page. Listing 3-5 shows the complete code for the App.xaml.cs file.

LISTING 3-5 Code-behind file for the *App* class: App.xaml.cs

```
using System;
using System.Collections.Generic;
using System.IO;
using System.Linq;
using Windows.ApplicationModel;
using Windows.ApplicationModel.Activation;
using Windows.Foundation;
using Windows.Foundation.Collections;
using Windows.UI.Xaml;
using Windows.UI.Xaml.Controls;
using Windows.UI.Xaml.Controls.Primitives;
using Windows.UI.Xaml.Data;
using Windows.UI.Xaml.Input;
using Windows.UI.Xaml.Media;
using Windows.UI.Xaml.Navigation;

// The Blank Application template is documented at http://go.microsoft.com/fwlink/?LinkId=234227

namespace MyFirstApp
{
    /// <summary>
    /// Provides application-specific behavior to supplement the default Application class.
    /// </summary>
    sealed partial class App : Application
    {
        /// <summary>
        /// Initializes the singleton application object.
        /// This is the first line of authored code
        /// executed, and as such is the logical equivalent of main() or WinMain().
        /// </summary>
        public App()
        {
            this.InitializeComponent();
            this.Suspending += OnSuspending;
        }

        /// <summary>
        /// Invoked when the application is launched normally by the end user.
        /// Other entry points will be used when the application is launched to open
        /// a specific file, to display, search results, and so forth.
        /// </summary>
        /// <param name="args">Details about the launch request and process.</param>
```

```csharp
protected override void OnLaunched(LaunchActivatedEventArgs args)
{
    Frame rootFrame = Window.Current.Content as Frame;

    // Do not repeat app initialization when the Window already has content,
    // just ensure that the window is active
    if (rootFrame == null)
    {
        // Create a Frame to act as the navigation context and navigate
        // to the first page
        rootFrame = new Frame();

        if (args.PreviousExecutionState == ApplicationExecutionState.Terminated)
        {
            //TODO: Load state from previously suspended application
        }

        // Place the frame in the current Window
        Window.Current.Content = rootFrame;
    }

    if (rootFrame.Content == null)
    {
        // When the navigation stack isn't restored navigate to the first page,
        // configuring the new page by passing required information as a navigation
        // parameter
        if (!rootFrame.Navigate(typeof(MainPage), args.Arguments))
        {
            throw new Exception("Failed to create initial page");
        }
    }
    // Ensure the current window is active
    Window.Current.Activate();
}


/// <summary>
/// Invoked when application execution is being suspended.  Application state is saved
/// without knowing whether the application will be terminated or
/// resumed with the contents
/// of memory still intact.
/// </summary>
/// <param name="sender">The source of the suspend request.</param>
/// <param name="e">Details about the suspend request.</param>
private void OnSuspending(object sender, SuspendingEventArgs e)
{
    var deferral = e.SuspendingOperation.GetDeferral();
    //TODO: Save application state and stop any background activity
    deferral.Complete();
}


/// <summary>
/// Invoked when the application is activated to display search results.
/// </summary>
/// <param name="args">Details about the activation request.</param>
protected async override void OnSearchActivated(Windows.ApplicationModel.Activation.
        SearchActivatedEventArgs args)
{
```

```
    // TODO: Register the Windows.ApplicationModel.Search.SearchPane.
        GetForCurrentView().QuerySubmitted
    // event in OnWindowCreated to speed up searches once the application is already
        running

    // If the Window isn't already using Frame navigation, insert our own Frame
    var previousContent = Window.Current.Content;
    var frame = previousContent as Frame;

    // If the app does not contain a top-level frame, it is possible that this
    // is the initial launch of the app. Typically this method and OnLaunched
    // in App.xaml.cs can call a common method.
    if (frame == null)
    {
        // Create a Frame to act as the navigation context and associate it with
        // a SuspensionManager key
        frame = new Frame();
        MyFirstApp.Common.SuspensionManager.RegisterFrame(frame, "AppFrame");

        if (args.PreviousExecutionState == ApplicationExecutionState.Terminated)
        {
            // Restore the saved session state only when appropriate
            try
            {
                await MyFirstApp.Common.SuspensionManager.RestoreAsync();
            }
            catch (MyFirstApp.Common.SuspensionManagerException)
            {
                //Something went wrong restoring state.
                //Assume there is no state and continue
            }
        }
    }

    frame.Navigate(typeof(SearchPeople), args.QueryText);
    Window.Current.Content = frame;

    // Ensure the current window is active
    Window.Current.Activate();
        }
    }
}
```

The *OnLaunched* method is the standard code suggested by the Windows Store Application template and is needed to activate the main page when the user launches the application. An application is "launched" when its state is not running.

The *OnSearchActivated* method is the code for the Search Contract default implementation. The code instantiates the designated page and calls the *Activate* custom method to pass the received arguments.

The *SearchActivatedEventArgs* used by the *OnSearchActivated* method and the *LaunchActivated EventArgs* used by the *OnLaunched* methods both implement the *IActivatedEventArgs* interface.

The first property of the interface is *Kind,* and it can be one of the values defined in the *Activation-Kind* enumeration. This property lets the developer ask for the kind of activation during launching; for instance, if the application is launched by the user, this property will be *ActivationKind.Launch.* However, if the application is launched by the system when the user designates it as search target, the property will be *ActivationKind.Search.* If the application is activated to receive something from other applications using a Share Contract, the property will be *ActivationKind.ShareTarget.*

The *QueryText* property of the *SearchActivatedEventArgs* contains the text entered by the user in the Search pane. This property is used in the default *OnSearchActivated* method during the navigation to the search page, as you can see in the following excerpt.

```
frame.Navigate(typeof(SearchPeople), args.QueryText);
Window.Current.Content = frame;

// Ensure the current window is active
Window.Current.Activate();
```

As you can see, the search terms are received in the *navigationParameter* parameter of the *LoadState* method of the SearchPeople.xaml.cs page and used to build the *QueryText* property of the user interface in the *DefaultViewModel* property of the page. Listing 3-6 shows the code for this method.

LISTING 3-6 Extract of SearchPeople.xaml.cs code behind

```
protected override void LoadState(Object navigationParameter, Dictionary<String, Object>
pageState)
{
    var queryText = navigationParameter as String;

    // TODO: Application-specific searching logic.  The search process is responsible for
    //       creating a list of user-selectable result categories:
    //
    //       filterList.Add(new Filter("<filter name>", <result count>));
    //
    //       Only the first filter, typically "All", should pass true as a third argument in
    //       order to start in an active state.  Results for the active filter are provided
    //       in Filter_SelectionChanged below.

    var filterList = new List<Filter>();
    filterList.Add(new Filter("All", 0, true));

    // Communicate results through the view model
    this.DefaultViewModel["QueryText"] = '\u201c' + queryText + '\u201d';
    this.DefaultViewModel["Filters"] = filterList;
    this.DefaultViewModel["ShowFilters"] = filterList.Count > 1;
}
```

The code in Listing 3-6 is relatively simple. The first line defines a local variable called queryText to host the text entered by the user in the search box. This text is passed in the search contract as the *QueryText* property of the *SearchActivatedEventArgs.*

The placeholder lets you choose the business logic to look for the text in your data and represents the most important part of this code.

The last three lines of code are useful if you decide to use the default layout to display the search results. The code assigns the text for the query, the filters list and a Boolean to indicate whether to show the filters list in the bindable dictionary (*IObservableMap* in fact derives from *IDictionary*). Let's try to implement the search by reusing the business layer you saw at the beginning of this chapter.

Implement the search logic

In the following procedure, you will implement the logic for retrieving the list of people. Although you can implement the logic using a LINQ (Language Integrated Query) query on the results from the business logic component *List* method, consider passing the search parameter to the business logic component to perform the search in lower layers. Generally speaking, it is a bad idea to filter the entire set of data in memory in the user interface layer. For the sake of simplicity, this sample application has no persistence layer. Thus, you will implement the search in memory inside the business layer.

1. Add a method to the business logic component (Biz.cs) to filter the data source using the following code:

```
public List<Person> GetPeople(String search)
{
        var list = this.GetPeople();
        return list.Where(p => p.FullName.Contains(search)).ToList();
}
```

2. Add a call to the new *GetPeople* method from the SearchPeople.xaml.cs *LoadState* method and assign the result to the *DefaultViewModel* property. Use the following code as a reference (the lines to add are in bold).

```
protected override void LoadState(Object navigationParameter,
    Dictionary<String, Object> pageState)
{
    var queryText = navigationParameter as String;

    // TODO: Application-specific searching logic.  The search process is
    //       responsible for
    //       creating a list of user-selectable result categories:
    //
    //       filterList.Add(new Filter("<filter name>", <result count>));
    //
    //       Only the first filter, typically "All", should pass true as a third
    //       argument
    //       in order to start in an active state.  Results for the active filter
    //       are provided in Filter_SelectionChanged below.

    var biz = new Biz();
    var people = biz.GetPeople(queryText);
    this.DefaultViewModel["Results"] = people;
```

```
        var filterList = new List<Filter>();
        filterList.Add(new Filter("All", 0, true));

        // Communicate results through the view model
        this.DefaultViewModel["QueryText"] = '\u201c' + queryText + '\u201d';
        this.DefaultViewModel["Filters"] = filterList;
        this.DefaultViewModel["ShowFilters"] = filterList.Count > 1;
}
```

3. Open SearchPeople.xaml and find the *GridView* control named resultGridView. Remove the *ItemTemplate* default definition and define a new one to show the person name for each result. The following code shows the complete control's definition:

```
<GridView
  x:Name="resultsGridView"
  AutomationProperties.AutomationId="ResultsGridView"
  AutomationProperties.Name="Search Results"
  TabIndex="1"
  Grid.Row="1"
  Margin="0,-238,0,0"
  Padding="110,240,110,46"
  SelectionMode="None"
  IsSwipeEnabled="false"
  IsItemClickEnabled="True"
  ItemsSource="{Binding Source={StaticResource resultsViewSource}}">
        <GridView.ItemTemplate>
            <DataTemplate>
                <TextBlock Text="{Binding FullName}" Margin="0,20,0,0"
                    Foreground="#7CFFFFFF" HorizontalAlignment="Left"  />
            </DataTemplate>
        </GridView.ItemTemplate>
        <GridView.ItemContainerStyle>
            <Style TargetType="Control">
                <Setter Property="Height" Value="70"/>
                <Setter Property="Margin" Value="0,0,38,8"/>
            </Style>
        </GridView.ItemContainerStyle>
</GridView>
```

4. Deploy the application and test a search from the Search pane, as you learned in the "Test the Default Search Component" procedure.

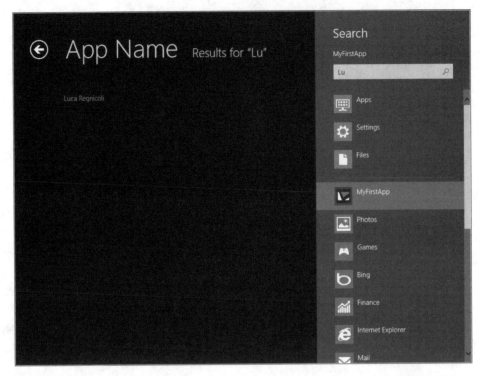

The last thing you need to do to complete the sample application is to change the *DefaultViewModel* property value to display the actual number of people retrieved by the search.

Modify the View Model properties

In this procedure, you will modify the code to show the actual number of people retrieved by the search. The procedure is very straightforward.

1. Modify the *LoadState* method as follows. The lines in bold represent the updated ones.

```
protected override void LoadState(Object navigationParameter,
    Dictionary<String, Object> pageState)
{
var queryText = navigationParameter as String;

// TODO: Application-specific searching logic.  The search process is responsible for
//       creating a list of user-selectable result categories:
//
//       filterList.Add(new Filter("<filter name>", <result count>));
//
//       Only the first filter, typically "All", should pass true as a third argument
//       in order to start in an active state.  Results for the active filter are
//       provided in Filter_SelectionChanged below.

var biz = new Biz();
var people = biz.GetPeople(queryText);
this.DefaultViewModel["Results"] = people;
```

```
var filterList = new List<Filter>();
filterList.Add(new Filter("All", people.Count, true));

// Communicate results through the view model
this.DefaultViewModel["QueryText"] = '\u201c' + queryText + '\u201d';
this.DefaultViewModel["Filters"] = filterList;
this.DefaultViewModel["ShowFilters"] = filterList.Count >= 1;
}
```

In practice, the first filter that shows the "All" keyword will contain the actual number of retrieved results and the *ShowFilters* boolean property indicates whether to show the various filters to the user. Obviously, you have to implement the various filters and the corresponding code.

2. Kill the application using the Task Manager because the process is probably already running from the previous procedure.

3. Deploy the application and test it again using the Search pane.

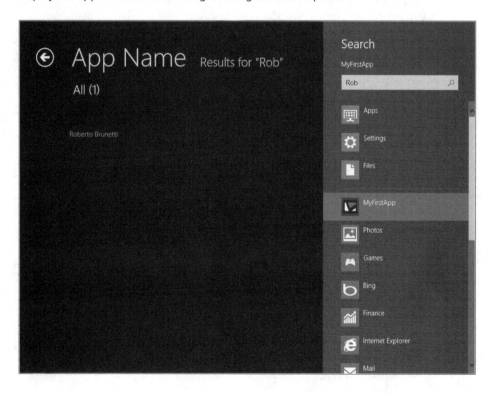

Summary

In this chapter, you saw the complete cycle for creating, testing, and deploying a simple Windows 8 application. You learned about the available templates and how to describe the application using the manifest. Finally, you added the code to implement the search contract using a provided template.

The next chapter is dedicated to application life cycle management. You will learn the details of the application manifest: how to package, test, and deploy an application, and how Windows 8 manages the launch, suspension, and termination of an application.

Quick reference

To	Do This
Arrange controls inside a flexible grid area	Use the *Grid* control.
Arrange child elements into a single line that can be oriented horizontally or vertically	Use the *StackPanel* control.
Deploy a Windows Store application	Use the deployment feature of Visual Studio 2012.
Deploy and test the application	In Visual Studio, press F5.
Implement the Search Contract	Use the SDK template called Search Contract that adds the search result page, the manifest declaration, and some sample code to the solution.
Define application features	Use the Visual Studio IDE Designer and open the Package.appxmanifest file.
Close an application	Stop the debugger, in case you are debugging it; or press Alt+F4; use the closing gesture; or use the new Task Manager to terminate the process.

CHAPTER 4

Application lifecycle management

After completing this chapter, you will be able to

- Understand the application manifest settings.

- Use the application manifest to modify application capability and appearance.

- Deploy and test an application.

- Understand the way Windows 8 manages the different running states of an application.

- Respond to launching, activation, suspending, and resuming events.

- Use the application data store to save data locally.

The preceding chapters showed how Microsoft Windows 8 provides a new user interface and a completely new user experience, while it offers a new set of application programming interfaces (APIs) called Windows Runtime APIs (WinRT) to interact with the operating system. You also developed a simple application in Chapter 3, "My first Windows 8 app."

This chapter introduces the complete application lifecycle in Windows 8: from deployment to launching to uninstallation. You will start by analyzing the various settings in the application manifest that let you define your application's appearance on the Start screen and inform Windows 8 about the WinRT features the application will use. You will also gain insight into how the WinRT manages the application lifecycle at runtime, launching, suspending, resuming, and terminating the application.

First, consider that a Windows 8 application cannot include an app.config file. This means that, as in a Microsoft Silverlight or Windows Presentation Foundation (WPF) Web Browser Application, you cannot use the classic .NET configuration mechanism to provide application and system settings. There are no *System.Configuration* namespace or equivalent classes in the WinRT APIs. The runtime system runs Windows Store applications in a sandboxed process like a Silverlight or WPF Web Browser Application. This means that users cannot navigate to the file system where the application is installed and change some files, because Windows 8 apps are mainly downloaded and installed from the Windows Store.

Application manifest

As in a Windows Phone 7.x project, many configuration settings and most deployment information are stored in a manifest file that the Windows Runtime calls Package.appxmanifest. This XML file describes various aspects of the project, as shown in the following listing, taken from a real Windows Store application.

```xml
<?xml version="1.0" encoding="utf-8"?>
<Package xmlns="http://schemas.microsoft.com/appx/2010/manifest">
  <Identity Name="ea15f786-9bb0-4d64-98b0-d251fa375633"
      Publisher="CN=Devleap" Version="1.0.0.1" />
  <Properties>
    <DisplayName>Learn with the Animals</DisplayName>
    <PublisherDisplayName>ThinkAhead</PublisherDisplayName>
    <Logo>Assets\Store_Logo.png</Logo>
  </Properties>
  <Prerequisites>
    <OSMinVersion>6.2.1</OSMinVersion>
    <OSMaxVersionTested>6.2.1</OSMaxVersionTested>
  </Prerequisites>
  <Resources>
    <Resource Language="x-generate" />
  </Resources>
  <Applications>
    <Application Id="App" Executable="$targetnametoken$.exe"
      EntryPoint="ThinkAhead.Windows8KidsGames.App">
      <VisualElements DisplayName="Learn with the Animals" Logo="Assets\logo.png"
        SmallLogo="Assets\small_logo.png" Description="Learn animal noises, names,
        guess their noises and names, try to read and try to write their names"
        ForegroundText="dark" BackgroundColor="#464646">
        <DefaultTile ShowName="noLogos" WideLogo="Assets\wide_logo.png" ShortName=
          "Learn with the Animals" />
        <SplashScreen Image="Assets\splash_screen.png" BackgroundColor="#b4dfba" />
        <InitialRotationPreference>
          <Rotation Preference="landscape" />
          <Rotation Preference="landscapeFlipped" />
        </InitialRotationPreference>
      </VisualElements>
    </Application>
  </Applications>
</Package>
```

The first section, called *Properties*, contains information used by the Windows Store, such as the title of the application, the name of the publisher, the official logo, and a brief description.

The last section, called *Capabilities*, contains every operating system feature the application will use on the user's PC or tablet. When the application code requests one of these features, the user receives a direct request to give the application specific permission to use the feature. The user can revoke this permission at any time: your code must fail gracefully if a user denies your application permission to use a capability.

This scheme has many similarities with a Windows Phone 7.x project, where the WMAppManifest.xml tells the operating system which capabilities the application requires to run. You can find more information on the application capabilities in Chapter 6, "Windows Runtime APIs."

Figure 4-1 shows the Manifest Designer that Microsoft Visual Studio 2012 provides to simplify the application definition. To open the designer, simply double-click the Package.appxmanifest file in Solution Explorer. The figure presents the real manifest for one of the authors' applications, called "Learn with the Animals." The Application UI tab lets you choose the Display Name of the application (name used for the Start screen), the description of the application, three logos for the application, and so on.

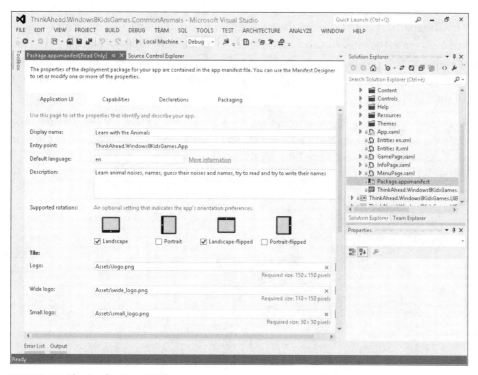

FIGURE 4-1 The Application UI tab.

The first tab of the Visual Studio Manifest Designer produces the following section in the application manifest.

```
<VisualElements DisplayName="Learn with the Animals" Logo="Assets\Logo.png"
  SmallLogo="Assets\SmallLogo.png" Description="Learn with the Animals"
  ForegroundText="light" BackgroundColor="#222222" ToastCapable="true">
    <LockScreen Notification="badgeAndTileText" BadgeLogo="Assets\BadgeLogo.png" />
    <DefaultTile ShowName="allLogos"  />
    <SplashScreen Image="Assets\SplashScreen.png" BackgroundColor="#000000" />
</VisualElements>
```

The *VisualElements* tag, as the name implies, defines the display name for the Windows 8 Start screen, the various logos for the tile (Logo), for the small tile (SmallLogo), and for the wide tile (WideLogo), as well as the supported rotation and the default one, the badge default logo, and the image for the splash screen.

All the required images referenced by the application package manifest are provided as placeholders by the Visual Studio templates for Windows Store applications, and are placed in the Assets folder of the project. The default template accepts an image for the application logo used for the default application tile (Logo.png), an image for the initial splash screen (SplashScreen.png), and a small logo image that is shown in the tile if the application changes its tile from code (SmallLogo.png). Last but not least, it also accepts the image used by Windows Store to represent the application (StoreLogo.png). As you can see from the Figure 4-1, you can also provide a wide logo to be displayed if the user chooses a wide tile for the application on the Start screen.

Figure 4-2 shows the application tile in the Windows 8 Start screen. The tile presents the image described in the application manifest as the *WideLogo* property and, as you will learn in Chapter 9, "Rethinking the UI for Windows 8 apps," the application can also modify the tile from code or create a secondary tile.

FIGURE 4-2 The "Learn with the Animals" wide tile on the Start screen.

Application package

The application manifest contains all the information the system uses to deploy the application on the target machine, which can be the local machine or the Windows 8 Simulator (useful for testing and debugging purposes), as well as all the information needed to package the application for the Windows Store.

When you run an application from Visual Studio using the F5 key, Visual Studio 2012 compiles the application, builds the application package, and asks the operating system to install the package on the developer machine, or on the Windows 8 Simulator.

Visual Studio lets you package and deploy the application on the Windows Store by using the Store menu, Create App Package feature. This menu item launches the Create App Packages wizard that helps you package the application and upload it to the store—or simply build the package to use it on a developer machine, as you can see from the options and descriptions in Figure 4-3.

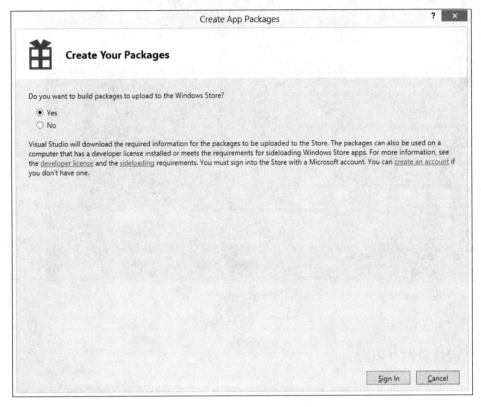

FIGURE 4-3 The Create App Packages wizard.

If you choose the first option to publish the application, you will be asked for the Windows Live ID you associated with your Windows Store account. In both cases, the last step of the wizard lets you choose which processor architecture you want to build the application for, and then creates the package (see Figure 4-4).

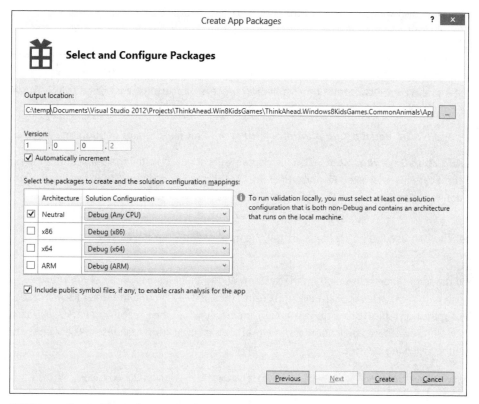

FIGURE 4-4 Create App Packages wizard lets you choose the output location, version, and configuration.

The package contains one binary file that represents the application and a folder with four different files:

- **<App Name_Version_Compilation>.appxupload** This is the real "package" and contains the compiled application that will be installed. For example, the application "Learn with the Animals," version 1.0.0.6 for the "Any CPU" is packaged in a file called LearnwiththeAnimals_1.0.0.6_AnyCPU.appxupload. This is the file for the Windows Store.

- **<App Name_Version_Compilation>.cer** This certificate is used to sign the application in the local development environment. The private key is contained in the .pfx file of the Visual Studio 2012 project. During the installation process this certificate is added to the Trusted Root Certification Authorities of the local machine.

- **<App Name_Version_Compilation>.appxsym** This file contains debugging symbols.

- **Add-AppxDevPakage.bat** This file contains the script to install the application, the signing certificate in the Trusted Root Certification Authorities, and all the dependencies the application needs to run.

 Note You can use the batch file to install the application on a developer machine manually.

When the application is installed on the system, Windows 8 creates a directory in the X:\ Users\<username>\AppData\Local\Packages\ using the Globally Unique Identifier (GUID) associated with the application. This GUID is generated automatically when the Create App Packages wizard creates a new Windows Store application and is stored in the application manifest in the Identity tag, as shown in the following excerpt:

```
<Identity Name="380ac04e-991e-4e5f-8758-5f56e68b0e94" Publisher="CN=DevLeap"
  Version="1.0.0.2" />
```

You can uninstall an application at any time by selecting its tile and choosing Uninstall from the Windows 8 Start screen. As shown in Figure 4-5, you can also unpin the application by clicking the Unpin From Start item in the App Bar. The unpin operation simply removes the tile from the Start screen; it does not uninstall the application from the system. You can reach the application again by pressing Windows+Q, and searching for the application among the installed apps.

FIGURE 4-5 Windows 8 Start screen App Bar.

The Windows Store

The Windows Store let users search, download, install, and review applications. You can upload your apps to the Windows Store by following some easy steps to make your applications available for every tablet and PC all around the globe.

The first step is to create a Windows Store account and bind it to a Windows Live ID. This procedure is quite straightforward and lets you define the publisher name—that is, the name of the application seller that the Windows Store screens display near the application name. The Windows Store lets users find applications by name, by keywords, and by publisher.

After creating an account, you can upload an application immediately, or you can reserve a name for an application you plan to develop within a year. If you plan to sell the application, you must also fill out a fiscal profile for the person or the company designated as the publisher. You will also need to fill out an IRS module related to your fiscal position. For example, if you are the publisher and you live outside of the United States, you will need to fill out the W8-BEN form. Fortunately, a wizard will guide you through the process of choosing the right module and filling it out online.

You *can* upload and sell an application before you have completed all the fiscal data, but you will receive no money until you have completed the fiscal data.

Aside from these "bureaucratic" tasks, the process of publishing an application is straightforward. The first thing you should do is verify that your application conforms to the Windows Store requirements locally. This step is not required, but it's very useful because you can validate your application quickly before performing any upload. To verify your application, use the application verifier (Windows Application Cert Kit) that validates an application for technical compliance with the Windows Store rules, as shown in Figure 4-6.

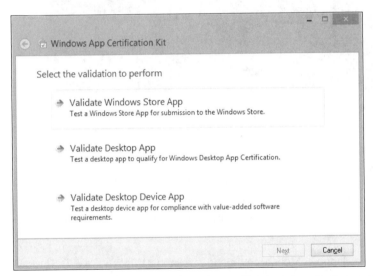

FIGURE 4-6 The Windows Application Cert Kit verifies that an application conforms to Windows Store rules.

The tool can also validate a desktop application or a desktop device application for Desktop App Certification. The Windows Application Cert Kit is installed on your system together with Visual Studio Express for Windows 8; you can launch it from the Start screen.

The next step lets you choose which application you want to validate (remember to first deploy it to the local system by compiling the project in release mode). The compliance validation begins by launching the application. It is very important that you do not interact with the application (and the system) during the validation process. The test also verifies whether the application can suspend and resume correctly, as well as close and terminate.

If your application does not pass all the tests performed by the Windows Application Cert Kit, there's no point in trying to upload the application package to the Windows Store; the store service runs the same verification process and your application cannot pass store certification if it is unable to pass local validation. At the end of the validation process you will receive a detailed report about any problems, presented as either errors or warnings. As stated, the local verification step is not required, but it's very useful.

After your application has completed local certification successfully, if you haven't already reserved a name for your app, you need to choose an application name before uploading the package.

For every application, you must provide such required information as the application name and the selling details (price, availability for country, trial versions), and you can include details about age rating (which is especially important if your app is a game), information cryptography mechanism, and some notes for the tester, as shown in Figure 4-7.

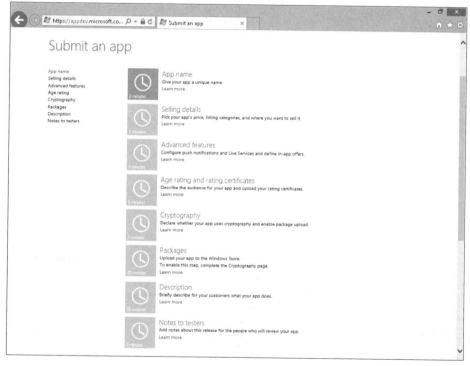

FIGURE 4-7 The Submit An App page allows you to fill in information about your application when submitting it to the Windows Store.

Next, you need to upload the package. You can build the package directly from Visual Studio 2012, as you saw in the previous section of this chapter, by choosing the option to associate the package with the application on the store. From a practical viewpoint, after you create an application using the Windows Store dashboard you can associate it with the Visual Studio project using the Store menu. This association modifies the application manifest using the publisher name and publisher ID taken from the store services.

From the Store menu, you can select Associate App With The Store menu item to bind the project to an application, and import the publisher name and certificate in the project. You can also make this association when building the application package, as shown in Figure 4-8.

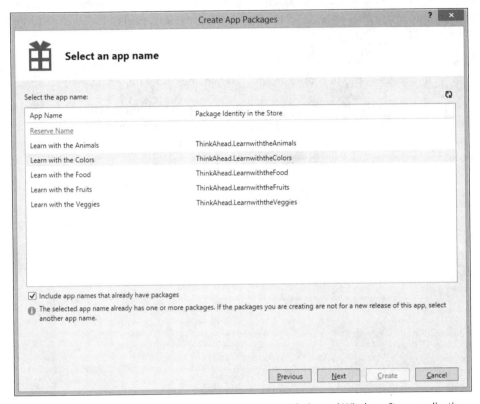

FIGURE 4-8 Associate an application Visual Studio project with the real Windows Store application.

After completing the upload operation, you will fill in an important form linked with the Description button that lets you define all of the marketing details for the application.

- Description of the application in plain text

- Two lines describing major application features

- Seven keywords

- The optional copyright information and license terms

- Eight optional screenshots, each one with a required description

- Some promotional images used by the system if your app is elected to be cited in the New Apps or Top Apps pages of the store

- Application minimum hardware requirements

- An email to be used for support requests

- A privacy policy

For example, Figure 4-9 shows some of the attributes used for the "Learn with the Colors" application, which is a Windows 8 app the authors published in the Windows Store.

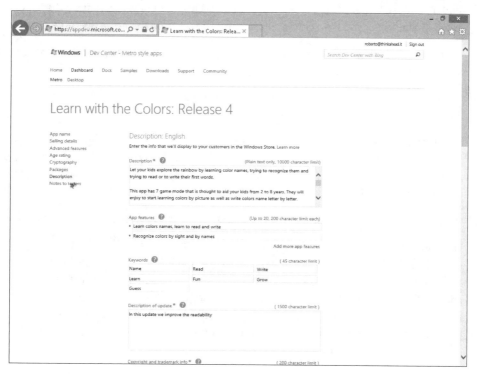

FIGURE 4-9 Attributes for the authors' "Learn with the Colors" app.

For each application, the store service provides statistics such as the store trend, the financial summary, the number of downloads, the reviews, and the rating information.

Launching

When you create a new Windows Store app using the Visual Studio template, you will end up with a solution containing one project with a default page called MainPage.xaml and a class that represents the application defined in the App.xaml.cs file. The Windows Runtime invokes the method called *OnLaunched* immediately after the creation of the application instance. You can override this method in your application to perform some activities.

Understanding the *OnLaunched* event

In this procedure, you will start coding event handlers for application events.

1. Create a new Application project. To do that, open Visual Studio 2012 and from the File menu, select New Project (the sequence can be File | New | Project for full-featured versions of Visual Studio). Choose Visual C# in the Templates tree and then Windows Store from the list of installed templates, and then choose Blank App (XAML) from the list of available projects.

2. Select version 4.5 as the target .NET Framework version for your new project (this step is not necessary in Visual Studio Express edition).

3. Name the new project **ALMEvents**, and then choose a location on your file system and accept the default solution name. When you have completed these actions, click OK.

    As you saw in Chapter 3, "My first Windows 8 app," the Windows Store Application template provides a default page (MainPage.xaml), an application entry point in the *App* class (App.xaml.cs), a default application description and a declaration in the Package.appxmanifest, as well as four default images representing logos and a splash screen.

4. Open App.xaml.cs in Visual Studio, and scroll down until you can see the *OnLaunched* method.

    The Windows Runtime calls this method when the user launches the application (an application is launched when a user clicks on the application tile). The default code inside the method simply instantiates a new *Frame* class, sets it as the current content, then navigates to the main page calling the *Navigate* method on the frame and passing the *MainPage* class. The last line activates the current content that is the Main Page. The code also contains a test to check for the presence of an existing frame (meaning the application is already running) that will be explained later in this chapter.

The following snippet shows the *OnLaunched* method.

```
protected override void OnLaunched(LaunchActivatedEventArgs args)
{
    Frame rootFrame = Window.Current.Content as Frame;

    // Do not repeat app initialization when the Window already has content,
    // just ensure that the window is active
    if (rootFrame == null)
    {
        // Create a Frame to act as the navigation context and navigate to the
        // first page
        rootFrame = new Frame();

        if (args.PreviousExecutionState == ApplicationExecutionState.Terminated)
        {
            //TODO: Load state from previously suspended application
        }

        // Place the frame in the current Window
        Window.Current.Content = rootFrame;
    }

    if (rootFrame.Content == null)
    {
        // When the navigation stack isn't restored navigate to the first page,
        // configuring the new page by passing required information as a
        navigation
        // parameter
        if (!rootFrame.Navigate(typeof(MainPage), args.Arguments))
        {
            throw new Exception("Failed to create initial page");
        }
    }
    // Ensure the current window is active
    Window.Current.Activate();
}
```

5. Add the following two lines right at the beginning of the method, before the rest of the code shown previously.

```
var dia = new Windows.UI.Popups.MessageDialog("App OnLaunched", "ALM Events");
dia.ShowAsync();
.....
```

The first line instantiates the *MessageDialog* class, passing to it the content and the title as string parameters. This class represents what in the past was typically called a "message box." The second line of code shows the message dialog in the default location and begins an asynchronous operation for processing the dialog, and then calls the *Start* method to start the operation.

6. Press F5 to start the application or deploy the application, as you learned in Chapter 3, and click or tap the application tile.

As you can see, the dialog is shown full screen and displays the title and the content passed as parameters in the class constructor.

7. Click or tap the Close button to close the dialog. You will see a completely black page because the default page doesn't present any content yet.

8. Click the Windows button to open the Start screen (you can also move the mouse in the lower-left corner of the screen and choose Start from the Start screen).

9. Scroll right until you find the ALM Events App and click the tile to launch it again. The application is already running, so you will not see the dialog; the Windows Runtime does not call the *OnLaunched* method for an application when that application instance is already loaded.

   This behavior is significantly different from previous versions of Windows, where the system started a new instance of the application each time the user launched it. In Windows 8, there can be only one instance of an application running; when a user launches an already running application, the Windows Runtime just brings the currently loaded application to the foreground.

10. Close the application by pressing Alt+F4 and repeat steps 6, 7, and 8 to verify the application flow again.

The parameter received by the *OnLaunched* method is of type *LaunchActivatedEventArgs*, a class that implements the *IActivatedEventArgs* interface you saw in Chapter 3. This interface is implemented by different classes that serve as event arguments for different activation events. The first property of the interface is *Kind* and can assume one of the values defined in the *ActivationKind* enumeration. This property lets the developer ask how the application was launched, for instance. When the application was launched by a user, this property will be *ActivationKind.Launch*. When the application was launched by the system when a user selected it as search target, the property will be *ActivationKind.Search*. When the application was activated so it could receive something from another application using a Share contract, the property will be *ActivationKind.ShareTarget*. In C# and VB there are two different methods in the base class to react to this activation. You will see these different methods later in this chapter.

Showing the launch kind

In this procedure, you will change the code of the previous procedure to show the type of activation.

1. Replace the code you inserted in the previous procedure for the *OnLaunched* method to create a message that contains the activation kind as follows. The lines in bold have to be inserted.

```
String message = "App Launched: " + args.Kind.ToString();
var dia = new Windows.UI.Popups.MessageDialog(message, "ALM Events");
dia.ShowAsync();

...
```

   The first line uses the *Kind* property of the event args to build the message text, and the second line presents it in a message dialog.

2. Run the application, deploying it from the Build menu. Then start the application by clicking the application tile in the Start screen. You will see the dialog presenting the text "App Launched: Launch."

3. Click Close, but do not shut down the application.

4. Go to the Start screen and click the application tile. Again, this time you will see no messages because the application is already running.

5. Close the application using Alt+F4.

Understanding the previous state

In this procedure, you will modify the code for the *OnLaunched* method to test the execution state for the previous launch of the application. If the user closed the application normally, the previous execution state will be *ClosedByUser*—letting you know that everything went well for the user. If the user has never launched the application, the previous execution state will be *NotRunning*.

1. Change the first line of the *OnLaunched* event to build a more detailed message that shows the activation kind and the previous execution state by replacing the first line of the method with the one shown in the following code excerpt (bold line):

```
String message = "App Launched: " + args.Kind.ToString() +
    " - Previous State: " + args.PreviousExecutionState.ToString();
var dia = new Windows.UI.Popups.MessageDialog(message, "ALM Events");
dia.ShowAsync();
...
```

2. Deploy the application using the Build | Deploy menu item.

3. Start the application by launching it from the Start screen.

4. Verify that the message displays "App Launched: Launch – Previous State: ClosedByUser," meaning the application was previously closed by you (if in fact you did close it in the previous procedure). The message will be "App Launched: Launch – Previous State: NotRunning" if the application was closed immediately before this launch. Try closing it and launching it from the Start screen quickly.

5. Close the application using Alt+F4.

6. Modify the MainPage.xaml by adding two buttons and their corresponding click events in the *Grid* control as follows.

```
<Grid Background="{StaticResource ApplicationPageBackgroundThemeBrush}">
    <StackPanel Orientation="Horizontal" VerticalAlignment="Top">
        <Button Click="Crash_Click" Content="Crash" />
        <Button Click="Close_Click" Content="Close" />
    </StackPanel>
</Grid>
```

The first button will be used to perform an invalid operation that causes the crash of the application. The second will be used to gracefully close the application from code.

7. Implement the event handlers for the *Crash_Click* and the *Close_Click* events (in bold) using the following code in the MainPage.xaml.cs file:

```
using System;
using System.Collections.Generic;
using System.IO;
using System.Linq;
using Windows.Foundation;
using Windows.Foundation.Collections;
using Windows.UI.Xaml;
using Windows.UI.Xaml.Controls;
using Windows.UI.Xaml.Controls.Primitives;
using Windows.UI.Xaml.Data;
using Windows.UI.Xaml.Input;
using Windows.UI.Xaml.Media;
using Windows.UI.Xaml.Navigation;

// The Blank Page item template is documented at http://go.microsoft.com/
fwlink/?LinkId=234238

namespace ALMEvents
{
    /// <summary>
    /// An empty page that can be used on its own or navigated to within a Frame.
    /// </summary>
    public sealed partial class MainPage : Page
    {
        public MainPage()
        {
            this.InitializeComponent();
        }

        private void Crash_Click(object sender, RoutedEventArgs e)
        {
            Int32 a = 10;
            Int32 b = 0;

            Int32 c = a / b;
        }

        private void Close_Click(object sender, RoutedEventArgs e)
        {
            Application.Current.Exit();
        }

        /// <summary>
        /// Invoked when this page is about to be displayed in a Frame.
        /// </summary>
        /// <param name="e">Event data that describes how this page was reached.  The
        Parameter
        /// property is typically used to configure the page.</param>
        protected override void OnNavigatedTo(NavigationEventArgs e)
        {
        }
    }
}
```

8. Deploy the application by right-clicking the project in the solution and choosing Deploy from the context menu.

9. Launch the application from the Start screen, click Close on the dialog, and then click the Crash button on the main page. The application should crash, returning you to the Start screen in a few seconds. Be patient.

10. Launch the application again from the Start screen. The dialog will show "NotRunning" as the previous state.

11. Close the dialog and then click the Close button on the main page to close the application gracefully.

12. Launch the application again from the Start screen to verify that the dialog shows "NotRunning" as the previous state.

13. Close the dialog and then close the application by using Alt+F4 or by swiping your mouse or finger from the upper-center of the screen to the lower-center of the screen to close the application in the canonical way.

14. Wait for at least 20 seconds and then launch the application again from the Start screen to verify that the dialog shows "ClosedByUser" as the previous state.

To summarize, an application receives a call to the *OnLaunched* method from the Windows Runtime when the user launches the application and the application is not already running. This method receives the launch kind and the previous state. You have also learned that there can be only one instance of a Windows Store app running in Windows 8.

Activation

If the user "launches" an application indirectly, using the Search contract, the application receives a call to the *OnSearchActivated* method as you saw in Chapter 3. The Windows Runtime terms this procedure "activation," as the name of the method implies. Activation is a more correct term because the application isn't launched directly by the user. The parameter args received by the *OnLaunched* method, as you saw in the preceding procedure, has a property called *Kind* that can assume the value of Search. But don't be confused by this; when the user selects the target of his or her search, the Windows Runtime invokes the *OnSearchActivated* method on the *App* class and never invokes the *OnLaunched* events. Both event arguments, as well as other event args for other activation methods, implement a common interface; this explains why both have the same property. The following procedure clarifies these concepts.

Understanding the *OnSearchActivated* Method

In this procedure, you will modify the code for the App.xaml.cs file to test the activation for search. You will use the Search Contract template proposed by Visual Studio and that you learned about in Chapter 3.

1. Implement the Search contract by right-clicking the project in the Solution Explorer and choose Add New Item.

   Scroll down until you find the Search contract item.

2. Click the Add button without changing the default name and select Yes when the dialog box asks you to add the requested files.

   You will not implement a real search page in this procedure, but just test the activation for searching.

   Adding the Search contract item modifies the Package.appxmanifest to declare the Search contract and adds the following line in the App.xaml.cs file.

```
protected async override void OnSearchActivated(
        Windows.ApplicationModel.Activation.SearchActivatedEventArgs args)
{
    // TODO: Register the
    // Windows.ApplicationModel.Search.SearchPane.GetForCurrentView().QuerySubmitted
    // event in OnWindowCreated to speed up searches once the application is already
    running

    // If the Window isn't already using Frame navigation, insert our own Frame
    var previousContent = Window.Current.Content;
    var frame = previousContent as Frame;

    // If the app does not contain a top-level frame, it is possible that this
    // is the initial launch of the app. Typically this method and OnLaunched
    // in App.xaml.cs can call a common method.
    if (frame == null)
    {
        // Create a Frame to act as the navigation context and associate it with
        // a SuspensionManager key
        frame = new Frame();
        ALMEvents.Common.SuspensionManager.RegisterFrame(frame, "AppFrame");

        if (args.PreviousExecutionState == ApplicationExecutionState.Terminated)
        {
            // Restore the saved session state only when appropriate try
            {
                await ALMEvents.Common.SuspensionManager.RestoreAsync();
            }
            catch (ALMEvents.Common.SuspensionManagerException)
            {
                //Something went wrong restoring state.
                //Assume there is no state and continue
            }
        }

        frame.Navigate(typeof(SearchResultsPage1), args.QueryText);
        Window.Current.Content = frame;

        // Ensure the current window is active
        Window.Current.Activate();
    }
```

3. Add the three bolded lines just at the beginning of the *OnSearchActivated* method.

```
protected async override void OnSearchActivated(
    Windows.ApplicationModel.Activation.SearchActivatedEventArgs args)
{
    String message = "App Activated by the Search Contract";
    var dia = new Windows.UI.Popups.MessageDialog(message, "ALM Events");
    dia.ShowAsync();

    ...
```

4. Deploy the application. If you haven't closed the application in the previous procedure yet, activate it and click the Close button or use the Task Manager to kill the application.

5. Press Windows+Q, type something in the search box, and select the ALMEvents App.

6. Verify that the dialog displays "App Activated by the Search Contract."

   You will not receive the dialog for the application launching because the application was not launched by the user but activated for a search. VB and C# application base classes expose different methods to respond to launch and search activations, whereas WinJS exposes just a generic activation function where you can test the activation kind property of the event args.

7. Close the application using Alt+F4.

If the user shares some content from another application, the target application receives a different activation called sharing target activation (*OnSharingTargetActivated* is the name of the corresponding method). You will learn about this kind of activation and the sharing contract in Chapter 6.

There are other types of activation, each one corresponding to an operation performed by the user. Table 4-1 summarizes the principal activation types.

TABLE 4-1 Windows Runtime activations

Method name	Description
Activated	Invoked when the application is activated by tile activation
File Activated	Invoked when the application is activated through file-open
File Picker Activated	Invoked when the application is activated through file-dialog association
Search Activated	Invoked when the application is activated through a search association
Sharing Target Activated	Invoked when the application is activated through sharing association

Because there are several types of activations, if you want to perform some actions not related to a specific type of activation, you can override the *OnInitialize* method of the application class. This method is called from the runtime immediately after the application instance has been created, and before the specific method for a particular activation kind.

Suspension

The Windows Runtime introduces a new concept for application lifecycle management (ALM) that consists of a two-phase process in which the application is suspended when the user leaves it to launch or activate a different app and resumed when the user switches back to it.

The idea behind this mechanism is to maintain system responsiveness even if the user launches many applications. Only the foreground application uses significant processor time, whereas other applications are suspended by the system. There can be a maximum of two running apps (when they are in snapped mode). Usually, when not in snapped mode, there will be only one foreground app. To avoid latency when the user returns to a previously launched application, the Windows Runtime freezes the application memory when suspending an application, and places it in a special idle state: no CPU-cycle, disk, or network access is given to a suspended application. The result is that the system remains fully responsive to the foreground application while the resume operation is practically instantaneous.

Verify application suspension

In this procedure, you will check the suspension state using the same application you have been building throughout this chapter.

1. Launch the application from the Start screen. Avoid using the Visual Studio 2012 debugger to test the standard suspension behavior because this behavior changes slightly while debugging.

2. Close the dialog that displays the launching message.

3. Press Alt+Tab or the Windows key to put the current application in the background.

4. Open the Task Manager, and wait until the application goes into the suspended status. To open the Task Manager, you can press Windows+Q and search for the term "Task Manager" in the Apps list, or you can activate the Desktop from the Start screen and right-click the taskbar.

Figure 4-10 shows the result of this procedure.

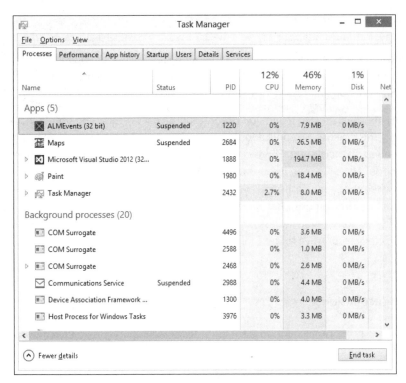

FIGURE 4-10 Using the Task Manager to determine application state and resources.

 Note Your screen may be slightly different depending on the columns shown by the Task Manager. For example, you must manually enable the Status column for it to be visible.

As you can see, the ALMEvents App (*PID 1220* in Figure 4-10) is placed in the suspended state. It uses no processor time or disk access at all, but, as previously stated, it uses 7.9 MB of frozen memory on our system. Obviously, this value may be different on your system.

Switch back to the application again (Alt+Tab) and note that the application resumes instantly without showing a launch message dialog (because it wasn't launched; it was just resumed from the suspended state).

The Windows Runtime will suspend the app after it has been switched into the background for at least 10 seconds. If you place an app in the background for fewer than 10 seconds and then return to it, the app will probably not be suspended.

The system informs the application immediately before the suspension manager starts its work. An application has only five seconds to perform any pre-suspension operations, and if an app requires more than five seconds to perform its pre-suspension operations, the Windows Runtime may terminate it forcibly.

It is very important to understand the complete flow of the suspension/resume process before coding against it. The system suspends your app whenever the user switches to another app or to the desktop. The system resumes your app whenever the user switches back to it. When the system resumes your app, the content of your variables and data structures will be the same as it was before the system suspended the app. The system restores the app exactly where it left off, so that, to the user, it appears as if it's been running in the background all along. There is no need to save any data the user has been working on during the suspension phase if the user comes back to the application. But, if the system does not have the resources to keep your app in memory, or needs more resources for other applications launched by the user, the system will terminate your app. Your app will not be notified of the termination because the Windows Runtime assumes you have already saved any needed data or state information during the suspension phase. When the user switches back to a suspended app that has been terminated, the app receives a different launch event, which is where you have to write the code that restores the application data.

Now that you have seen the complete flow, let's add some code to the application you are developing in this chapter to follow the operations.

Using the *Suspending* event

In this procedure, you will modify the code for App.xaml.cs to intercept the suspension and display a message dialog. This is not what you would do in a real application, but it is a helpful experiment to make sure you understand the complete process.

1. Open the App.xaml.cs file.

2. In the constructor, the Visual Studio Blank App template prepares the code to hook up the *Suspending* event as follows.

```
public App()
{
    InitializeComponent();
    this.Suspending += OnSuspending;
}
```

3. Use the following code for the event handler for the *Suspending* event. Replace the existing code.

```
void OnSuspending(object sender,SuspendingEventArgs e)
{
    String message = "App Suspending";
    var dia = new Windows.UI.Popups.MessageDialog(message, "ALM Events");
    dia.ShowAsync();
}
```

4. Deploy the application and launch it from the Start screen.

5. Close the dialog that displays the launching.

6. Click the Windows key to put the current application in the background.

7. Open Task Manager and wait until the application has been suspended.

8. When the application has been suspended, press Alt+Tab again to return to the application and verify that the message shows "App Suspending."

This dialog was shown during application suspension but because the application was not in the foreground anymore, you saw nothing during the system operation. When you reactivate the application, the Windows Runtime resumes the application as it was prior to the suspension, which is why you can see the dialog on the screen only during the resuming operation.

In practice, the dialog is visible because the application has been resumed exactly where it was left off; the last thing the application did before the suspension was process the call to display this message. You did not see this message during the suspension because the application was already sent to the background.

An incorrect suspension example

As mentioned earlier, an application has only five seconds to respond to the suspension event. If the application requires more time, the Windows Runtime kills the application. In this procedure, you will test this behavior.

1. Close the application if you left it open in the previous procedure.

2. Open the App.xaml.cs file and comment out the existing code of the *OnSuspending* method and insert the bolded line from the following excerpt.

```
void OnSuspending(object sender,SuspendingEventArgs e)
{
    //String message = "App Suspending";
    //var dia = new Windows.UI.Popups.MessageDialog(message, "ALM Events");
    //dia.ShowAsync();
    while(true);
}
```

This code simply loops indefinitely—so it exceeds the five-second limit; the pre-suspension code runs "too long" for the system, so it will kill the application after the allotted time.

3. Deploy the application.

4. Open an instance of the Task Manager and minimize it.

5. Go to the Start screen using the Windows key and launch the application.

6. Maximize the Task Manager.

You can verify that after some time (maybe 20 seconds or more depending on the system) the application disappears from the application list: this means that the application was killed by the system because the code for the suspending event exceeded the maximum allowed time.

7. Launch the application again and verify the message in the dialog: it indicates the previous state as "Terminated" because the application was terminated (killed) by the Windows Runtime. This procedure can be slightly unpredictable because the runtime can decide to terminate the application later, which makes debugging code in the *OnLaunched* event quite difficult and time consuming if you are trying to test for a previous termination. But don't worry, at the end of this chapter you will learn how you can simulate suspension, resuming, and termination from Visual Studio 2012 during a debugging phase.

Requesting more suspension time

If your application can't save its state and data in five seconds and needs some more time—for example, to persist some temporary data via web services or in the cloud—you can inform the system that you are executing an asynchronous operation. Call the *SuspendingOperation.GetDeferral* method to indicate that the app is saving its application data asynchronously. When the operation completes, the handler calls the *SuspendingDeferral.Complete* method to indicate that the app's application data has been saved. If the app does not call the *Complete* method, the system assumes the app is not responding and terminates it. When that happens, the next time the user launches the application they should not rely on the validity of the saved application data.

The *SuspendingOperation* has a deadline time. Make sure all your operations are completed by that time. You can ask the system for the deadline using the *Deadline* property of the *SuspendingOperation*.

In this procedure you will change the code for the event handler so it writes the suspension time on disk using an asynchronous deferred operation. Theoretically, this operation cannot last longer than five seconds, but this example shows the correct code to implement an asynchronous operation.

1. Comment out the line that performs the endless loop.

2. Add the code shown in bold in the following block.

```
void OnSuspending(object sender, SuspendingEventArgs e)
{
    //String message = "App Suspending";
    //var dia = new Windows.UI.Popups.MessageDialog(message, "ALM Events");
    //dia.ShowAsync().Start();
    // while(true);;

    var deferral = e.SuspendingOperation.GetDeferral();


    var settingsValues = Windows.Storage.ApplicationData.Current.LocalSettings.
    Values;
    if (settingsValues.ContainsKey("SuspendedTime"))
    {
        settingsValues.Remove("SuspendedTime");
    }
    settingsValues.Add("SuspendedTime", DateTime.Now.ToString());
    // Perform the aysnc operation
    deferral.Complete();

    }
```

The first uncommented line gets the deferral from the suspending operation property of the *SuspendingEventArgs* class. At the end, the code reports the completion of the deferred operation to the system.

The code gets the *LocalSettings* property of the application data and inserts a key called *Suspended-Time* with the current time in the collection. The *LocalSettings* class lets the developer save simple key/value pairs in the local application data folder. As you will learn in Chapter 10, "Architecting a Windows 8 app," the Windows Runtime denies access to the classic file system and instead provides a local or roaming space, called *application data*, that applications can use to store data. This kind of storage is similar in many aspects to the *IsolatedStorage* provided by the Silverlight and the Windows Phone runtime. You can use a *RoamingSettings* property instead of the *LocalSettings* property if you want to be able to share your app data across multiple devices. *RoamingSettings* is a cloud-based isolated storage, which relates the data to the current user's Windows Live ID account.

 Warning Remember that the *entire method* must return before the deadline.

You can also hook the suspending event inside the code of an application page, which is very useful for saving the state of the page during the suspension so that you can restore it in case of termination. Be aware that the *Suspending* event is not raised in the UI thread, so if you have to perform some UI operations you have to use a dispatcher.

You can debug the code for the suspending method as usual, and you can also force a suspension during a debugging session from Visual Studio. You will try this functionality during the next procedure.

Resume

In the "Suspending" section of this chapter, you implemented a suspension event handler in the application class to calculate and save the current suspension time to the application data store.

In this procedure you will read the saved time from the application data store during the resume operation from the application class and then you will implement the code to show that same data within a page.

The resume operation is useless if the application was suspended by the system because the memory dedicated to the application is just frozen and not cleared. However, if the system needed more memory and decided to terminate the application, the resume operation is the right place to read the data saved in the suspension procedure.

You can intercept the resume operation by hooking up the *Resuming* event of the application class if you need to perform some application operations. For instance, you can save the page that the user was on before the suspension and, if the application was terminated, open that page instead of the default one. That's what the following code sample does.

```
using System;
using System.Threading;
using System.Threading.Tasks;
using Windows.ApplicationModel.Activation;
using Windows.UI.Xaml;

namespace ALMEvents
{
    sealed partial class App : Application
    {
        public App()
        {
            InitializeComponent();
            this.Suspending += OnSuspending;
            this.Resuming += OnResuming;
        }

        private static String currentPage;

        private void OnSuspending(object sender, Windows.ApplicationModel.SuspendingEventArgs e)
        {
            var def = e.SuspendingOperation.GetDeferral();

            var settingsValues = Windows.Storage.ApplicationData.Current.LocalSettings.Values;
            if (settingsValues.ContainsKey("Page"))
            {
                settingsValues.Remove("Page");
            }
            settingsValues.Add("Page", currentPage);

            def.Complete();

        }

        void OnResuming(object sender, object e)
        {

            var settingsValues = Windows.Storage.ApplicationData.Current.LocalSettings.Values;
            if (settingsValues.ContainsKey("Page"))
            {
                if (settingsValues["Page"] == "CustomerDetails")
                {
                    // Activate the Customer Details Page
                }
            }
        }
    }
}
```

The code is straightforward. The *OnSuspending* event handler saves the name of the current page in the local application data store and the *OnResuming* event handler reads that value when the application is resumed from a terminated state.

An application can leverage the resuming operation, performing some actions even if the application was not terminated. For example, you can request data taken from a web service or remote source if the suspend operation occurred some minutes before the resume, letting your app present fresh content to the user.

Refresh data during resume

In this procedure, you will modify the code for the MainPage.xaml.cs file to display the launch time, the suspended time, and the resuming time.

1. Open the MainPage.xaml file and add three *TextBlock* controls. The first one will display the time the page was first opened, the second will display the suspension duration, and the third will display the resumed time. Use the following code as a reference.

    ```
    <Page
        x:Class="ALMEvents.MainPage"
        xmlns="http://schemas.microsoft.com/winfx/2006/xaml/presentation"
        xmlns:x="http://schemas.microsoft.com/winfx/2006/xaml"
        xmlns:local="using:ALMEvents"
        xmlns:d="http://schemas.microsoft.com/expression/blend/2008"
        xmlns:mc="http://schemas.openxmlformats.org/markup-compatibility/2006"
        mc:Ignorable="d">

        <Grid Background="{StaticResource ApplicationPageBackgroundThemeBrush}">
            <StackPanel Orientation="Vertical" VerticalAlignment="Top" Margin="10,01,10,10">
                <Button Click="Close_Click" Content="Close" />
                <TextBlock Name="firstTime" FontSize="24" Margin="10,10,10,10" />
                <TextBlock Name="suspendTime" FontSize="24" Margin="10,10,10,10" />
                <TextBlock Name="resumeTime" FontSize="24" Margin="10,10,10,10" />
            </StackPanel>
        </Grid>
    </Page>
    ```

2. Open the MainPage.xaml.cs file. Use the following code as a reference to hook up the resuming event to display the suspended time restored from the application state and the resumed time.

    ```
    using System;
    using System.Collections.Generic;
    using System.IO;
    using System.Linq;
    using Windows.Foundation;
    using Windows.Foundation.Collections;
    using Windows.UI.Xaml;
    using Windows.UI.Xaml.Controls;
    using Windows.UI.Xaml.Controls.Primitives;
    using Windows.UI.Xaml.Data;
    using Windows.UI.Xaml.Input;
    using Windows.UI.Xaml.Media;
    using Windows.UI.Xaml.Navigation;
    ```

```csharp
// The Blank Page item template is documented at http://go.microsoft.com/
fwlink/?LinkId=234238

namespace ALMEvents
{
    /// <summary>
    /// An empty page that can be used on its own or navigated to within a Frame.
    /// </summary>
    public sealed partial class MainPage : Page
    {
        public MainPage()
        {
            this.InitializeComponent();

            firstTime.Text = "Ctor : " + DateTime.Now.ToString();

            App.Current.Resuming += Current_Resuming;

        }

        void Current_Resuming(object sender, object e)
        {
            this.Dispatcher.RunAsync(Windows.UI.Core.CoreDispatcherPriority.Normal,
                () =>
                {
                    var settingsValues =
                        Windows.Storage.ApplicationData.Current.LocalSettings.Values;

                    if (settingsValues.ContainsKey("SuspendedTime"))
                    {
                        suspendTime.Text = "Suspended : " +
                            settingsValues["SuspendedTime"].ToString();
                    }
                    resumeTime.Text = "Resumed :" + DateTime.Now.ToString();
                });
        }

        private void Close_Click(object sender, RoutedEventArgs e)
        {
            Application.Current.Exit();
        }


        /// <summary>
        /// Invoked when this page is about to be displayed in a Frame.
        /// </summary>
        /// <param name="e">Event data that describes how this page was reached.  The
        Parameter
        /// property is typically used to configure the page.</param>
        protected override void OnNavigatedTo(NavigationEventArgs e)
        {
        }
    }
}
```

In the constructor of the *MainPage* class, the second line of code assigns the current time to the first *TextBlock*. This code executes only when the application instantiates the page—that is, when the user launches the application or when the application is resumed from a terminated state. The code is not executed when the application is resumed from the suspended state.

The *Current_Resuming* event handler reads the value of the *SuspendedTime* key in the application data store and assigns it to the second *TextBlock*, and then assigns the current time to the last *TextBlock*. This code is not executed in the UI thread, which is why the code is executed by a dispatcher.

3. Deploy the application.

4. Launch the application from the app tile on the Start screen and close the initial dialog box.

5. Click the Windows Key and go to the Desktop.

6. Open the Task Manager and wait until the application has been suspended by the system.

   Minimize the Task Manager.

7. Return to the application by pressing Alt+Tab.

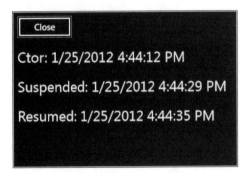

8. Close the application using the Close button.

To facilitate debugging the suspending and resuming event, Visual Studio includes two menu items that let you ask the Windows Runtime to suspend and resume the application during a debugger session. This feature is very useful because it lets you avoid using the Task Manager as you have been doing so far, and because it lets you invoke this event sequence as needed.

Use Visual Studio to debug suspend and resume

In this procedure, you will use Visual Studio to debug the suspending and resuming events.

1. Open the App.xaml.cs file and place a breakpoint in the first line of the *OnSuspending* method.

2. Open MainPage.xaml.cs and place a breakpoint in the first line of the *Current_Resuming* method.

3. Press F5 to start a debugging session and wait until the application is visible on the screen.

4. Press Alt+F4 to return to Visual Studio. In the Debug Location toolbar, choose Suspend. If this toolbar is not visible, you can enable it using the View menu, choosing the Toolbars item, and then selecting the Debug Location item.

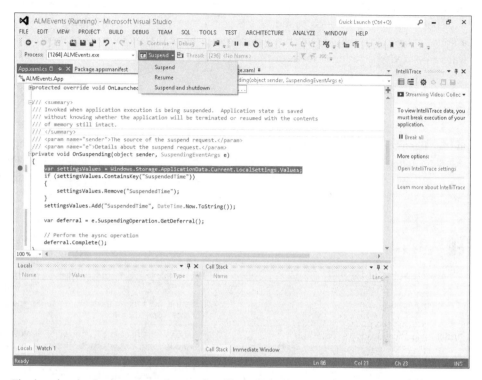

The breakpoint in the suspend event handler will be hit. Press F5 to continue. The breakpoint in the resume event handler will be hit soon because the application is taken in the foreground by Visual Studio when you pressed F5.

5. Press F5 again. Verify that the application is visible and presents the three labels with different times.

6. Press Alt+F4 to return to Visual Studio, and use the Debug Location toolbar to select Resume to verify you can directly debug the resume procedure without the need to debug the suspend procedure first. You can also click the Resume button on the debug toolbar.

7. Using the Debug Location toolbar, select Suspend And Shutdown. The application will first go into the suspended state and then be terminated by the runtime. Using this option you can debug the code for the *OnLaunched* event to test a previous termination.

In short, the system suspends your app whenever the user switches to another app or to the desktop, and resumes your app whenever the user switches back to it. When the system resumes your app, the content of your variables and data structures is the same as it was before the system suspended the app. The system restores the app exactly where it left off, so that it appears to the user as if it's been running in the background. However, the app may have been suspended for a significant amount of time, so it should refresh any displayed content that might have changed while the app was suspended, such as news feeds or the user's location.

Summary

In this chapter, you saw the complete application lifecycle at runtime. You saw how to package and install an application in the local system and how to create a package suitable for the Windows Store. Then you saw the various events that the Windows Runtime fires to launch, activate, suspend, resume, and terminate a Windows 8 app.

Quick reference

To	Do this
Create the Application Package	Use the Store menu from Visual Studio, and choose Create App Package.
Install an application locally for testing	You can use the classic F5 button to deploy and run the app automatically, or choose Deploy from the project contextual menu, or you can create the App Package and launch the batch file.
Save temporary data	Use the *Suspending* event from the application class.
Test Suspend and Resume	Debug the application and use the Suspend and Resume buttons on the Visual Studio Debug Location toolbar.
Uninstall an application	Go to the Start screen, right-click the tile, and choose uninstall. You can also swipe down with your finger on the tile to activate the lower toolbar.

CHAPTER 5

Introduction to the Windows Runtime

After completing this chapter, you will be able to

- Understand the architecture of the Windows Runtime (WinRT).

- Leverage the new Windows 8 APIs across multiple languages.

- Create custom WinMD libraries.

This chapter provides an introduction to the Windows Runtime application programming interfaces (APIs), which are the new APIs that sit at the very base of every Microsoft Windows 8 app.

Overview of the Windows Runtime

Microsoft Windows, since its earliest version, has always provided developers with libraries and APIs to interact with the operating system. However, before the release of Windows 8, those APIs and libraries were often complex and painful to use. Moreover, while working in .NET Framework using C# or VB.NET, you often had to rely on COM (Component Object Model) Interop and Win32 interoperability via P/Invoke (Platform Invoke) in order to directly leverage the operating system. For example, consider Listing 5-1.

LISTING 5-1 A sample code excerpt leveraging Win32 in C#

```
[DllImport("avicap32.dll", EntryPoint="capCreateCaptureWindow")]
static extern int capCreateCaptureWindow(
  string lpszWindowName, int dwStyle,
  int X, int Y, int nWidth, int nHeight,
  int hwndParent, int nID);

[DllImport("avicap32.dll")]
static extern bool capGetDriverDescription(
  int wDriverIndex,
  [MarshalAs(UnmanagedType.LPTStr)] ref string lpszName,
  int cbName,
  [MarshalAs(UnmanagedType.LPTStr)] ref string lpszVer,
  int cbVer);
```

This sample C# code imports a couple of Win32 APIs into the .NET world to leverage the video capture features of your PC. As you can see, the code is not tricky and the syntax can be prone to easy errors.

Microsoft acknowledged the complexity of the previously existing scenario and made a huge investment in Windows 8 and the Windows Runtime (WinRT) to simplify the interaction with the native operating system. In fact, the WinRT is a set of fresh, new APIs that were reimagined from the developer perspective to make easy, simple, and fast what previously was too complex. Moreover, the WinRT is built so that it supports the idea of developing Windows 8 apps with many of the available programming languages and environments, such as HTML5/WinJS, CLR, and C++.

Listing 5-2 shows the same code used in Listing 5-1, but rewritten using WinRT and C# instead.

LISTING 5-2 A sample code excerpt leveraging WinRT in C#

```
using Windows.Media.Capture;

var camera = new CameraCaptureUI();
camera.PhotoSettings.CroppedAspectRatio = new Size(4, 3);

var file = await camera.CaptureFileAsync(CameraCaptureUIMode.Photo);

if (file != null)
{
    var bitmap = new BitmapImage() ;
    bitmap.SetSource(await file.OpenAsync(FileAccessMode.Read));
    Photo.Source = bitmap;
}
```

The preceding code illustrates how the syntax is clearer and easier to write, as well as easier to read and maintain in the future, when leveraging WinRT. In this last example, Photo is a XAML *Image* control.

As mentioned before, if you prefer to write code using WinJS and HTML5, the code will be similar to the C# version, as you can see in Listing 5-3.

LISTING 5-3 Sample code excerpt leveraging WinRT in WinJS

```
var camera = new capture.CameraCaptureUI();

camera.captureFileAsync(capture.CameraCaptureUIMode.photo)
    .then(function (file) {
        if (file != null) {
            media.shareFile = file;
        }
    });
```

Basically, WinRT is a rich set of APIs built upon the Windows 8 operating system that provides direct and easy access to all the main primitives, devices, and capabilities for any language available for developing Windows 8 apps. WinRT is available only for building Windows 8 apps. Its main goal is to unify the development experience of building a Windows 8 app, regardless of which programming language you choose.

Figure 5-1 shows the overall architecture of WinRT.

Windows Runtime Architecture

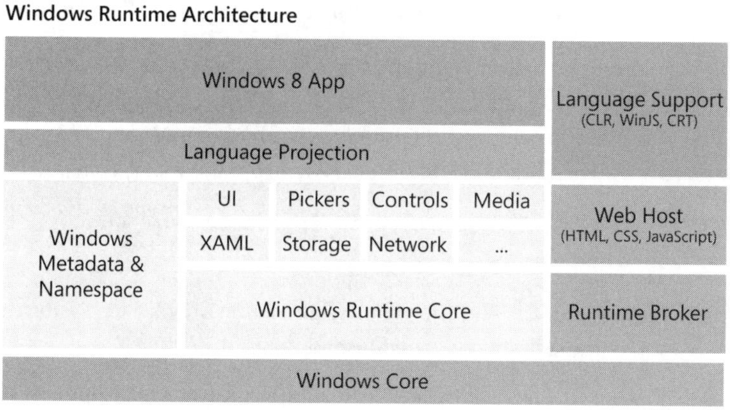

FIGURE 5-1 High-level architecture of WinRT.

WinRT sits on top of the Windows Runtime core engine, which is a set of C++ libraries that bridge WinRT with the underlying operating system. On top of the WinRT core, there is a rich set of specific libraries and types that interact with the various tools and devices available in any Windows 8 app. For example, there is a library that works with the network and another that reads and writes from the storage (local or remote). There is a set of pickers to pick up items (files, pictures, and so on.) and there are a bunch of classes to leverage media services, and so on. All these types and libraries are defined in a structured set of namespaces and are described by a set of metadata called Windows Metadata (WinMD). All metadata information is based on a new file format, which is built upon the *Common Language* infrastructure (CLI) metadata definition language (ECMA-335).

As already stated, the WinRT core engine is written in C++ and internally leverages a proprietary set of data types. For example, there is the notion of *HSTRING*, which is the name of the type representing a text value in WinRT. Also, there are numeric types like *INT32* and *UINT64*, enumerable collections represented by *IVector<T>*, enums, structures, runtime classes, and so on.

In order to be able to consume all this stuff from any supported programming language, WinRT provides a projection layer that shuttles types and data between WinRT and the target language. For example, the WinRT *HSTRING* type will be translated into a *System.String* of .NET for a common language runtime (CLR) app, or to a *Platform::String* for a C++ app.

Next to this layered architecture there is a "Runtime Broker," which acts as a bridge between the operating system and the host executing Windows 8 apps, whether those are CLR, HTML5/WinJS, or C++ apps.

To better understand the architecture and philosophy behind WinRT, in the following procedure your code will consume WinRT from a CLR Windows 8 app.

Using WinRT from a CLR Windows 8 app

In this procedure, you will use the WinRT Camera APIs to capture an image from a C# Windows 8 app.

1. Create a new Application project. To do that, open Microsoft Visual Studio 2012, and from the File menu, select New Project (the sequence can be File | New | Project for full featured versions of Visual Studio). Choose Visual C# in the Templates tree and then Windows Store from the list of installed templates. Then select Blank App (XAML) from the list of available projects.

    Select version 4.5 as the target .NET Framework version for your new project (this is not necessary in Visual Studio Express edition).

2. Name the new project **WinRTFromCS**, and then choose a location on your file system and accept the default solution name. When you have finished, click OK.

3. As you saw in Chapter 3, "My first Windows 8 app," the Windows Store Application template provides a default page (MainPage.xaml), an application entry point in the *App* class (App.xaml.cs), a default application description and a declaration in the Package.appxmanifest file, as well as four default images representing logos and a splash screen.

4. In Solution Explorer, double-click MainPage.xaml.

    This file contains the layout of the user interface. The window, named Design View, shows two different views of this file: the Design and the XAML view.

5. Scroll down the MainPage.xaml source code and insert a *Button* control inside a *StackPanel* control, as illustrated in the bolded lines of the following code excerpt.

    ```
    <Page x:Class="WinRTFromCS.MainPage"
        xmlns="http://schemas.microsoft.com/winfx/2006/xaml/presentation"
        xmlns:x="http://schemas.microsoft.com/winfx/2006/xaml"
        xmlns:local="using:WinRTFromCS"
        xmlns:d="http://schemas.microsoft.com/expression/blend/2008"
        xmlns:mc="http://schemas.openxmlformats.org/markup-compatibility/2006"
        mc:Ignorable="d">
        <Grid Background="{StaticResource ApplicationPageBackgroundThemeBrush}">
            <StackPanel>
                <Button Click="UseCamera_Click" Content="Use Camera" />
            </StackPanel>
        </Grid>
    </Page>
    ```

6. Right-click the *UseCamera_Click* attribute of the *Button* element and select Navigate To Event Handler.

7. Replace the event handler code with the following code.

    ```
    private async void UseCamera_Click(object sender, RoutedEventArgs e)
    {
        var camera = new Windows.Media.Capture.CameraCaptureUI();
        var photo = await camera.CaptureFileAsync(
                Windows.Media.Capture.CameraCaptureUIMode.Photo);
    }
    ```

Notice the *async* keyword (which will be explained in Chapter 8, "Asynchronous patterns") and the two lines of code inside the event handler that instantiate an object of type *CameraCaptureUI* and invoke its *CaptureFileAsync* method.

8. Insert a breakpoint at the first line of code (the one starting with *var camera* = ...) and start debugging the app. When the breakpoint is reached the call stack window reveals that the app is called by External Code, which is native code.

```
Call Stack
  Name
  WinRTFromCS.exe!WinRTFromCS.MainPage.ChooseFiles_Click(object sender, Windows.UI.Xaml.RoutedEventArgs e) Line 40
  [External Code]
```

If you try to step into the code of the *CameraCaptureUI* type constructor you will see that it is not possible in managed code because the type is defined in WinRT, which is unmanaged.

9. Stop the app by stopping the debugger or pressing Alt-F4 to close the app window.

Using WinRT from a C++ Windows 8 app

In this procedure, you will use the WinRT Camera APIs to capture an image from a C++ Windows 8 app. First, you need to create a fresh app, using C++ this time.

1. Create a new Application project. To do that, open Visual Studio 2012, and from the File menu, select New Project (the sequence can be File | New | Project for full featured versions of Visual Studio). Choose Visual C++ from the Templates tree and then Windows Store from the list of installed templates. Then choose Blank App (XAML) from the list of available projects.

2. Name the new project **WinRTFromCPP**, then choose a location on your file system and leave the provided solution name. When you have finished, click OK.

3. In Solution Explorer, double-click MainPage.xaml.

4. Scroll down the MainPage.xaml source code and insert a Button control inside a StackPanel control, as illustrated in the bold lines of the following code excerpt.

```
<Page x:Class="WinRTFromCPP.MainPage"
    xmlns="http://schemas.microsoft.com/winfx/2006/xaml/presentation"
    xmlns:x="http://schemas.microsoft.com/winfx/2006/xaml"
    xmlns:local="using:WinRTFromCPP"
    xmlns:d="http://schemas.microsoft.com/expression/blend/2008"
    xmlns:mc="http://schemas.openxmlformats.org/markup-compatibility/2006"
    mc:Ignorable="d">
    <Grid Background="{StaticResource ApplicationPageBackgroundThemeBrush}">
        <StackPanel>
            <Button Click="UseCamera_Click" Content="Use Camera" />
        </StackPanel>
    </Grid>
</Page>
```

5. Right-click the UseCamera_Click attribute of the Button element and select Navigate To Event Handler.

6. Replace the event handler code with the following code.

```
void WinRTFromCPP::MainPage::UseCamera_Click(Platform::Object^ sender,
    Windows::UI::Xaml::RoutedEventArgs^ e) {
    auto camera = ref new Windows::Media::Capture::CameraCaptureUI();
    camera->CaptureFileAsync(Windows::Media::Capture::CameraCaptureUIMode::Photo);
}
```

7. Insert a breakpoint at the first line of code (the one starting with *auto camera* = …) and start debugging the app. As you can see, you will be able to step into the native code of the *CameraCaptureUI* constructor, as well as into the code of the *CaptureFileAsync* method.

8. Stop the app by stopping the debugger or pressing Alt-F4 to close it.

By experimenting with this exercise you may also notice that the names of the types, as well as the names of the methods and enums, are almost the same in C# and in C++. Nevertheless, each individual language has its own syntax, code casing, and style. However, through this procedure, you have gained hands-on experience with the real nature of WinRT: a multi-language API that adapts its syntax and style to the host language and maintains a common set of behavior capabilities under the covers. What you have just seen is the result of the language projection layer defined in the architecture of WinRT.

To take this exercise one step further, you can create the same example you did in C# and C++ using HTML5/WinJS. If you do that, you will see that the code casing will adapt to the JavaScript syntax.

Windows Runtime under the covers

The language projection of WinRT is based on a set of new metadata files, called Windows Metadata (WinMD). By default, those files are stored under the path <OS Root Path>\System32\WinMetadata, where <OS Root Path> should be replaced with the Windows 8 root installation folder (normally C:\Windows). The following is a list of the default contents of the WinMD folder.

- Windows.ApplicationModel.winmd

- Windows.Data.winmd

- Windows.Devices.winmd

- Windows.Foundation.winmd

- Windows.Globalization.winmd

- Windows.Graphics.winmd

- Windows.Management.winmd

- Windows.Media.winmd

- Windows.Networking.winmd

- Windows.Security.winmd

- Windows.Storage.winmd

- Windows.System.winmd

- Windows.UI.winmd

- Windows.UI.Xaml.winmd

- Windows.Web.winmd

Note that the folder includes a Windows.Media.winmd file, which contains the definition of the *CameraCaptureUI* type that you used in the previous exercise.

You can inspect any WinMD file using the Intermediate Language Disassembler (ILDASM) tool available in the Microsoft .NET SDK, which ships with Microsoft Visual Studio 2012 and that you can also download as part of the Microsoft .NET Framework SDK. For example, Figure 5-2 shows the ILDASM tool displaying the content outline of the Windows.Media.winmd file, which contains the definition of the *CameraCaptureUI* type that you used in the previous exercise.

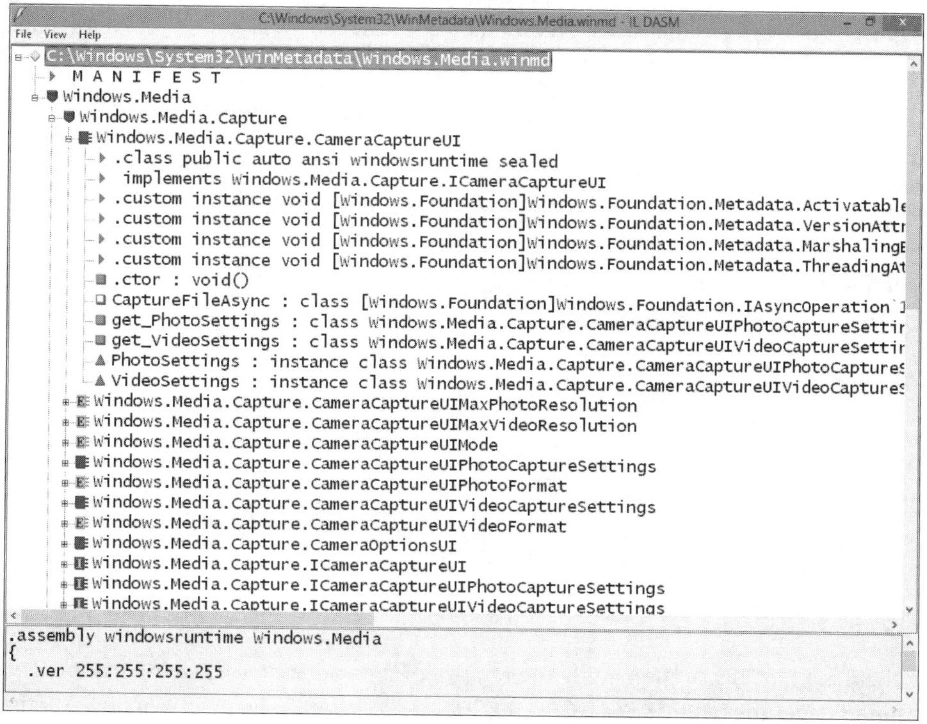

FIGURE 5-2 The ILDASM tool showing part of the Windows.Media.winmd file, which contains the definition of the *CameraCaptureUI* type.

At the top there is a file *MANIFEST*, which defines the name, version, signature, and dependencies of the current WinMD file. Moreover, there is a hierarchy of namespaces grouping various types. Each single type defines a class from the WinRT perspective. In Figure 5-3, you can clearly identify the *CaptureFileAsync* method (*CameraCaptureUI* type) you used in the previous example. By double-clicking the method in the outline, you can see its definition, which is not the source code of the method but rather the metadata mapping it to the native library that will be leveraged under the cover. In the following code excerpt, you can see the metadata definition of the *CaptureFileAsync* method defined for the *CameraCaptureUI* type.

```
.method public hidebysig newslot virtual final
        instance class [Windows.Foundation]Windows.Foundation.IAsyncOperation`1<class
[Windows.Storage]Windows.Storage.StorageFile>
        CaptureFileAsync([in] valuetype Windows.Media.Capture.CameraCaptureUIMode mode) runtime
managed {
    .override Windows.Media.Capture.ICameraCaptureUI::CaptureFileAsync
} // end of method CameraCaptureUI::CaptureFileAsync
```

The language projection infrastructure will translate this neutral definition into the proper format for the target language.

Whenever a language needs to access a WinRT type, it will inspect its definition through the corresponding WinMD file and will use the *IInspectable* interface, which is implemented by any single WinRT type. The *IInspectable* interface is an evolution of the already well-known *IUnknown* interface declared many years ago in the COM world.

Figure 5-3 shows a graphical schema of the structure of every single WinRT object.

Windows Runtime Object

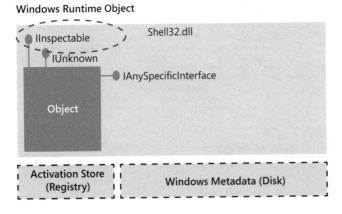

FIGURE 5-3 WinRT object schema.

First, there is a type declaration inside the registry of the operating system. All the WinRT types are registered under the path HKEY_LOCAL_MACHINE\SOFTWARE\Microsoft\WindowsRuntime\ ActivatableClassId.

For example, the *CameraCaptureUI* type is defined under the following path:

```
HKEY_LOCAL_MACHINE\SOFTWARE\Microsoft\WindowsRuntime\ActivatableClassId\Windows.Media.Capture.
CameraCaptureUI
```

The registry key contains some pertinent information, including the activation type (in process or out of process), as well as the full path of the native dynamic-link library (DLL) file containing the implementation of the target type.

The type implements the *IInspectable* interface, which provides the following three methods:

- *GetIids* Gets the interfaces that are implemented by the current WinRT class

- *GetRuntimeClassName* Gets the fully qualified name of the current WinRT object

- *GetTrustLevel* Gets the trust level of the current WinRT object

By querying the *IInspectable* interface, the language projection infrastructure of WinRT will translate the type from its original declaration into the target language that is going to consume the type.

As illustrated in Figure 5-4, the projection occurs at compile time for a C++ app consuming WinRT, and it will produce native code that will not need any more access to the metadata. In the case of a CLR app (C#/VB), it happens during compilation into IL code, as well as at runtime through a runtime callable wrapper. However, the cost of communication between CLR and the WinRT metadata is not so different than the cost of talking with the CLR metadata in general. Lastly, in the case of an HTML5/WinJS app it will occur at runtime through the Chakra engine.

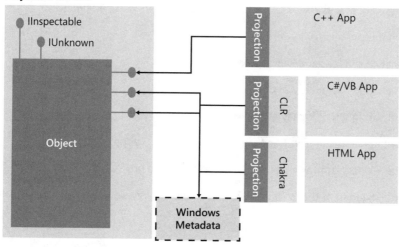

FIGURE 5-4 How data moves between C++, the CLR, HTML/WinJS, and WinRT.

The overall architecture of WinRT is also versioning compliant. In fact, every WinRT type will be capable of supporting a future version of the operating system and of the Windows Runtime engine by simply extending the available interfaces implemented and providing the information about the new extensions through the *IInspectable* interface.

Windows Runtime design requirements

To support the architecture of WinRT and the language projection infrastructure, every Windows 8 app—regardless of the programming language used to write it—runs in a standard code execution profile that is based on a limited set of capabilities. To accomplish this goal, the WinRT product team defined the minimum set of APIs needed to implement a Windows 8 app. For example, the Windows 8 app profile has been deprived of the entire set of console APIs, which are not needed in a Windows 8 app. The same happened to ASP.NET, for instance—the list of .NET types removed is quite long. Moreover, the WinRT product team decided to remove all the old-style, complex, and/or dangerous APIs and instead provide developers with a safer and easier working environment. As an example, to access XML nodes from a classic .NET application, you have a rich set of APIs to choose from (XML Document Object Model, Simple API for XML, LINQ to XML in .NET, and so on). The set also depends on which programming language you are using. In contrast, in a Windows 8 app written in CLR (C#/VB) you have only the LINQ to XML support, while the XML Document Object Model has been removed.

Furthermore, considering a Windows 8 app is an application that can execute on multiple devices (desktop PCs, tablets, ARM-based devices, and Windows Phone 8 mobile phones), all the APIs specific to a particular operating system or hardware platform have been removed.

The final result is a set of APIs that are clear, simple, well-designed, and portable across multiple devices. From a .NET developer perspective, the Windows 8 app profile is a .NET 4.5 profile with a limited set of types and capabilities, which are the minimum set useful for implementing a real Windows 8 app.

Consider this: the standard .NET 4.5 profile includes more than 120 assemblies, containing more than 400 namespaces that group more than 14,000 types. In contrast, the Windows 8 app profile includes about 15 assemblies and 70 namespaces that group only about 1,000 types.

The main goals in this profile design were to:

- Avoid duplication of types and/or functionalities.

- Remove APIs not applicable to Windows 8 apps.

- Remove badly designed or legacy APIs.

- Make it easy to port existing .NET applications to Windows 8 apps.

- Keep .NET developers comfortable with the Windows 8 app profile.

Figure 5-5 shows a diagram of the main .NET APIs available in a Windows 8 app.

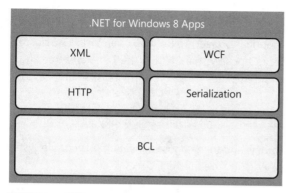

FIGURE 5-5 .NET APIs available to a Windows 8 application.

For example, the Windows Communication Foundation (WCF) APIs exist, but you can use WCF only to consume services, therefore leveraging a reduced set of communication bindings. You cannot use WCF in a Windows 8 app to host a service—for security reasons and for portability reasons.

Creating a WinMD library

The previous sections contained some information about the WinRT architecture and the WinMD infrastructure—which allows the language projection of WinRT to make a set of APIs available to multiple programming languages. In this section, you will learn how to create a library of APIs of your own, making that library available to all other Windows 8 apps through the same projection environment used by WinRT.

Internally, the WinRT types in your component can use any .NET Framework functionality that's allowed in a Windows 8 app. Externally, however, your types must adhere to a simple and strict set of requirements.

- The fields, parameters, and return values of all the public types and members in your component must be WinRT types.

- Public structures may not have any members other than public fields, and those fields must be value types or strings.

- Public classes must be *sealed* (*NotInheritable* in Visual Basic). If your programming model requires polymorphism, you can create a public interface and implement that interface on the classes that must be polymorphic. The only exceptions are XAML controls.

- All public types must have a root namespace that matches the assembly name, and the assembly name must not begin with "Windows."

In the following exercise, you will create a *WinMD* library and share it across all the languages supported by Windows 8 apps.

Using C# to create a *WinMD* library sharable with C++ and HTML5/WinJS

1. Create a new Windows Runtime Component project. To do that, open Visual Studio 2012, and from the File menu, select New Project. Choose Visual C# from the Templates tree and then Windows Store from the list of installed templates. Then choose Windows Runtime Component from the list of available projects

2. Select version 4.5 as the Microsoft .NET Framework target version for your new project.

3. Name the new project **WinMDCSLibrary**, and then choose a location on your file system and leave the provided solution name. When you have finished, click OK.

4. Right-click the project icon in the Solution Explorer and choose Properties. The project Output Type is Windows Runtime Component, which means that the project will create not only a DLL, but also a WinMD file for sharing the library with any Windows 8 app written with any language.

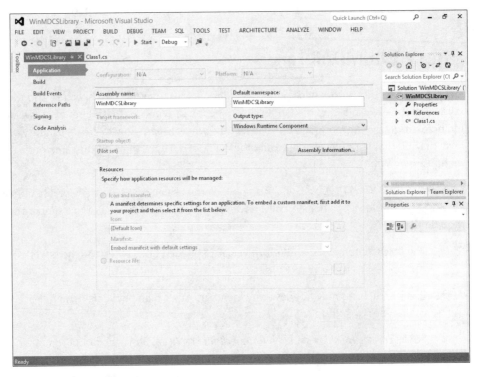

5. Close the Project Properties window.

6. In the Solution Explorer, right-click the Class1.cs file and select Rename. Enter the new name **SampleUtility.cs** and when prompted by Visual Studio, confirm that you want to also rename the class and not just the file.

7. Add the following *using* statement at the beginning of the file, before the class declaration.

```
using System.Text.RegularExpressions;
```

8. Insert the following code into the class file.

```
public Boolean IsMailAddress(String email)
{
    Regex regexMail = new Regex(@"\b[A-Z0-9._%+-]+@[A-Z0-9.-]+\.[A-Z]{2,4}\b");
    return(regexMail.IsMatch(email));
}
```

9. Build the project by right-clicking the project icon in the Solution Explorer and choosing Build.

10. Check the output by right-clicking the project icon in the Solution Explorer and choosing Open Folder In File Explorer.

11. Browse to the bin\Debug subfolder.

12. As you can see in the output folder, there is a WinMDCSLibrary.winmd file.

   Open the file with ILDASM, just to check its content and to see that the file defines the *WinMDCSLibrary.SampleUtility* class.

Next you will consume this C#-based Windows Runtime Component from C++.

Consuming a *WinMD* library created with C# from C++

1. Open the solution defined in the previous exercise, if it is not already open.

2. Add a new Application project. To do that, from the File menu, select Add New Project. Choose Visual C++ from the Templates tree and then Windows Store from the list of installed templates. Finally, choose Blank App (XAML) from the list of available projects.

3. Name the new project **WinMDCPPConsumer**, and then choose a location on your file system. When you have finished, click OK.

4. In Solution Explorer, right-click the WinMDCPPConsumer project and select the References menu item.

5. In the WinMDCPPConsumer Property Pages window, select Add New Reference.

6. In the left pane of the Add Reference window, select Solution, and then select Projects.

7. In the right pane, select the WinMDCSLibrary project and click OK twice.

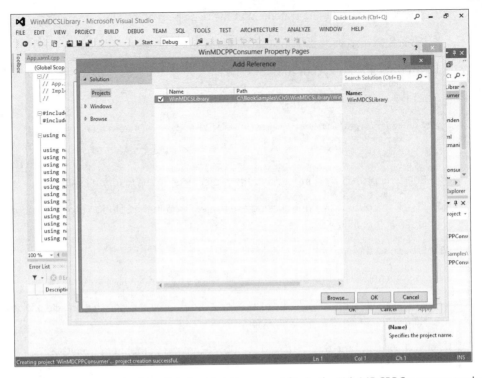

8. In Solution Explorer, double-click the MainPage.xaml file in the WinMDCPPConsumer project.

    This file contains the layout for the user interface. The window, named Design View, shows two different views of this file: the Design view and the XAML view.

9. Scroll down the MainPage.xaml source code and insert a *Button* control inside a *StackPanel* control, as illustrated in the bold lines of code in the following excerpt.

```
<Page x:Class="WinRTFromCS.MainPage"
    xmlns="http://schemas.microsoft.com/winfx/2006/xaml/presentation"
    xmlns:x="http://schemas.microsoft.com/winfx/2006/xaml"
    xmlns:local="using:WinRTFromCS"
    xmlns:d="http://schemas.microsoft.com/expression/blend/2008"
    xmlns:mc="http://schemas.openxmlformats.org/markup-compatibility/2006"
    mc:Ignorable="d">
    <Grid Background="{StaticResource ApplicationPageBackgroundThemeBrush}">
        <StackPanel>
            <Button Click="ConsumeWinMD_Click" Content="Consume WinMD Library" />
        </StackPanel>
    </Grid>
</Page>
```

10. Right-click the *ConsumeWinMD_Click* attribute of the *Button* element and select Navigate To Event Handler.

11. Replace the event handler code with the following code.

```
void WinMDCPPConsumer::MainPage::ConsumeWinMD_Click(Platform::Object^ sender,
    Windows::UI::Xaml::RoutedEventArgs^ e) {
    auto utility = ref new WinMDCSLibrary::SampleUtility();
    bool result = utility->IsMailAddress("paolo@devleap.com");
}
```

Build the whole solution.

12. Place a breakpoint in the *IsMailAddress* method of WinMDCSLibrary and start the C++ project in debug mode, configuring "Mixed (Managed and Native)" in the debugging properties of the WinMDCPPConsumer project.

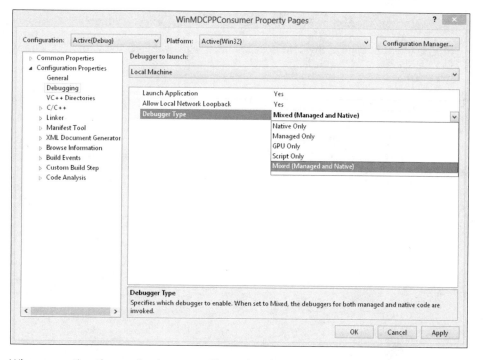

When executing the application, you will see that the debugger will step into the C# code starting from the C++ code.

13. After debugging, close the sample C++ app by pressing Alt-F4 or stopping the app execution in Visual Studio.

Do not close Visual Studio.

Next, you'll consume the same component in HTML5/WinJS.

Consuming a *WinMD* library created with C# from HTML5/WinJS

1. Open the C# solution you defined previously, if it's not already open.

2. Add a new HTML5/WinJS Application project. To do that, from the File menu, select Add New Project. Choose JavaScript from the Templates tree and then Windows Store from the list of installed templates. Finally, choose Blank App from the list of available projects.

3. Name the new project **WinMDJSConsumer**, and then choose a location on your file system and accept the default solution name. When you have finished, click OK.

4. In the Solution Explorer, right-click the References folder of the WinMDJSConsumer project and select Add Reference.

5. In the left pane of the Reference Manager window, select Solution and then select Projects.

6. In the right pane of the Reference Manager window, select the WinMDCSLibrary project and click OK.

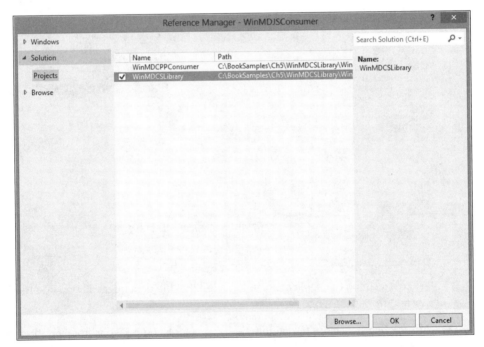

7. In Solution Explorer, double-click the Default.html file of the WinMDJSConsumer project. This file contains the layout for the user interface.

8. Replace the HTML body of the Default.html page with the following code:

```
<body>
    <p><button id="consumeWinMDLibrary">Consume WinMD Library</button></p>
</body>
```

9. Open the Default.js file, which is in the js folder of the project, and place the following event handler inside the file, just before the *app.start()* method invocation.

```
function consumeWinMD(eventInfo) {
    var utility = new WinMDCSLibrary.SampleUtility();
    var result = utility.isMailAddress("paolo@devleap.com");
}
```

Notice that the case of the *IsMailAddress* method, defined in C#, has been translated into *isMailAddress* in JavaScript thanks to the language projection infrastructure provided by WinRT.

10. Next, insert the following lines of code into the function associated with the *app.onactivated* event, just before the end of the *if* statement.

```
// Retrieve the button and register the event handler.
var consumeWinMDLibrary = document.getElementById("consumeWinMDLibrary");
consumeWinMDLibrary.addEventListener("click", consumeWinMD, false);
```

Here's how the complete code of the Default.js file should look after you have made the edits.

```
// For an introduction to the Blank template, see the following documentation:
// http://go.microsoft.com/fwlink/?LinkId=232509
(function () {
    "use strict";

    WinJS.Binding.optimizeBindingReferences = true;

    var app = WinJS.Application;
    var activation = Windows.ApplicationModel.Activation;

    app.onactivated = function (args) {
        if (args.detail.kind === activation.ActivationKind.launch) {
            if (args.detail.previousExecutionState !==
            activation.ApplicationExecutionState.terminated) {
                // TODO: This application has been newly launched. Initialize
                // your application here.
            } else {
                // TODO: This application has been reactivated from suspension.
                // Restore application state here.
            }
            args.setPromise(WinJS.UI.processAll());

            // Retrieve the button and register our event handler.
            var consumeWinMDLibrary = document.getElementById("consumeWinMDLibrary");
            consumeWinMDLibrary.addEventListener("click", consumeWinMD, false);
        }
    };

    app.oncheckpoint = function (args) {
        // TODO: This application is about to be suspended. Save any state
        // that needs to persist across suspensions here. You might use the
        // WinJS.Application.sessionState object, which is automatically
        // saved and restored across suspension. If you need to complete an
        // asynchronous operation before your application is suspended, call
        // args.setPromise().
    };
```

```
function consumeWinMD(eventInfo) {
    var utility = new WinMDCSLibrary.SampleUtility();
    var result = utility.isMailAddress("paolo@devleap.com");
}

app.start();
})();
```

11. Build the solution.

12. Place a breakpoint in the *IsMailAddress* method of WinMDCSLibrary and start the HTML5/
    WinJS project in debug mode, configuring "Mixed (Managed and Native)" in the debugging
    properties of the WinMDJSConsumer project.

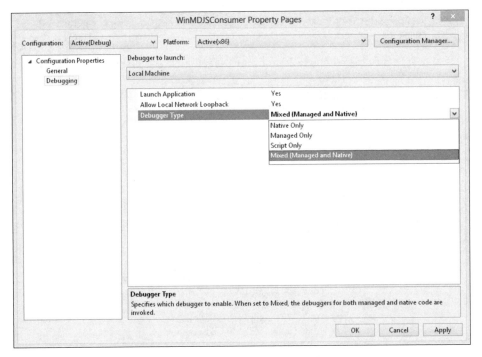

As the code executes, the debugger will step into the C# code starting from the JavaScript
code.

13. After debugging, close the sample HTML5/WinJS app by pressing Alt-F4 or by stopping the
    execution in Visual Studio.

Windows Runtime app registration

Whenever you create a Windows 8 app and launch it through the Visual Studio 2012 debugger, you'll
find that it is placed as a Tile into the Start screen of Windows 8. For example, if you followed all the
previous exercises, your Windows 8 Start screen will have the tiles shown in Figure 5-6.

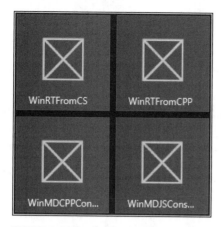

FIGURE 5-6 Tiles for the sample project in the Windows 8 Start screen.

In fact, every single time you execute a project from Visual Studio 2012, it automatically adds your app to the Start screen. Under the covers, your app is registered into the Windows Registry, using some information defined in the Package.appxmanifest file available in your project. If you double-click that file, for example in the WinMDJSConsumer project you defined in the last exercise, you will be prompted with a graphical editor/designer as in Figure 5-7, which shows the Packaging tab of the designer.

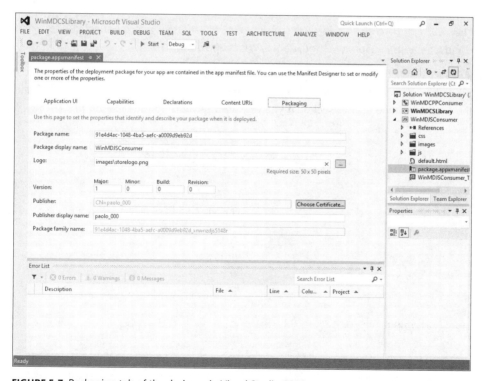

FIGURE 5-7 Packaging tab of the designer in Visual Studio 2012.

The *Package* name property contains the unique name used to identify the package on any target device. You should provide a human-friendly name to this property instead of using the default GUID generated by Visual Studio 2012. In addition, the Package display name will be shown in the app's tile on the Start screen. In the designer, you can supply a logo, version number, and the publisher display name as additional information used to describe the package and the app better.

When you register (in this case, execute an app for the first time from Visual Studio 2012) a Windows 8 app, the system reads the packaging information and writes some information into the Windows Registry. Execute the following instructions to better understand what happens *under* the cover.

1. Supply the value **WinMDJSConsumer** to the *Package* name property of the WinMDJSConsumer project in the Package.appxmanifest file.

2. Execute the WinMDJSConsumer Windows 8 app.

3. Close the app by pressing Alt-F4.

4. Open the Registry Editor by pressing Windows+Q and typing **Regedit**, select the Registry Editor tool on the search result page and when asked, execute it with elevated privileges.

Under the HKEY_CLASSES_ROOT\Extensions\ContractId\Windows.Launch key you will find a sub-key named *PackageId*. That key contains a sub-key called *WinMDJSConsumer_1.0.0.0_x86__xnwnzd-js5148r,* which is the name of the package, followed by its build version, the target platform, and an alphanumeric code describing the publisher.

That key will, in turn, contain a sub-key named *ActivatableClassId*, which defines the sub-key app (for CLR and C++ apps) or App.wwa (for HTML5/WinJS apps).

Under HKEY_CURRENT_USER\Software\Classes\ActivatableClasses\Package there will be a corresponding *ActivatableClasses* key that will define the packages, under the *Package* sub-key. Figure 5-8 shows the registry outline for this section if you executed the apps in the previous exercises.

FIGURE 5-8 The Registry editor, showing entries made by registering the example apps in this chapter.

When you start a new app instance or resume an already executing instance by clicking or tapping its tile in the Start screen, the operating system will read the server sub-key of the package defined in the *ActivatableClasses* and will locate the path of the process to execute from the *ExePath* key. Notice that the WinMDJSConsumer App has an *ExePath* corresponding to the standard HTML5 app host, which is C:\Windows\syswow64\wwahost.exe.

In contrast, the WinMDCPPConsumer App has an *ExePath* value of *<Path of your exercises>*\AppX\ WinMDCPPConsumer.exe.

Both apps will have a key named *CustomAttributes*, under the *App* key that is a child of the *ActivatableClassId* sub-key of each package.

The *CustomAttributes* key contains an *AppObject.EntryPoint* string value, which defines the entry point of the app. For the C++ App that assumes the value *WinMDCPPConsumer.App* (the main class). But the HTML5/WinJS App will have a value of Default.html (the default HTML page).

Summary

In this chapter, you have seen what the Windows Runtime is, how it works, and a high-level view of its architecture. You also learned what a Windows 8 app profile is, and how to create a custom Windows Runtime Component library that you or other developers can consume from multiple languages, all while leveraging the language projection features of WinRT.

Quick reference

To	Do this
Get a picture from the camera of a Windows 8 device	Using C# code, instantiate the *CameraCaptureUI* class and invoke the *CaptureFileAsync* method.
Inspect the content of a WinMD file	Use the ILDASM tool available in the .NET Framework SDK.
Debug a solution based on a mixture of CLR and C++ code	Configure the debugging options to support "Mixed (Managed and Native)" debug.
Understand what apps are registered in the Start screen of Windows 8	Inspect the Windows Registry under the key HKEY_CLASSES_ROOT\Extensions\ContractId\Windows.Launch.

CHAPTER 6

Windows Runtime APIs

After completing this chapter, you will be able to

- Interact with Windows Runtime APIs from a Windows 8 app.

- Use some of the available date, time, and file pickers.

- Interact with the webcam to take photos and videos.

- Implement the Share contract to share information between applications.

Chapter 5, "Introduction to the Windows Runtime," covered the Windows Runtime (WinRT) architecture and the basic types, how to write code using the multilanguage features, and the concept of language projection. This chapter shows you how to interact with the user-related WinRT APIs such as File Picker and Webcam, and the APIs that you need to implement the Share contract.

Pickers

Windows 8 has two types of pickers. One has been in common use since the 1990s; it lets users choose something such as a date, a file, or a printer. This type of picker normally corresponds to user controls that are part of the framework or the programming environment. For example, ASP.NET provides the *DatePicker Calendar* Control, Windows Presentation Foundation (WPF) exposes a *DatePicker* control, and Windows Forms provided common dialog controls that let users pick files or printers from the operating system.

In Windows 8, you can find these kinds of controls as part of the Extensible Application Markup Language (XAML) framework or as part of the WinJS (Windows Library for JavaScript) library for HTML Windows 8 UI style apps (Windows Store app or simply Windows 8 app). To use them, you simply drag the controls from the Microsoft Visual Studio toolbox to the window editing surface or by coding their definition declaratively in XAML or HTML code.

The other types of pickers in Windows 8 are provided not by user controls, but rather via APIs exposed by WinRT. You can use them directly in your Windows 8 UI style applications or Windows 8 UI style class libraries without having to add any external references because they are part of the environment. For example, you can invoke these APIs to retrieve a file path for a document directly from code. It's important to realize that the WinRT APIs are accessible from any Windows 8 UI style application—so you can access them using Microsoft C# or Microsoft Visual Basic code from a .NET Windows 8 UI style app, or using JavaScript code from HTML Windows 8 UI style apps.

A picker has its own user interface that adheres to the Windows 8 UI design language that you learned about in Chapter 2, "Windows 8 UI style," and neither the layout nor the appearance can be modified from code; instead, your applications can customize only some settings.

To get a feel for how this works, in the next exercise you'll start by coding the File Picker.

Using the File Picker

In this procedure, you will use the *FileOpenPicker* class, which allows a user to choose a file from the document library.

1. Create a new Application project. To do that, open Visual Studio 2012, and from the File menu, select New Project (the sequence can be File | New | Project for full-featured versions of Visual Studio). Choose Visual C# from the Templates tree and then Windows Store from the list of installed templates. Finally, choose the Blank App (XAML) project type from the list of available projects.

   Select version 4.5 as the Microsoft .NET Framework target version for your new project (this is not necessary in the Visual Studio Express edition).

2. Name the new project **FilePicker**, and then choose a location on your file system without changing the default solution name. When you have finished, click OK.

   As you saw in Chapter 3, "My first Windows 8 app," the Windows Store application template provides a default page (MainPage.xaml), an application entry point in the *App* class (App. xaml.cs), a default application description and a declaration in the Package.appxmanifest file, as well as four default images representing logos and a splash screen.

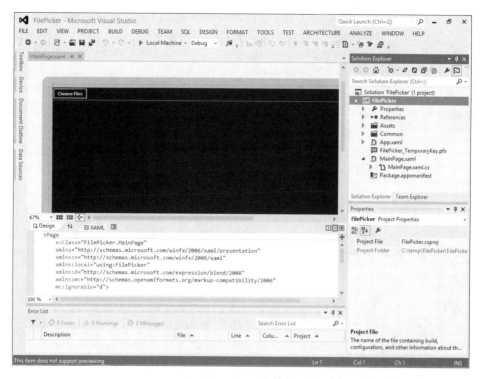

3. Scroll down in the MainPage.xaml source code and insert a *ListBox* control and a *Button* control inside a *StackPanel* control, as illustrated in the bold lines of the following code excerpt.

```
<Page x:Class="FilePicker.MainPage"
    xmlns="http://schemas.microsoft.com/winfx/2006/xaml/presentation"
    xmlns:x="http://schemas.microsoft.com/winfx/2006/xaml"
    xmlns:local="using:FilePicker"
    xmlns:d="http://schemas.microsoft.com/expression/blend/2008"
    xmlns:mc="http://schemas.openxmlformats.org/markup-compatibility/2006"
    mc:Ignorable="d">

    <Grid Background="{StaticResource ApplicationPageBackgroundThemeBrush}">
        <StackPanel>
            <Button Click="ChooseFiles_Click" Content="Choose Files" />
            <ListBox x:Name="filesList"  />
        </StackPanel>
    </Grid>

</Page>
```

The *ListBox* control will be filled with the file names chosen by the user through the *FileOpenPicker* picker; the button will simply fire the code to start the picker and bind the selected files in the *ListBox*.

4. Open the MainPage.xaml.cs file and add the method *ChooseFiles_Click,* which implements the event handler for the button. You can also double-click the button in the integrated development environment (IDE) designer. Add the *async* keyword to the method because pickers use the asynchronous pattern of .NET 4.5.

 Note You will learn all the details of this asynchronous technique in Chapter 8, "Asynchronous patterns."

The code here represents the complete method definition:

```
private async void ChooseFiles_Click(object sender, RoutedEventArgs e)
{
}
```

5. Add the following code to the method to open the File Picker and retrieve the selected files.

```
var picker = new Windows.Storage.Pickers.FileOpenPicker();
picker.FileTypeFilter.Add("*");

var files = await picker.PickMultipleFilesAsync();

filesList.Items.Clear();
foreach (var file in files)
    filesList.Items.Add(file.Name);
```

The first line of code creates an instance of the *FileOpenPicker* class and assigns it to the local variable named *picker.* Then the code adds a filter on the file type that the picker will show to the user (all files in this case).

The third line of code is the most important: it asks the *FileOpenPicker* class to let the user choose multiple files. It then *awaits*—waits for method completion in an asynchronous way, without blocking the current thread—the result. This new *async* pattern lets you write code that resembles synchronous code, simplifying coding and debugging. The *async* pattern eliminates the need to define callbacks and use the *IAsyncResult* interface.

When a user has chosen some files (or has clicked the Cancel button on the picker) the code continues by simply clearing and then filling *ListBox* with the selected files.

The complete code for MainPage.xaml.cs should look like the following.

```
using System;
using System.Collections.Generic;
using System.IO;
using System.Linq;
using Windows.Foundation;
using Windows.Foundation.Collections;
using Windows.UI.Xaml;
using Windows.UI.Xaml.Controls;
using Windows.UI.Xaml.Controls.Primitives;
using Windows.UI.Xaml.Data;
```

```
using Windows.UI.Xaml.Input;
using Windows.UI.Xaml.Media;
using Windows.UI.Xaml.Navigation;

// The Blank Page item template is documented at http://go.microsoft.com/
fwlink/?LinkId=234238

namespace FilePicker
{
    /// <summary>
    /// An empty page that can be used on its own or navigated to within a Frame.
    /// </summary>
    public sealed partial class MainPage : Page
    {
        public MainPage()
        {
            this.InitializeComponent();
        }

        private async void ChooseFiles_Click(object sender, RoutedEventArgs e)
        {
            var picker = new Windows.Storage.Pickers.FileOpenPicker();
            picker.FileTypeFilter.Add("*");
            var files = await picker.PickMultipleFilesAsync();

            filesList.Items.Clear();

            foreach (var file in files)
                filesList.Items.Add(file.Name);
        }

        /// <summary>
        /// Invoked when this page is about to be displayed in a Frame.
        /// </summary>
        /// <param name="e">Event data that describes how this page was reached.
            The Parameter
        /// property is typically used to configure the page.</param>

        protected override void OnNavigatedTo(NavigationEventArgs e)
        {
        }
    }
}
```

Before running the project, remember that Visual Studio first deploys your application to Windows 8 and then starts it. Thus, after you run an app from Visual Studio, you will find the default app Tile on the Start screen. As you learned in Chapter 3, the default value for the *Show Name* property in the application manifest is *All Logos*. Before moving on, choose the behavior you want for your app tile by opening the Package.appxmanifest file in the designer, and choosing the property *Show Name*.

 Note Please refer to Chapter 3, "My first Windows 8 app," and Chapter 4, "Application lifecycle management," for a description of the structure of the manifest.

The following graphic shows the user interface for the main page of the application.

6. Click Choose Files and use the Windows 8 File Picker to select some files.

   You can simply click or tap on a file to select or clear it. The following graphic shows the File Picker on the desktop with the Logo.png and SmallLogo.png files selected.

The top of the picker shows the user the selected directory, the applied sorting, and a link to select all the files in that folder. The content pane shows the available files where you enter selections by simply clicking or tapping on them. The bottom line of the picker shows the selected files, the Cancel button, and the Open button.

7. Select some files and then click Open.

As you have seen so far, the steps and the code to use a picker such as the File Picker are really simple.

You can define the text for the Open button using the *CommitButtonText* property, provide a default start location using the *SuggestedStartLocation* property, and use the *PickSingleFileAysnc* property if the user has to select a single file.

You also can change the viewing mode from list to thumbnail; this is the only allowed customization for the user interface. Add the following line of code just before the *PickMultipleFileAsync* call to modify the view mode.

```
private async void ChooseFiles_Click(object sender, RoutedEventArgs e)
{
    var picker = new Windows.Storage.Pickers.FileOpenPicker();
    picker.FileTypeFilter.Add("*");

    picker.ViewMode = Windows.Storage.Pickers.PickerViewMode.Thumbnail;

    var files = await picker.PickMultipleFilesAsync();

    filesList.Items.Clear();

    foreach (var file in files)
        filesList.Items.Add(file.Name);
}
```

The last thing to notice before moving to the Webcam API is that you haven't modified the manifest file to allow the access to the library. When you open the Capabilities tab on the Package. appxmanifest designer while in step 7, you may notice a *Document Library* property. It is not necessary to grant this capability, nor the *Music Library* or the *Picture Library* property, because they are not related to the *FileOpenPicker*.

Webcam

WinRT provides a very simple API to interact with the webcam from .NET, C++, or JavaScript code. As with other WinRT APIs, you do not need any references to class libraries to use the Webcam API. The .NET for Windows Store apps reference is added automatically when you create a new Windows Store App project in Visual Studio. If you don't have a Webcam attached to your system, move on to the next example in the chapter because this example won't be able to demonstrate the device capabilities for you.

Using the Webcam

In this procedure, you will start using the Webcam API to let the user take a photo (or a video) and return it to the Windows 8 UI style application.

1. Create a new Application project. To do that, open Visual Studio 2012, and from the File menu, select New Project. Choose Windows Store from the list of installed templates, and then choose Blank App (XAML) from the list of available projects.

2. Select version 4.5 as the .NET Framework target version for your new project.

3. Name the new project **Webcam**, and then choose a location on your file system and a solution name. When you're finished, click OK.

4. Open the MainPage.xaml page and add a *Button* and an *Image* control. The button will fire the code to start the webcam, and the image will display the photo that the user will take. The following code shows the complete XAML code for MainPage.xaml. The lines in bold show what you need to add to the page.

```
<Page x:Class="Webcam.MainPage"
    xmlns="http://schemas.microsoft.com/winfx/2006/xaml/presentation"
    xmlns:x="http://schemas.microsoft.com/winfx/2006/xaml"
    xmlns:local="using:Webcam"
    xmlns:d="http://schemas.microsoft.com/expression/blend/2008"
    xmlns:mc="http://schemas.openxmlformats.org/markup-compatibility/2006"
    mc:Ignorable="d">

    <Grid Background="{StaticResource ApplicationPageBackgroundThemeBrush}">
        <StackPanel>
            <Button Click="TakePhoto_Click" Content="Take Photo"/>
            <Image x:Name="image" Height="800" />
        </StackPanel>
    </Grid>

</Page>
```

5. Implement the event handler for the button click event using the following code as a reference:

```csharp
using System;
using System.Collections.Generic;
using System.IO;
using System.Linq;
using Windows.Foundation;
using Windows.Foundation.Collections;
using Windows.Media.Capture;
using Windows.Storage;
using Windows.UI.Xaml;
using Windows.UI.Xaml.Controls;
using Windows.UI.Xaml.Controls.Primitives;
using Windows.UI.Xaml.Data;
using Windows.UI.Xaml.Input;
using Windows.UI.Xaml.Media;
using Windows.UI.Xaml.Media.Imaging;
using Windows.UI.Xaml.Navigation;

// The Blank Page item template is documented at http://go.microsoft.com/
fwlink/?LinkId=234238

namespace Webcam
{
    /// <summary>
    /// An empty page that can be used on its own or navigated to within a Frame.
    /// </summary>

    public sealed partial class MainPage : Page
    {
        public MainPage()
        {
            this.InitializeComponent();
        }

        private async void TakePhoto_Click(object sender, RoutedEventArgs e)
        {
            var camera = new CameraCaptureUI();
            var img = await camera.CaptureFileAsync(CameraCaptureUIMode.Photo);
            if (img != null)
            {
                var stream = await img.OpenAsync(FileAccessMode.Read);
                var bitmap = new BitmapImage();
                bitmap.SetSource(stream);
                image.Source = bitmap;
            }
        }
```

```
/// <summary>
/// Invoked when this page is about to be displayed in a Frame.
/// </summary>
/// <param name="e">Event data that describes how this page was reached.
/// The Parameter
/// property is typically used to configure the page.</param>

protected override void OnNavigatedTo(NavigationEventArgs e)
{
}
        }
    }
}
```

The first line of code in the *TakePhoto_Click* method creates an instance of the *CameraCaptureUI* class and the second line waits for the completion of its method, *CaptureFileAsync*, which, as you can imagine, captures the stream using the *async* pattern, which prevents blocking the UI thread. The method accepts the *CameraCaptureUIMode* parameter, which can assume the value of *Photo*, *Video*, or *PhotoOrVideo*. In the presented example, the webcam will be activated to take a photo.

The *CaptureFileAsync* method returns an instance of the *StorageFile* WinRT class representing the captured stream as a file. This file can be opened as a stream using the *OpenAsync* method: the method returns an instance of *IRandomAccessStream* interface that can be used to set the source for a *BitmapImage* instance. Finally, the instance of the bitmap can be assigned to the *Source* property of the XAML *Image* control.

6. Modify the application manifest to set the *Show Name* property accordingly to your preferences, just as you did in the previous procedure, and then press F5.

If you click Take Photo, the webcam screen will occupy the entire screen, but you won't be able to take a photo—in fact the default message is very clear and informs you that this app needs the user's permission to use the camera. The reason is very simple: you cannot use the Webcam API without declaring the webcam capability in the application manifest. Obviously, if you have no camera attached to your PC, the application will first ask you to connect the device.

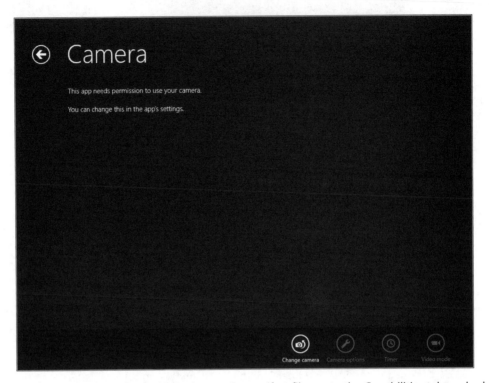

7. Stop the application, open the Package.appxmanifest file, go to the Capabilities tab, and select Webcam from the Capabilities list.

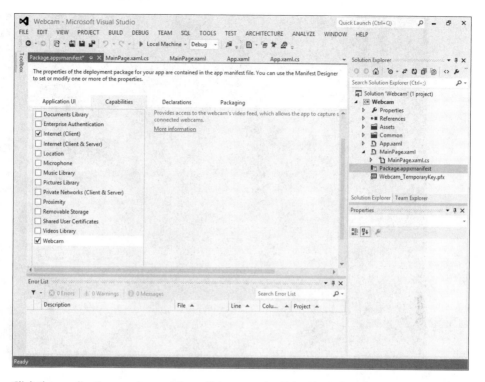

8. Click the application again, and then click or tap the Take Photo button. A message box (displayed in Windows 8 UI style) will ask you if this application can use the webcam.

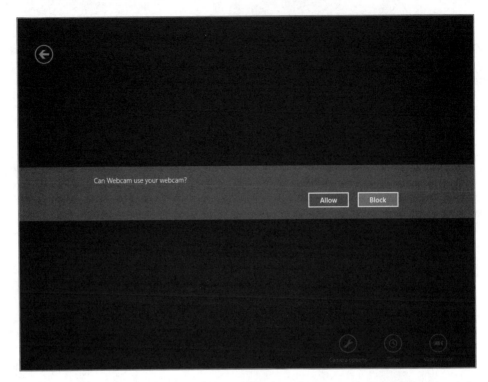

This request is the standard mechanism that Windows 8 uses to ask the user for permission to use a specific application capability. In practice, the application needs to declare its capabilities in the manifest and the user has to provide permission to the application explicitly for each capability. If the user blocks a capability, the corresponding feature cannot be used. In the application you are building, the webcam shows a black screen in which the user cannot do anything but click Back to return to the application.

The system retains the user's choice forever; however, users can remove a specific permission at any time for any application or restore a permission at any time, as you will see in the following steps.

9. Click the Block button in the screen represented in the previous image. The user can do nothing with the camera in this app.

10. Move the mouse to the lower-right corner to view the Charms and select Settings. A panel appears on the right of the screen with some settings in the lower section, such as the network joined by the system, the volume level, the language, and a button to turn off/sleep/restart the system.

11. In the upper section of the panel, you can see the application name, the user currently using the application, the version of the application, and the Permissions for the webcam. The following graphic shows the permissions for the Webcam App.

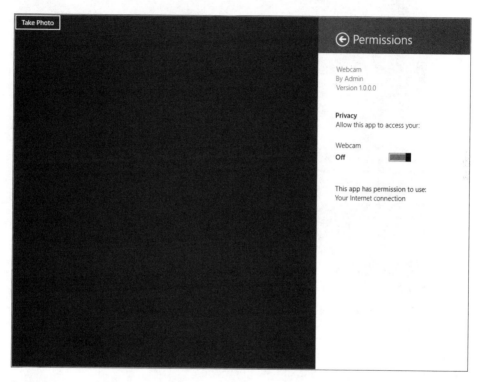

As you can see, the lower section of the pane presents the two capabilities requested in the application manifest: Internet Connection and Webcam.

12. By using the slider next to the Webcam item, grant the app permission to use the webcam. Immediately, you will be able to preview the image taken from the webcam in the remaining part of the screen.

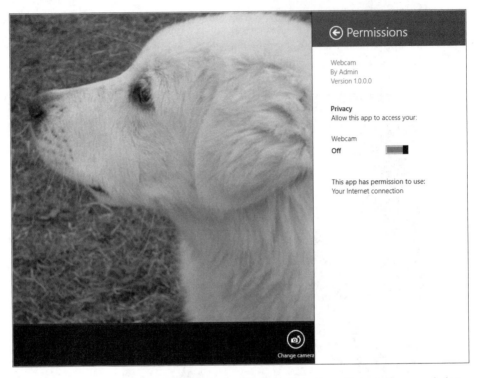

You can turn the Webcam permission on or off at any time to verify how the permission mechanism works.

13. Tap or click the screen to take the photo and go to the confirmation screen, where you can crop the photo, accept it, or take a new one.

14. Accept the photo by clicking OK. The webcam dialog box will return the photo to the application, which, in turn, will display it on the main page.

The *CameraCaptureUI* class exposes some properties to define the settings to take photos and some properties to adjust the settings for taking videos. For instance, with the first, you can set the *AllowCropping* property to *True* or *False*, and you can set the format and the resolution for the image. With the latter, you can set the resolution for the video, the maximum duration, and the format.

If you want to record the audio as well, you need to specify the Microphone capability in the application manifest.

Sharing contracts

In Chapter 3, you implemented the Search contract feature to let the user search data inside your application.

A contract regulates the interaction between an application and the operating system. Every application that implements a Windows 8 contract can use the corresponding operating system feature.

The Sharing contract regulates data exchange between applications. Chapter 1, "Introduction to Windows Store apps," introduced and demonstrated the use of the Sharing contract to show how data can be passed from one application to another without direct communication. The operating system acts as a bridge between the source application and the target application, invoking the necessary APIs on both of them.

The source app needs to do the following:

- Register itself with the Data Transfer Manager, which is the operating system component that manages the information exchange between the application and the target application.

- Implement an event handler to reply to sharing requests. When the user chooses to share something, she activates the Share pane by using the Share charm. The operating system asks the source application to prepare the data package invoking an event on the source application; this corresponding event handler is the place where you prepare the data package. The source application can request a sharing operation directly from code without the user needing to use the Share charm.

The package specifies the type of resources it contains. The operating system lists all the target applications that can receive the same type of resources. For instance, if the source application shares images, the operating system will enumerate all the possible target applications that can receive images.

The target app needs to:

- Define the sharing target declaration inside the application manifest.

- Declare the types of resources that it can receive. This information is used by the operating system to create the list of applications that can receive the content shared by the source application.

- Implement the sharing target activation, a special kind of application activation that receives the data package. This activation is requested by the operating system when the user chooses the application as the target for sharing operations.

- Provide the page to be displayed in the pane filled with the information about the received data. For instance, a social application can display the received image and ask the user for a description and a tag before posting it to the social network.

- Implement the logic to process the data. Following the preceding example, the application can post the image to Facebook. This process can be done in an asynchronous way if the operations are time-consuming.

- Report the completion of the operation.

As you learned in Chapter 1, some native Windows 8 applications can be used as sources and others can be used as targets. For instance, the Windows 8 UI style version of Windows Internet Explorer can act as a source application, sharing the text the user has selected on a page to Mail, the preinstalled email application, which can receive the text and send it to a recipient.

Let's see an example of using the native applications, and then you will implement a source application from scratch by using a very simple but effective application.

Using native applications

In this procedure, you start using the Windows 8 UI style version of Internet Explorer to share some information with Mail.

1. Open Internet Explorer from the Start screen. Be careful—do not use the classic Win32 version of Internet Explorer (which you can find on the classic taskbar, just in case you have activated the "old desktop" of Windows 8 from the Desktop tile).

2. Open any website (for example, *http://www.devleap.com/*) in the address bar. If you use that site, the text will appear in Italian. Select *EN* in the top menu.

3. Select some text on the home page and position the cursor in the lower-right corner of the screen (or press Windows+C) to open the Charm (or flip your finger from the right corner toward the center of the screen).

4. Choose Share from the menu or the Charm.

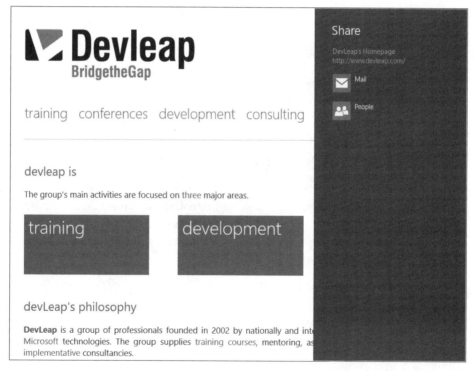

As you can see, the Windows 8 version of Internet Explorer has no window at all, nor a menu item or an address bar: it fills the entire surface of the screen. The Share pane appears on the right side of the screen.

You cannot customize the Share pane because it is an operating system component. On the top, it displays the information that comes from the source application, and immediately below that, it lists all the applications that are capable of receiving the content.

5. Select Mail to open the target application. The target application will receive the data package sent from Internet Explorer via the Data Transfer Manager. Mail will present the shared text with the hyperlink and show the Send Mail button. The target application page is displayed in the foreground, letting the user see the source application in the background. If you have not configured Mail in your system, the following graphic shows how this looks in action.

The target application is responsible for presenting the content on the Share pane and informing users about the operations available for that content. This is a good example of a target application because Mail receives the data package and processes it, sending the resulting email to the target recipients.

Now that you have seen the complete flow, you'll implement a sharing source application of your own from scratch.

Implement a source application

In this procedure, you will implement a simple source application that can share textual content.

1. Create a new Application project. To do that, open Visual Studio 2012, and from the File menu, select New Project. Choose Windows Store from the list of installed templates, and then choose Blank App (XAML) from the list of available projects.

2. Select version 4.5 as the .NET Framework target version for your new project.

3. Name the new project **SharingSource**, and then choose a location on your file system and a solution name. When you're finished, click OK.

4. Open the MainPage.xaml page and add a *ListView* control, using the following code as a guide:

```
<Page x:Class="SharingSource.MainPage"
    xmlns="http://schemas.microsoft.com/winfx/2006/xaml/presentation"
    xmlns:x="http://schemas.microsoft.com/winfx/2006/xaml"
    xmlns:local="using:SharingSource"
    xmlns:d="http://schemas.microsoft.com/expression/blend/2008"
    xmlns:mc="http://schemas.openxmlformats.org/markup-compatibility/2006"
    mc:Ignorable="d">

    <Grid Background="{StaticResource ApplicationPageBackgroundThemeBrush}">
        <ListView x:Name="list" DisplayMemberPath="FullName"
                SelectedValuePath="FullName" />
    </Grid>

</Page>
```

5. Fill the *ListView* control with some people's names using code similar to the following in the constructor of the *MainPage* class:

```
public sealed partial class MainPage : Page
{
    public MainPage()
    {
        this.InitializeComponent();

        list.ItemsSource = new List<object>()
        {
            new { FullName = "Roberto Brunetti " },
            new { FullName = "Paolo Pialorsi" },
            new { FullName = "Marco Russo" },
            new { FullName = "Luca Regnicoli" },
            new { FullName = "Vanni Boncinelli" },
            new { FullName = "Guido Zambarda" },
            new { FullName = "Katia Egiziano" },
            new { FullName = "Jessica Faustinelli" }
        };
    }
```

6. Test the application to verify that you can see the names on the page and that you can select one of them.

7. Add the code to respond to the sharing event that the operating system will fire on the applications using the *DataTransferManager* WinRT class. Use this code inside the constructor of the class, just below the *InitializeComponent* method call:

```
DataTransferManager.GetForCurrentView().DataRequested +=

    new TypedEventHandler<DataTransferManager,
        DataRequestedEventArgs>(MainPage_DataRequested);
```

8. Add the *using* statement to the namespace that provides the *DataTransferManager* class as follows:

```
using Windows.ApplicationModel.DataTransfer;
```

9. Implement the *MainPage_DataRequested* method using the following code:

```
void MainPage_DataRequested(DataTransferManager sender, DataRequestedEventArgs
    args)
{
    args.Request.Data.Properties.Title = "DevLeap Sharing";
    if (list.SelectedItem != null)
    {
        args.Request.Data.Properties.Description = "DevLeap is sharing his
            crew member " + list.SelectedValue.ToString();
        args.Request.Data.SetText(list.SelectedValue.ToString());
    }
    else
    {
        args.Request.FailWithDisplayText("You have selected no one");
    }
}
```

The method sets the *Request* property of the received event arguments: it represents the data package to pass to the Data Transfer Manager that, in turn, sends it to the target application.

The first line sets the *Title* property of the data package. If no item was selected in the list, then the package shows text indicating a failure in data sharing because there is nothing to share.

If a name is selected, the source application sets the description of the data package and, more importantly, uses the *SetText* method to indicate that the package contains a set of characters and defines the desired text; the first one is very important because the Share pane will list all the registered applications that can receive text.

You can use *SetBitmap*, *SetHtml*, *SetStorageItems*, *SetUri*, *SetRtf,* and some other self-explaining methods.

10. Run the application, open the Charm, and choose Share.

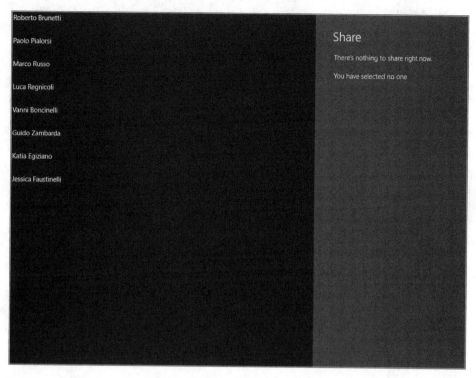

The message "There's nothing to share right now" is the default text that the Share pane shows the user when the source application uses the *FailWithDisplayText* method. The text provided by the source application is shown immediately below the default error message.

11. Select the first name from the list and share the content again. Now the Share pane shows several applications and presents the text provided by the code you implemented.

12. Select Mail.

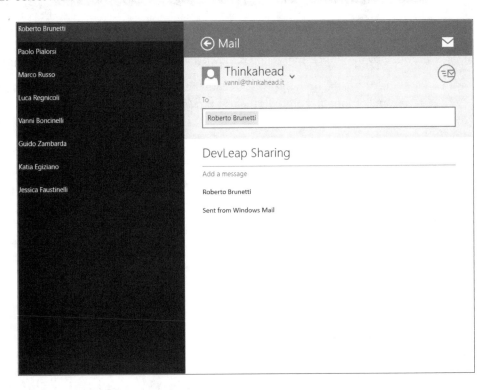

You also can activate the sharing operation from the code of the source application using the *ShowSendUI* or the *ShowShareUI* static methods of the *DataTransferManager* class.

Implementing a target application

In this procedure, you will implement a simple target application that displays the textual content shared by some other application. Remember that any app that can share textual content will be able to share it with the application that you are about to implement in this procedure; this is because the Sharing contract regulates the data exchange between applications so they don't need to know anything about each other in advance. You will implement an HTML Windows 8 UI style application to see how to interact with WinRT APIs from JavaScript and how to create a simple HTML page to show the text shared by some other applications. It's important to note that you could do the same thing using XAML and C# or Visual Basic.

1. Create a new Application project. To do that, open Visual Studio 2012, and from the File menu, select New Project. Choose JavaScript from the Templates tree and then Windows Store from the list of installed templates. Then choose Blank App from the list of available projects.

2. Name the new project **SharingTarget**, and then choose a location on your file system and a solution name. When you're finished, click OK. Use the following graphic as a reference.

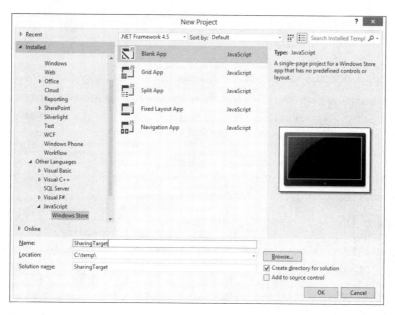

3. Open the manifest by double-clicking the Package.appxmanifest file and selecting the Declaration tab.

4. Select Share Target from the list of Available Declarations and click Add. This setting is necessary for this application to be considered a share target.

5. Click the Add New button in the Data Formats pane and type **Text** in the Data Format text box. This setting tells the Share pane that this application supports only text.

6. Leave other settings at their default values and save the manifest. You must have a manifest configured like the one illustrated in the following graphic.

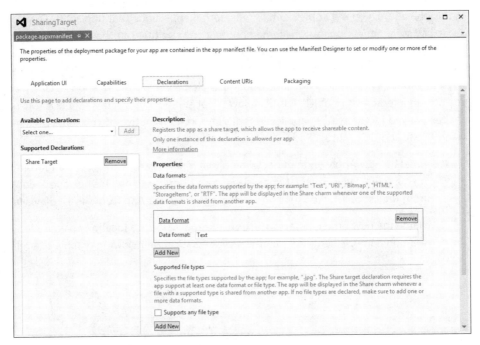

7. Deploy the application to test it. You have not provided a user interface yet, but the steps you have completed so far will suffice for the application to be listed as a target when you try to share text from other applications.

8. Open Windows 8 Internet Explorer from the Start screen. You may see the home page of the site used in the previous procedure. If not, type an address (such as *http://www.devleap.com/*) in the address bar.

9. Select the first line of text and activate the Share pane.

10. Verify that the application (SharingTarget if you have carefully followed this procedure) will appear in the list.

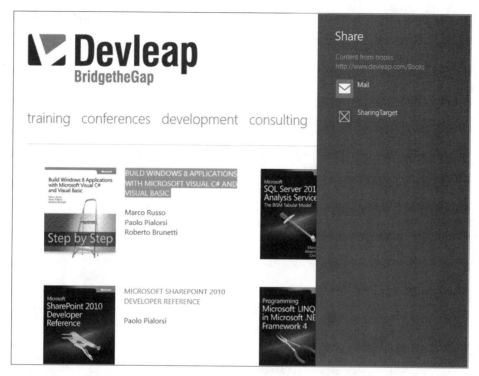

If you select your application in the Share pane, you will see a blank page (with the default "content goes here" text) because you have not implemented the page yet. It's time to do that.

Implementing a result page

In this procedure, you will develop an HTML Windows 8 UI style application. The page that displays when the user selects this application as the target for a sharing operation will be implemented in HTML5, using the WinRT APIs from JavaScript.

It is beyond the scope of this book to analyze or explain in detail how to build an HTML Windows 8 UI style application, but for this exercise, you will use the simplest way to build this page.

1. Replace the default body content (the paragraph) with an *H1, H2,* and *H3* HTML tag inside the body of the default page as follows:

```
<body>
    <h1 />
    <h2 />
    <h3 />
</body>
```

The manifest references the default page, which represents the starting point for the app.

2. Open the default.js file, which is available in the *js* folder of the project, and add the following variable declaration, just after the app variable declaration:

```
var shareOperation;
```

3. This variable will be used in the next steps to hold information about the data shared.

4. Within the same default.js file, add a script excerpt in the *app.onactivated* event handler. The code excerpt implements the activation of the application by using the WinRT environment, in case of a request for sharing contents. The following code illustrates how the *app.onactivated* event handler should be after modification.

```
app.onactivated = function (args) {
if (args.detail.kind === activation.ActivationKind.launch) {
    if (args.detail.previousExecutionState !==
        activation.ApplicationExecutionState.terminated) {
        // TODO: This application has been newly launched. Initialize
        // your application here.
    } else {
        // TODO: This application has been reactivated from suspension.
        // Restore application state here.
    }
    args.setPromise(WinJS.UI.processAll());
} else if (args.detail.kind ==
        Windows.ApplicationModel.Activation.ActivationKind.shareTarget) {
    shareOperation = args.detail.shareOperation;


    if (shareOperation.data.contains(
        Windows.ApplicationModel.DataTransfer.StandardDataFormats.text)) {
        document.querySelector('h1').textContent =
            shareOperation.data.properties.title;
        document.querySelector('h2').textContent =
            shareOperation.data.properties.description;


        shareOperation.data.getTextAsync().then(function (text) {
            if (text !== null) {
                document.querySelector('h3').textContent = text;
            }
        });
    }
}
}
};
```

You can see the inserted code in bold. App activation can occur via the application tile on the Start screen or—as in the page you are building—when the user selects an application as a search target. The just added *else if* statement in the *onactivated* event handler tests this condition by analyzing the *kind* property of the detail of the received event arguments.

If the condition is met, the code fills the HTML header elements with the properties of the received Data Package. In the source application that you built in the previous procedures, you filled the same properties during the share operation.

5. Deploy the application again and test it as a share target from Internet Explorer as you did in steps 8–10 of the preceding procedure. You do not need to open the share target application, as you did not have to open Mail in the previous example. The system activates the share target automatically as you will see during the sharing operation in the next step.

6. Open the Share App that you built in this chapter from the Start screen, select a name from the list, and activate the Sharing charm as you learned (swipe your finger from the right towards the center of the screen, and then choose Share). When the Share pane opens, choose SharingTarget as the target application for the sharing operation and you will see the page that you built filled with the shared information.

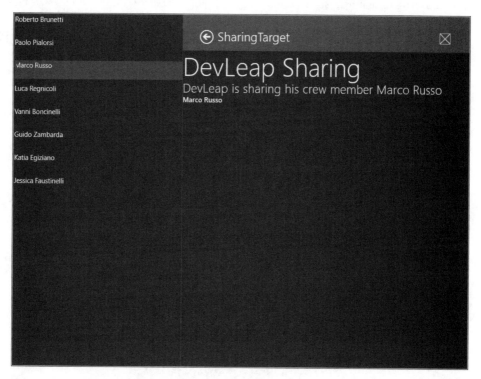

Sharing is a powerful technique for sending and receiving information to and from applications using a common contract defined by WinRT.

Summary

In this chapter, you saw some WinRT APIs at work. You started with the *FileOpenPicker* class, which lets the user choose and send file information to the calling application. Next, you implemented a simple application using the *CameraCaptureUI* class to take and retrieve photos from the webcam. The last example features two different applications: the first one lets the user choose a person from a list and share his or her full name to other applications. The second application represents the target application and was built using HTML and JavaScript. Every WinRT API can be called from any language.

Quick reference

To	Do this
Use APIs that access the system	Specify the corresponding capabilities in the application manifest.
Block or allow capabilities for one application	Open the settings pane for the application and set the slider for every capability accordingly.
Interact with the webcam	Specify the Web capability and use the *CameraCaptureUI* class settings, the video and photo attributes, and then the *CaptureFileAsync* method.
Create a source application for sharing content	Use the *DataTransferManager* to create the data package and respond to the sharing event.
Receive content from other applications	Use the Share Target declaration in the application manifest and intercept the activation for the sharing operation.

CHAPTER 7

Enhance the user experience

After completing this chapter, you will be able to

- Draw an application using Microsoft Visual Studio 2012 visual tools.

- Create an application layout.

- Customize the appearance of controls.

Understanding the XAML layout system is fundamental to position and arrange elements in a Windows Store app. The base class for all elements that provide layout support is *Panel* and the platform includes a suite of derived panel classes that enable many complex layouts. This chapter provides an introduction to the available layout *Panel* elements.

Styling and templating refer to a suite of features that allow developers and designers to create visually compelling effects and to create a consistent appearance for their applications. Another feature of the XAML styling model is the separation of presentation and logic. This means that designers can work on the appearance of an application by using only XAML at the same time that developers work on the programming logic using C# or Visual Basic (VB). This chapter focuses on the styling and templating aspects of the application.

Draw an application using Visual Studio 2012

Visual Studio 2012 contains many different tools to create a Windows Store app graphically and interactively.

In the introductory section of this chapter, you will learn how to use the Visual Studio 2012 designer in order to add controls to the page structure and customize the properties using the appropriate graphic palettes.

Create a graphical application in Visual Studio 2012

1. Create a new Application project. To do that, open Visual Studio 2012, and from the File menu, select New Project (the sequence can be File | New | Project for full-featured versions of Visual Studio). Choose Visual C# from the Templates tree and then Windows Store from the list of installed templates. Finally, choose the Blank App (XAML) project type from the list of available projects.

2. Select version 4.5 as the .NET Framework version for your new project.

3. Name the new project **Panels**, and then choose a location on your file system and a solution name. When you're finished, click OK. As you saw in Chapter 3, "My first Windows 8 app," the Windows Store application template provides a default page (MainPage.xaml), an application entry point in the App class (App.xaml.cs), a default application description and a declaration in the Package.appxmanifest file, as well as four default images representing logos and a splash screen.

4. In the Solution Explorer, double-click the MainPage.xaml file.

   This file contains the layout of the user interface. The window, named Design View, shows two different views of the file.

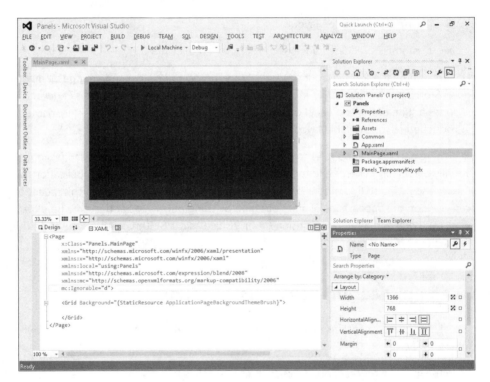

The top panel, named Design, contains the graphical display of the page, whereas the bottom panel, named XAML, shows the XAML code of the same page.

In the next procedure, you will use the Design View window to add a control to the user interface of an application and customize some of its properties using the designer and the Properties window.

Create the user interface

1. Click the Toolbox tab that appears on the left of the form in the Design View window.

2. Expand the Common XAML Controls section.

This section contains the most common controls; you can click the All XAML Control section to visualize the full list of controls provided by the platform.

3. In the Common XAML Controls section, drag the *TextBlock* control onto the page.

> **Tip** If you dragged a different control, you can delete it from the page by selecting the item within the design area and clicking Delete.

This operation creates a *TextBlock* control within the page and the Toolbox disappears temporarily. If you want the Toolbox to always be visible, just click Auto Hide on the right-hand side of the title bar.

> **Tip** The thumbtack (push pin) provides a visual cue as to whether the Toolbox (or any other window for that matter) will automatically hide itself when not in use.

Click the *TextBlock* control in the form and drag it wherever you prefer. Notice that you may need to click away from the control and then click it again before the Design View window allows you to move it.

The bottom panel of the Design View contains the markup code of the layout you have just created. It includes a description of a *TextBlock* control with its properties: *Margin*, *Text*, *HorizontalAlignment*, and *VerticalAlignment*.

The XAML code of the *TextBlock* control should look like the following:

```
<TextBlock HorizontalAlignment="Left" Height="54" Width="250" Margin="216,171,0,0"
 TextWrapping="Wrap" Text="TextBlock" VerticalAlignment="Top"/>
```

The *Margin* property may be different depending on where you placed the control on the page, such as the *Height* and the *Width* properties that depend on your actions on the designer. The XAML pane and the Design View window have a two-way relationship. You can edit the XAML code from the XAML pane and see the changes reflected in the Design View window, and vice versa. Practice changing the *Margin* property in the XAML panel. You will notice a visual change in the position of the control in the Design View window.

4. On the View menu, click Properties.

It is possible to set any property by using the XAML code, but it is definitely easier to use the Properties window for this task. The Properties window shows the properties of the currently selected control; in fact, if you click the *TextBlock* control in the Design View window, you'll see the properties of that control. However, if you click outside the *TextBlock* you will notice the Properties window displaying the properties of the parent Grid.

5. Click the *TextBlock* control in the Design View window. The Properties window will display the properties for the *TextBlock* control again.

6. In the Properties window, expand the *Text* property and change the *FontSize* property to 16 px. This property is located next to the drop-down list box containing the name of the font.

7. In the XAML pane below the Design View window, examine the text that defines the *TextBlock* control. If you scroll to the end of the line, you should see the text *FontSize="16"*. Changes performed using the Properties window will be reflected in the XAML source code automatically and, consequently, also in the Design View window.

8. Set the value of the *FontSize* property in the XAML panel to 24; you will notice a visual change in the Design View window, as well as a change in the drop-down list box of the Properties window.

9. Open the Common section of the Properties window and change the value of the *Text* property from *TextBlock* to *Hello Windows 8 App!*

 Note If you choose to organize the property names in alphabetical order, you will not find the Common section or any other categories, so you have to find the property in the list (the *Text* property in this case) and change its value as described in the procedure.

10. On the Build menu, click Build Solution, and verify that the project builds successfully.

11. On the Debug menu, click Start Debugging.

12. Return to Visual Studio 2012 by pressing ALT+TAB. On the Debug menu, click Stop Debugging.

Create the layout of a Windows 8 application

The objects derived from the *Panel* class are responsible for the placement of controls. These objects act as containers of user interface elements, and each of them has its specificities and behaviors. In this section, you will learn them and use them from within a Windows 8 application.

Use the *Canvas* panel

The aim of the *Canvas* control is to place its child elements through coordinates that are relatives to the parent *Canvas*.

1. Create a new Application project. To do that, open Visual Studio 2012 and, from the File menu, select New Project. Choose Windows Store from the list of installed templates, and then choose Blank App (XAML) from the list of available projects.

2. Select version 4.5 as the .NET Framework version for your new project.

3. Name the new project **Canvas**, and then choose a location on your file system and a solution name. When you're finished, click OK.

4. Click the Toolbox tab that appears in the left-hand side of the form in the Design View window.

5. Expand the All XAML Controls section.

6. Click the *Canvas* control and drag it within the form.

7. Using the designer surface, modify the dimensions and position of the *Canvas* control until you get something that resembles the following graphic.

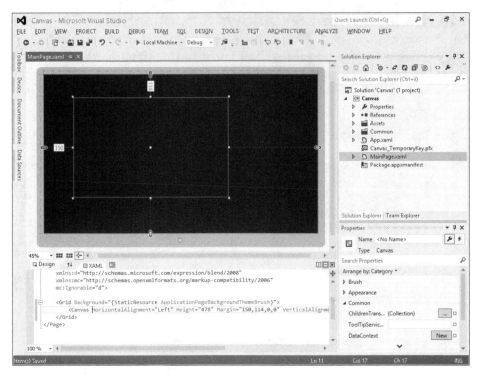

8. From the Toolbox tab, choose a *Button* control and drag it within the existing *Canvas*.

9. Modify the *Margin*, *Height,* and *Width* properties as you like.

10. Repeat steps 8 and 9 two more times to obtain a total of three *Button* controls contained within the *Canvas* panel. The following graphic shows a possible composition of the above-mentioned controls, but feel free to express your creativity by arranging them in different orders or modifying their dimensions.

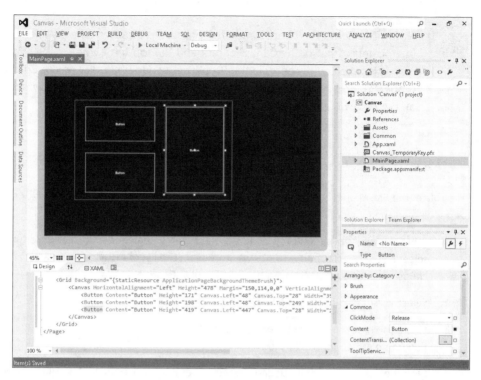

11. Click any of the three *Button* controls in the Design View window.

12. In the Properties window, expand the Layout category and modify the *Left* property by setting a higher value. You will notice a change in the placement of the selected control.

13. In the XAML panel, take a look at the source code of the *Button* controls. In addition to the classic properties, you can see the new properties *Canvas.Left* and *Canvas.Top*.

    These properties are also called "attached properties" because they do not belong to the object model of the target element, but are rather "attached" to the control itself by the parent control. Their purpose is to provide an indication to the parent panel about the position of the control. In our scenario, the Canvas panel exposes the attached *Canvas.Left* and *Canvas.Top* properties; their role is to allow the absolute positioning of the child controls.

Note The *Canvas.Left* and *Canvas.Top* properties represent the distance between the top-left corner of the Canvas parent and the top-left corner of the control. By modifying the *Left* property in the Properties window, you act on the *Canvas.Left* property, and by modifying the *Top* property in the Properties window, you operate on the *Canvas.Top* property.

Use the *StackPanel* panel

The role of the *StackPanel* control is to position the child elements below each other or side by side depending on the *Orientation* property.

1. Create a new Application project. To do that, open Visual Studio 2012 and from the File menu select New Project. Choose Windows Store from the list of installed templates, and then choose Blank App (XAML) from the list of available projects.

2. Select version 4.5 as the .NET Framework version for your new project.

3. Name the new project **StackPanel**, and then choose a location on your file system and a solution name. When you're finished, click OK.

4. Click the Toolbox tab that appears on the left of the form in the Design View window.

5. Expand the Common XAML Controls section.

6. Click the *StackPanel* control and drag it within the form.

7. Modify the dimensions and position of the *StackPanel* control until you get something that resembles the following graphic.

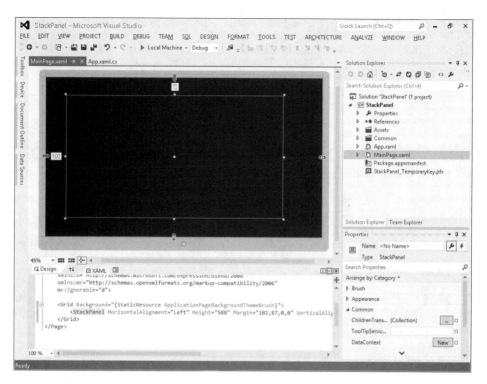

8. In the Toolbox Tab, select a *Button* control and drag it within the *StackPanel*.

9. Modify the *Margin*, *Height*, and *Width* properties as you like. For a better result to the proce-dure, set the *Height* property about one quarter of the *StackPanel* height (about 150 pixels).

10. Click the *Button* control in the Design View window.

11. Press Ctrl+C to copy the control. Press Ctrl+V. You will notice a new *Button* control placed right under the preceding button.

12. Press Ctrl+V two more times. You will notice two other *Button* controls placed according to the *StackPanel* behavior. You will find the result of these steps in the StackPanelVertical sample.

13. In the Design View window, select the *StackPanel* control by clicking inside the area defined by the control, but not on any of the buttons. Press Delete.

14. Click the Toolbox tab that appears on the left-hand side of the form in the Design View window.

15. Expand the All XAML Controls section.

16. Click the *StackPanel* control and drag it within the form.

17. Modify the dimensions and position of the *StackPanel* control until you get something similar to the previous graphic.

18. From the Properties window, set the *Orientation* property to *Horizontal*.

19. From the Toolbox tab, select a *Button* control and drag it within the preceding *StackPanel*.

20. Modify the *Margin, Height,* and *Width* properties as you like. For a better result to the procedure, set to *Width* property about one quarter of the *StackPanel* height (about 250 pixels).

21. Click the *Button* control in the Design View window and press Ctrl+C to copy the control.

22. Press Ctrl+V. You will notice a new *Button* control positioned next to the preceding button.

23. Press Ctrl+V two more times. You will notice two more *Button* controls being positioned according to the *StackPanel* behavior. You will find the result of these steps in the StackPanel-Horizontal sample.

24. On the Debug menu, click Start Debugging.

Use the *ScrollViewer* panel

The role of the *ScrollViewer* control is to enable scrolling (both vertical and horizontal) in the case of overflow of the content (that is, when its content exceeds the size of the *ScrollViewer* control).

1. Create a new Application project. To do that, open Visual Studio 2012 and from the File menu select New Project. Choose Windows Store from the list of installed templates, and then choose Blank App (XAML) from the list of available projects.

2. Select version 4.5 as the .NET Framework version for your new project.

3. Name the new project *ScrollViewer*, and then choose a location on your file system and a solution name. When you're finished, click OK.

4. Click the Toolbox tab that appears on the left-hand side of the form in the Design View window.

5. Expand the All XAML Controls section.

6. Click the *StackPanel* control and drag it within the form.

7. Modify the dimensions and position of the *StackPanel* control until you get something that resembles the following graphic.

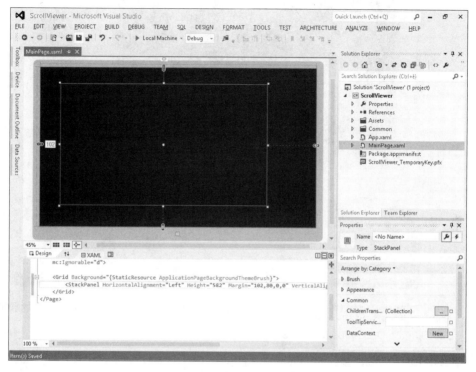

8. From the Toolbox tab, select a *Button* control and drag it within the preceding *StackPanel*.

9. Modify the *Margin*, *Height,* and *Width* properties as you like. For a better result to the procedure, set the *Height* property to about 215 pixels.

10. Click the *Button* control in the Design View window and press Ctrl+C to copy the control.

11. Press Ctrl+V. You will notice a new *Button* control placed below the preceding button.

12. Press Ctrl+V two more times until you get something similar to the following graphic.

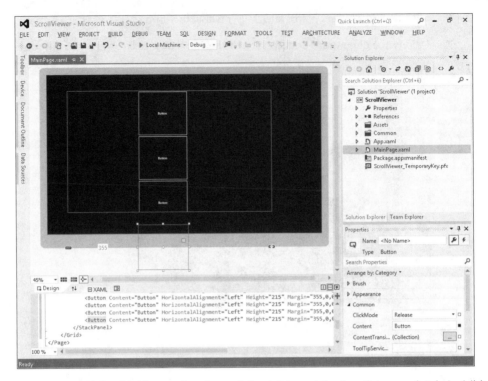

Do not worry if the third button is only partially visible and the fourth is completely invisible.

13. On the Debug menu, click Start Debugging.

14. You will notice that at runtime the third button is partially visible (but still clickable), whereas the fourth button is completely invisible and therefore not usable.

15. Return to Visual Studio 2012. On the Debug menu, click Stop Debugging.

16. Right-click the *StackPanel* control in the Design View window, and then select Group Into | ScrollViewer.

17. Click the *StackPanel* node in the XAML pane.

18. In the Properties window, expand the *Layout* property and click Set To Auto next to the *Width* property.

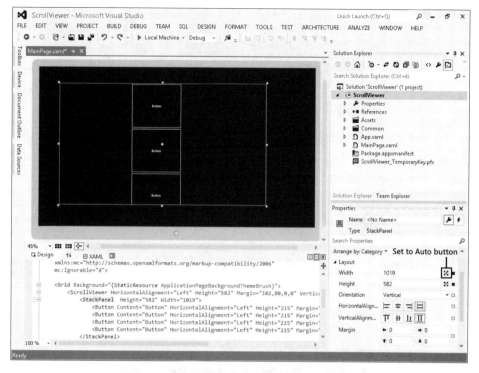

19. Click the Set To Auto button next to the *Height* property.

20. On the Debug menu, click Start Debugging.

21. Place the mouse over a button and scroll between the various *Button* controls.

 Note The controls of the platform have been designed to natively support different types of input; therefore it is possible to scroll using touch gestures, digital pen, mouse, and keyboard (in the latter case, using the arrow keys or the Page Up and Page Down keys).

22. Return to Visual Studio 2012 by pressing Alt+Tab. On the Debug menu, click Stop Debugging.

Use the *Grid* panel

The purpose of the *Grid* control is to place its child elements in rows and columns.

1. Create a new Application project. To do that, open Visual Studio 2012 and from the File menu, select New Project. Choose Windows Store from the list of installed templates, and then choose Blank App (XAML) from the list of available projects.

2. Select version 4.5 as the .NET Framework version for your new project.

3. Name the new project **Grid**, and then choose a location on your file system and a solution name. When you're finished, click OK.

4. Click the Toolbox tab that appears on the left-hand side of the form in the Design View window, expand the Common XAML Control section, and click the *Grid* control and drag it on the form.

   Modify the dimensions and position of the *Grid* control until you get something similar to the following graphic.

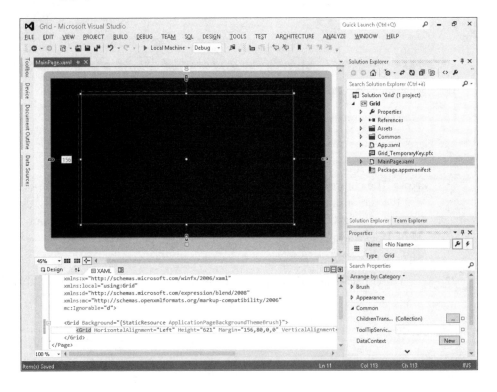

5. In the Design View window, place the mouse pointer within the area between the top margin of the *Grid* control and the dotted border positioned a few pixels above the *Grid* control. You will notice that the pointer has changed its shape into a column delimiter.

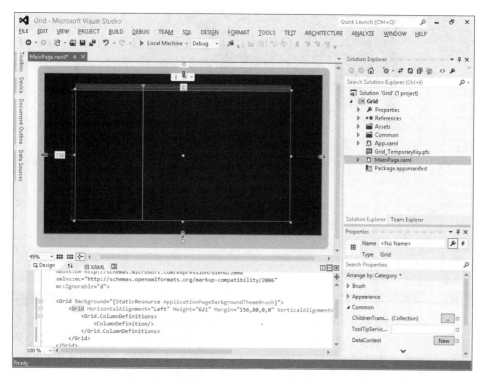

6. Place the mouse at about one-third of the length and click. You can see the Design View window at the end of the operation in the following screenshot.

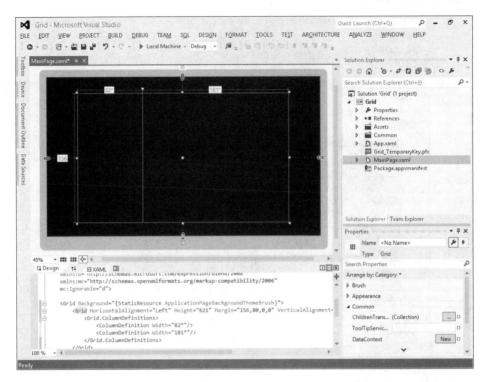

As a result of this action, two columns have been created inside the *Grid* control. The first column has a width equal (in our case) to *82** and the second column to *181**. Do not worry if your numerical values are different. By observing the XAML View, you will find that the XAML code is similar to the following code:

```
<Grid HorizontalAlignment="Left" Height="620" Margin="156,80,0,0" VerticalAlignment="Top"
    Width="1052">
        <Grid.ColumnDefinitions>
            <ColumnDefinition Width="82*"/>
            <ColumnDefinition Width="181*"/>
        </Grid.ColumnDefinitions>
</Grid>
```

The *Grid* control uses the *ColumnDefinitions* property to define the number of columns and their properties. In the Design View window, you can add more columns at your will.

7. Hover the mouse a few pixels below the triangle-shaped icon that represents the boundary of a column. You will see the pointer of the mouse assuming the shape of two arrows pointing, respectively, to the left and right. While holding the left mouse button, move the mouse left or right to resize the column. Release the left button to confirm the position.

8. Hover the mouse a few pixels below the triangle-shaped icon (as to resize a column), double-click to delete the column, and then delete all the additional columns until you get something resembling the previous screenshot.

9. In the Toolbox window, select a *Button* control and drag it into the second column of the *Grid*.

Take a look at the markup code of the *Button* control in the XAML View and notice the attached property *Grid.Column="1"*; this property is used by the parent *Grid* control to position the button in the second column. In case you want to place the *Button* control in the first column, simply change the code to *Grid.Column="0"*.

> **Note** For the platform, omitting the *Grid.Column* property is the same as writing *Grid.Column="0"*.

10. In the Design View window, drag the *Button* control inside the first column.

11. Place your mouse over the label that represents the width of the column (in our case, this is the label that shows the number *82**) and you'll notice a new drop-down list above the column.

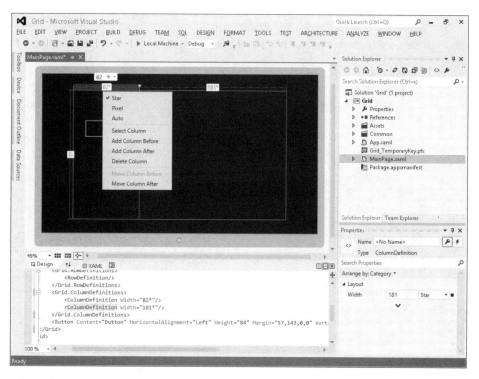

The main role of this drop-down list is to allow you to edit the properties of a *ColumnDefinition*. The *ColumnDefinition* class defines column-specific properties, like *Width*, that apply to *Grid* controls.

12. In the drop-down list, select Pixel. The underlying label will show a value without the * character (in our case, the value is *328*).

This operation resulted in the creation of a *ColumnDefinition* with a fixed width of, in our case, 328 pixels.

13. From the drop-down list, select Auto to set the column width to the width of its children controls automatically. In this scenario, the actual width of the column will be the sum of the width of the button and its margins.

14. From the drop-down list, select Star to return to the initial situation. Do not worry if the numerical values are different, just make sure that the *ColumnDefinition* elements have their *Width* property set to *Star*; that is, their value contains the * character.

The Star option allows us to create columns with proportional width; this ratio will be maintained even at runtime. This option is very useful if you want to create user interfaces capable of adapting to different client screen resolution.

In this procedure, you have created two columns with the value, in our case, of *82** and *181*. (In your case, the actual values might be different.) From the runtime perspective, it means that if the first column is 82 times a "logical unit," the second column will be 181 times that same unit—thus maintaining an identical ratio.

15. In the XAML View, modify the *Width* property of the two *ColumnDefinition* elements as follows (the property to edit is highlighted in bold):

```
<Grid.ColumnDefinitions>
    <ColumnDefinition Width="1*"/>
    <ColumnDefinition Width="2*"/>
</Grid.ColumnDefinitions>
```

This way, you can be sure that the width of the second column will always be double the width of the first column.

16. In the Design View window, place the mouse pointer into the area between the left edge of the *Grid* control and the dotted line that is just a few pixels from the left of the *Grid* control. You will notice that the pointer changes its shape into a row delimiter.

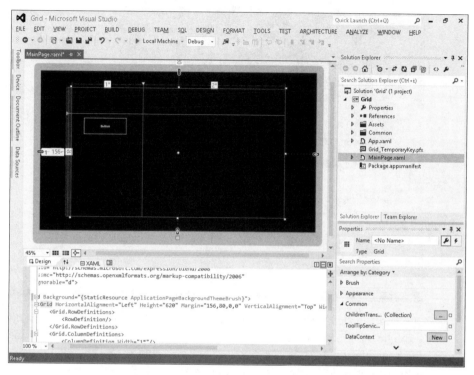

Stop the mouse at around a quarter of the height and left-click. In the following graphic, you can see the Design View window at the end of the operation.

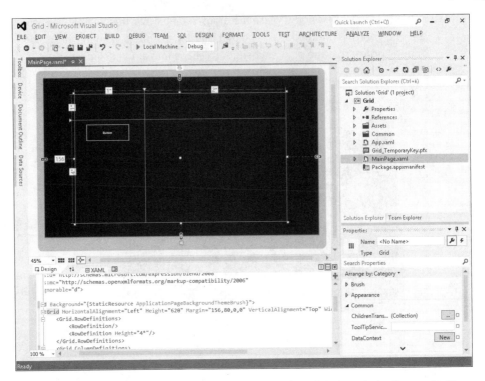

This operation led to the creation of two rows inside the *Grid* control, the first one with a width (in this example) of *1** and the second column with a width of *4**. If you take a look at the XAML View, you will notice that the XAML code of the *Grid* control is similar to the follow-ing code (the code produced by the last operation is highlighted in bold):

```
<Grid HorizontalAlignment="Left" Height="620" Margin="156,80,0,0" VerticalAlignment="Top"
    Width="1054">
        <Grid.RowDefinitions>
            <RowDefinition/>
            <RowDefinition Height="4*"/>
        </Grid.RowDefinitions>
        <Grid.ColumnDefinitions>
            <ColumnDefinition Width="1*"/>
            <ColumnDefinition Width="2*"/>
        </Grid.ColumnDefinitions>
        <Button Content="Button" HorizontalAlignment="Left" Height="84"
            Margin="57,18.556,0,0" VerticalAlignment="Top" Width="217" Grid.Row="1"/>
</Grid>
```

The *Grid* control uses the *RowDefinitions* property to define the rows and their properties.

Notice that the first *RowDefinition* does not have any *Height* property defined. In that case, the platform assumes *Height="*"* or *Height="1*"*, which is the same.

> **Note** A *ColumnDefinition* with no *Width* property is the same as a *ColumnDefinition* with *Width="*"* or, if you prefer, *Width="1*"*.

If you take a look at the markup code of the *Button* control in the XAML View, you can see the attached property *Grid.Row = "1"*; this property is used by the parent *Grid* control to position the child control in the specified row. If you need to place the *Button* control in the first line, you should specify *Grid.Row = "0"*.

> **Note** From the platform perspective, omitting the *Grid.Row* property equates to *Grid.Row="0"*.

17. In the Design View window, add as many rows as you like.

Position the mouse a few pixels to the right of the triangle-shaped icon that represents the demarcation of a row and you'll see that the pointer of the mouse takes the shape of two arrows pointing upwards and downwards. Holding the left mouse button, drag the mouse up or down to resize the affected row. Release the left mouse button to confirm the position.

18. Place the mouse a few pixels to the right of the triangle-shaped icon (as you would do to resize the row), double-click to delete the row, and then delete all the additional rows until you obtain something that resembles the previous graphic.

19. Place your mouse over the label that represents the height of the first line (in our scenario, it's the label with the value of *1**) and you'll notice a new drop-down list next to the row. The main purpose of this drop-down list is to allow you to modify the *Height* property of a *RowDefinition*. Opening the drop-down list will reveal a view similar to the following graphic.

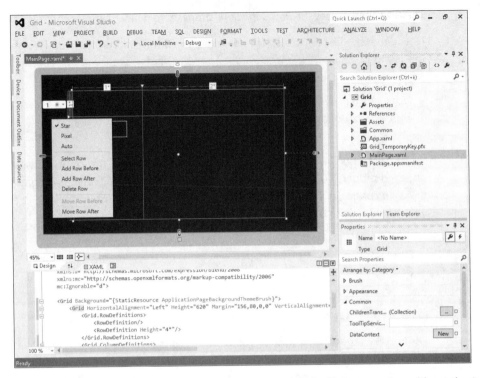

20. In the drop-down list, select Pixel, and the underlying label will show a value without the * character (for instance, the value could be 124).

This operation allows you to create a *RowDefinition* with a fixed width of 124 pixels.

21. From the drop-down list, select Auto to automatically set the row height; it will be the height of its child controls to determine the actual height of the *RowDefinition*. In this sample scenario, there aren't any children controls yet, therefore it seems that the row has been deleted, so just look at the XAML View to ensure the presence of both rows. Press Ctrl+Z to undo the last operation.

22. In the drop-down list, select Star to step back to the initial situation. Do not worry if the numerical values are different, just make sure that the *Height* property of both *RowDefinition* elements is set to *Star*; that is, its value presents the * character.

The Star option allows creating rows with proportional height, and this ratio will be maintained at runtime as well. This option is extremely important to design user interfaces capable of adapting to different client screen resolutions.

In this procedure, you have created two rows with the values of *1** and *4**. At runtime, it means that if the height of the first row is one "logic unit" high, the second row is four times higher—thus preserving the same fixed ratio.

23. In the Toolbox window, select a *Button* control and drag it into the second column and second row of the *Grid* control.

24. Modify the *Margin, Height,* and *Width* properties as you like. The XAML code of the new *Button* control should look like the following code:

```
<Button Content="Button" HorizontalAlignment="Left" Height="84" Margin="241,198,0,0"
    VerticalAlignment="Top" Width="217" Grid.Row="1" Grid.Column="1"/>
```

Notice that the two attached properties, *Grid.Row* and *Grid.Column,* will be used by the parent *Grid* control to position the control properly.

25. On the Debug menu, click Start Debugging.

Use the *Border* panel

The *Border* class is not derived from the *Panel* base class; it cannot contain a list of user interface controls but it can contain a single child element. The purpose of the *Border* control is to draw a frame around a single child control, and it is mostly used for creating an appealing graphic effect around elements like round corners.

1. Create a new Application project. To do that, open Visual Studio 2012 and, from the File menu, select New Project. Choose Windows Store from the list of installed templates, and then choose Blank App (XAML) from the list of available projects.

2. Select version 4.5 as the .NET Framework version for your new project.

3. Name the new project **Border**, and then choose a location on your file system and a solution name. When you're finished, click OK.

4. Click the Toolbox tab that appears in the left-hand side of the form in the Design View window.

5. Click the *Border* control and drag it within the form.

6. Modify the dimensions and position of the *Border* control until you get something that resembles the following graphic.

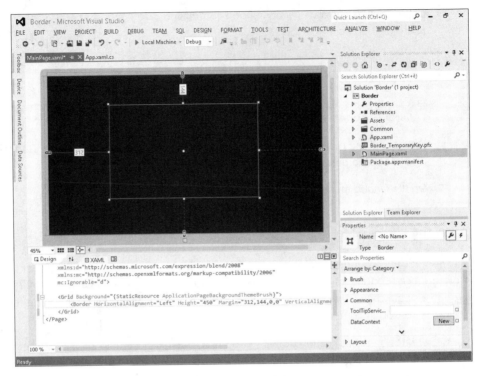

7.   In the Design View window, click the *Border* control.

8.   In the Properties window, expand Brush, and then click BorderBrush | Solid Color Brush. The underlying palette will display a color picker.

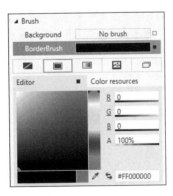

9.   Click and drag the mouse inside the color picker, halting on whatever color you like (a light color, such as white, will look better).

10. Once you have finished, the palette will show the preview of the selected color within the rectangle next to the *BorderBrush* property, the color code (in this example, #FFFFFFFF), and various shades of red, green, blue, and alpha (the alpha is the transparency of the color). If you choose white, the palette will look like the following graphic.

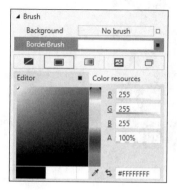

Note A higher transparency number produces an opaque color, whereas a lower number produces a more transparent color (one where the background can show through).

11. In the Properties window, expand the *Appearance* property group and set the *BorderThickness* property by assigning the value *10* to *Left* and *Right*, *20* to the *Top*, and *40* to the *Bottom*.

12. In the Properties window, set the *CornerRadius* property to the following values: *20,20,40,40*.

The *CornerRadius* property represents the radii of a border's corners: the first value (*20*, in the preceding example) specifies the radius of the top-left corner; the second value (*20*) specifies the radius of the top-right corner; the third (*40*) specifies the radius of the bottom-right corner; and the fourth (*40*) specifies the radius of the bottom-left corner.

Note If only a single value is specified, that measure is applied to *all* of the *TopLeft*, *TopRight*, *BottomRight*, and *BottomLeft* corners of the *CornerRadius*.

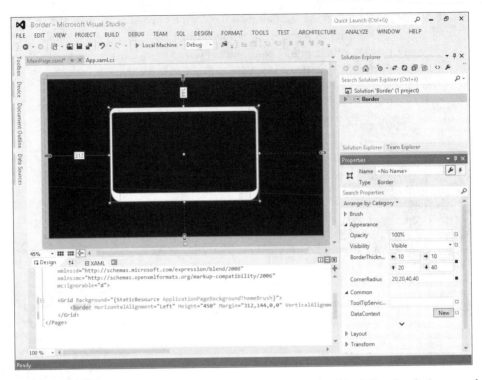

13. On the Debug menu, click Start Debugging. The application will look like the designer surface shown in the previous graphic.

Use the *Margin* property

The *Margin* property describes the distance between an element and its child or peers. The use of this property enables very fine control of an element's rendering position.

1. Create a new Application project. To do that, open Visual Studio 2012 and from the File menu, select New Project. Choose Windows Store from the list of installed templates, and then choose Blank App (XAML) from the list of available projects.

2. Select version 4.5 as the .NET Framework version for your new project.

3. Name the new project **Margin**, and then choose a location on your file system and a solution name. When you're finished, click OK.

4. Click the Toolbox tab that appears on the left-hand side of the form in the Design View window.

5. Expand the Common XAML Controls section.

6. Click the *Button* control and drag it within the form.

7. In the XAML View, set the *Height* property with a value of *200*. Set the *Width* property with a value of *450*. Set the *Margin* property with values of *300,200,0,0*.

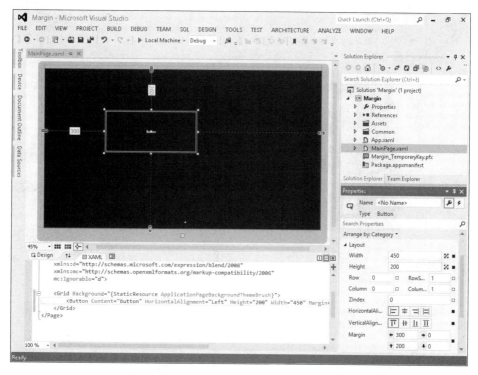

8. In the Properties window, expand the *Layout* property group and take a look at the *Margin* property—where the value *300* represents the left margin, the subsequent value *200* defines the top margin, and the other two values represent the right and bottom margin, respectively. A value of *0* means that the margins have not been defined.

9. In the Design View window, follow the dashed line that starts from the right side of the button to the right side of the parent *Grid* control to find an icon shaped like an anchor. Click the icon.

   By doing this, you have set a fixed margin with a specific value (for example *616*, in the current sample, but in your application the actual values might be different).

10. In the Properties window, expand the *Layout* property group and make sure that the *Width* property is set to *Auto*. If it is not, click Set To Auto next to the *Width* property.

    Attributing a value of *Auto* to the *Width* property (or omitting that property from the XAML code) shifts the task of assigning a width to the control onto the *Margin* property. In other words, at runtime the *Button* control will expand and collapse in compliance with the "contract" imposed by the *Margin* property; that is, a left margin of 300 pixels and a right margin of 616 pixels.

11. In the Visual Studio 2012 toolbar, click the drop-down list by the Local Machine button to open the menu shown in the following image.

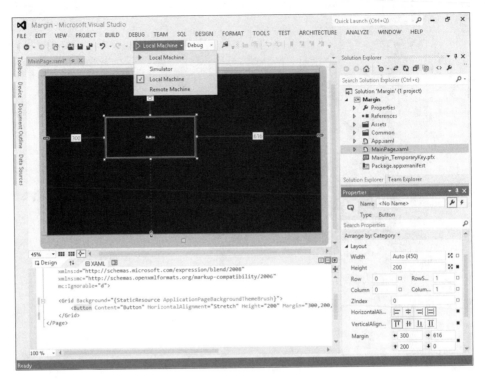

12. Select Simulator and then click the green play icon.

Visual Studio 2012 will start the Windows 8 Simulator and then will run the application within that virtual environment.

13. In the simulator, click Change Resolution (positioned in the right toolbar of simulator) and select the first entry "10.6 1024 × 768."

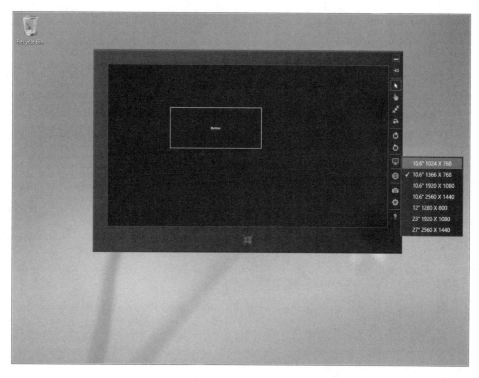

Notice that the button width varies according to the screen resolution.

14. Try other resolutions and notice the changes in the button width.

15. Return to Visual Studio 2012. On the Debug menu, click Stop Debugging.

16. In the Design view, follow the dotted line running from the underside of the button to the lower edge of the parent *Grid* control and you will find an icon with the shape of an anchor. Click that icon.

By doing this, you have set a fixed bottom margin with a specific value, which is 368 in the current example—but in your environment it might be different.

17. Drag the *Button* control towards the bottom-right margin of the parent *Grid* control.

    Notice how the *Margin* property varies while you are dragging the control.

18. Click the anchor-shaped icon that represents the top margin.

    Notice how the solid line changes its shape into a dashed line—this means that the margin value has been set to zero.

19. Click the anchor-shaped icon that represents the left margin.

    Notice how the solid line changes its shape into a dashed line—this means that the margin value has been set to zero.

20. Set the *Margin* property through the XAML View to the following values: *0,0,80,80*.

21. Make sure that the *Width* property of the *Button* control is set to any value other than zero (for example, *450*).

22. On the Debug menu, click Start Debugging.

23. In the simulator, click Change Resolution and select whatever resolution you prefer.

24. Try other resolutions and observe the button: its dimensions, as well as its right and bottom margins, remain constant.

25. Return to Visual Studio 2012. On the Debug menu, click Stop Debugging.

Customize the appearance of controls

In the previous examples, you have set the various properties control by control. However, leveraging the features of the XAML platform, it is possible to centralize the layout definition of the various controls to improve the maintainability of the solution and create a consistent appearance for the product.

Another feature of the XAML styling model is the separation between presentation and logic. It means that designers can focus on the appearance of the application, whereas developers can take care of the application logic.

You will start this section by reusing a style that is already included in the Visual Studio 2012 project. Then you will customize that style. Lastly, you will create a new style from scratch and use templates to redefine the structure of a control.

Use a predefined style

A *Style* element is a container of property values. In this procedure, you will use a *Style* element that is already included in the Visual Studio 2012 project template.

1. Create a new Application project. To do that, open Visual Studio 2012 and, from the File menu, select New Project. Choose Windows Store from the list of installed templates, and then choose Blank App (XAML) from the list of available projects.

2. Select version 4.5 as the .NET Framework version for your new project.

3. Name the new project **UsingStyles**, and then choose a location on your file system and a solution name. When you're finished, click OK.

4. Click the Toolbox tab that appears on the left-hand side of the form in the Design View window.

5. Expand the Common XAML Controls section.

6. Click the *TextBlock* control and drag it within the form.

7. In the XAML View, set the *Margin* property to *200,100,0,0*.

8. In the Design View, select the *TextBlock* control and open the contextual menu by right-clicking.

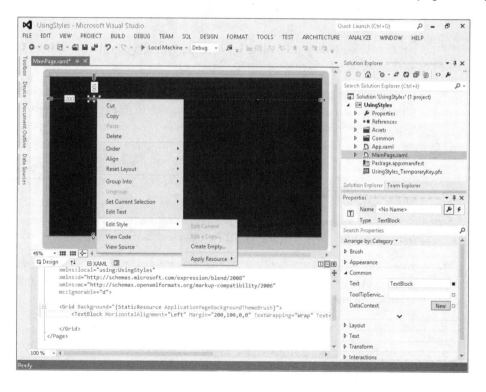

9. Select Edit Style | Apply Resource. Then select PageHeaderTextStyle in the inner menu.

In the XAML View, take a look to the XAML code of the *TextBlock* control—it should look like the following code:

```
<TextBlock HorizontalAlignment="Left" Margin="200,100,0,0" TextWrapping="Wrap"
    Text="TextBlock" VerticalAlignment="Top"
    Style="{StaticResource PageHeaderTextStyle}"/>
```

The previous operation has set the *Style* property with a reference to a shared resource called PageHeaderTextStyle.

10. In the Solution Explorer window, expand the Common directory and double-click the StandardStyles.xaml file.

11. Press Ctrl+F and, in the textbox, type **PageHeader**. Visual Studio 2012 will shift the focus to the definition of the style named PageHeaderTextStyle. The markup code should look like the following:

```
<Style x:Key="PageHeaderTextStyle" TargetType="TextBlock"
    BasedOn="{StaticResource HeaderTextStyle}">
    <Setter Property="TextWrapping" Value="NoWrap"/>
    <Setter Property="VerticalAlignment" Value="Bottom"/>
    <Setter Property="Margin" Value="0,0,30,40"/>
</Style>
```

As you can see, a style is just a container of property settings—as the properties *TextWrapping*, *VerticalAlignment*, and *Margin* illustrate.

Starting from the first line of code for the style, you can find its name, expressed by the *x:Key* attribute, the kind of controls that can use it (*TextBlock*, in this case), and finally the *BasedOn* attribute, which indicates from which style it derives (it means that the PageHeaderTextStyle style will inherit all the settings of the base style, plus its own personal settings).

Customize a predefined style

A *Style* element is a container of property values. In this procedure, you will customize a *Style* element that is already included in the Visual Studio 2012 project template.

1. Create a new Application project. To do that, open Visual Studio 2012 and, from the File menu, select New Project. Choose Windows Store from the list of installed templates, and then choose Blank App (XAML) from the list of available projects.

2. Select version 4.5 as the .NET Framework version for your new project.

3. Name the new project **CustomStyles**, and then choose a location on your file system and a solution name. When you're finished, click OK.

4. Click the Toolbox tab that appears on the left-hand side of the form in the Design View window.

5. Expand the Common XAML Controls section.

6. Click the *TextBlock* control and drag it within the form.

7. In the XAML View, set the *Margin* property to *200,100,0,0*.

8. In the Design View, click the *TextBlock* control and right-click to open the contextual menu. From the menu, select Edit Style | Apply Resource | PageHeaderTextStyle.

9. In the Design View, click the *TextBlock* control and right-click to open the contextual menu. From that menu, select Edit Style | Edit Current.

    Replace the following PageHeaderTextStyle style definition:

```
<Style x:Key="PageHeaderTextStyle" TargetType="TextBlock"
    BasedOn="{StaticResource HeaderTextStyle}">
    <Setter Property="TextWrapping" Value="NoWrap"/>
    <Setter Property="VerticalAlignment" Value="Bottom"/>
    <Setter Property="Margin" Value="0,0,30,40"/>
</Style>
```

    with this code:

```
<Style x:Key="PageHeaderTextStyle" TargetType="TextBlock"
    BasedOn="{StaticResource HeaderTextStyle}">
    <Setter Property="Foreground" Value="Red"/>
    <Setter Property="TextWrapping" Value="NoWrap"/>
    <Setter Property="VerticalAlignment" Value="Bottom"/>
    <Setter Property="Margin" Value="0,0,30,40"/>
</Style>
```

    The new line of code that will customize the control's foreground color is highlighted in bold.

10. In Solution Explorer, double-click MainPage.xaml.

    Notice how the foreground color of the *TextBlock* control is now red.

11. Click the Toolbox tab.

12. Expand the Common XAML Controls section.

13. Click the *TextBlock* control and drag it within the form, then move it under the previously added control.

14. Click the new *TextBlock* control and right-click to open the contextual menu. In the menu, select Edit Style | Apply Resource | PageHeaderTextStyle.

    Observe the new control again: the foreground color is red, meaning that it uses the custom definition of a predefined style.

15. On the Debug menu, click Start Debugging. The result is shown in the following graphic.

Customize the copy of a predefined style

A *Style* element is a container of property values. In this procedure, you will customize a copy of a *Style* element that is already included in the Visual Studio 2012 project template.

1. Create a new Application project. To do that, open Visual Studio 2012 and from the File menu, select New Project. Choose Windows Store from the list of installed templates, and then choose Blank App (XAML) from the list of available projects.

2. Select version 4.5 as the .NET Framework version for your new project.

3. Name the new project **CopyStyles**, and then choose a location on your file system and a solution name. When you're finished, click OK.

4. Click the Toolbox tab that appears on the left-hand side of the form in the Design View window.

5. Expand the Common XAML Controls section.

6. Click the *TextBlock* control and drag it within the form.

7. In the XAML View, set the *Margin* property to *200,100,0,0*.

8. In the Design View, click the *TextBlock* control and right-click to open the contextual menu. In the menu, select Edit Style | Apply Resource | PageHeaderTextStyle.

9. In the Design View, click the *TextBlock* control and right-click to open the contextual menu. In that menu, select Edit Style | Edit A Copy to open the Create Style Resource modal window.

10. In the *Name* property field, type **MyPageHeaderTextStyle** and make sure that This Document is selected. Click OK.

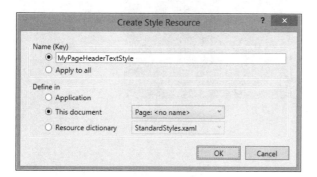

11. Replace the PageHeaderTextStyle style definition that follows:

```
<Style x:Key="MyPageHeaderTextStyle" TargetType="TextBlock"
    BasedOn="{StaticResource HeaderTextStyle}">
    <Setter Property="TextWrapping" Value="NoWrap"/>
    <Setter Property="VerticalAlignment" Value="Bottom"/>
    <Setter Property="Margin" Value="0,0,30,40"/>
</Style>
```

with this code:

```
<Style x:Key="MyPageHeaderTextStyle" TargetType="TextBlock"
    BasedOn="{StaticResource HeaderTextStyle}">
    <Setter Property="Foreground" Value="Red"/>
    <Setter Property="TextWrapping" Value="NoWrap"/>
    <Setter Property="VerticalAlignment" Value="Bottom"/>
    <Setter Property="Margin" Value="0,0,30,40"/>
</Style>
```

The new line of code that will customize the control's foreground color is highlighted in bold.

Notice how the foreground color of the *TextBlock* control is now red.

12. Click the Document Outline tab.

13. Click the Return Scope To [Page] button positioned right by the style name (MyPageHeaderTextStyle). The following graphic shows the Document Outline tab.

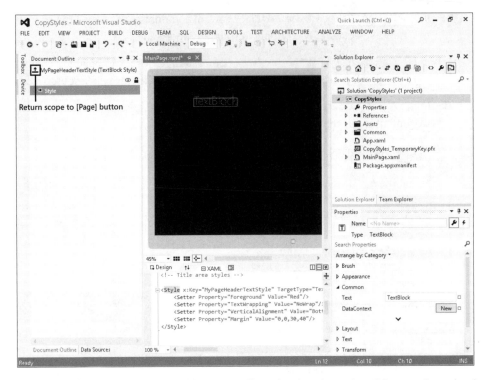

This operation is quite important because it allows leaving the style editing mode and going back to the design layout mode.

14. Click the Toolbox tab.

15. Expand the Common XAML Controls section.

16. Click the *TextBlock* control, drag it within the form, and then move it below the previously added control.

17. Click the *TextBlock* control you just added, and then right-click to open the contextual menu. Select Edit Style | Apply Resource | MyPageHeaderTextStyle. Your new style has been created by starting from a predefined one.

18. On the Debug menu, click Start Debugging. The result will look similar to the final graphic in the previous procedure.

Create a new style

A *Style* element is a container of property values. In this procedure, you will create a new style from scratch.

1. Create a new Application project. To do that, open Visual Studio 2012 and from the File menu, select New Project. Choose Windows Store from the list of installed templates, and then choose Blank App (XAML) from the list of available projects.

2. Select version 4.5 as the .NET Framework version for your new project.

3. Name the new project **NewStyles**, and then choose a location on your file system and a solution name. When you're finished, click OK.

4. Click the Toolbox tab that appears on the left-hand side of the form in the Design View window.

5. Expand the Common XAML Controls section.

6. Click the *TextBlock* control and drag it within the form.

7. In the XAML View, set the *Margin* property to *200,100,0,0*.

8. In the Design View, click the *TextBlock* control, and right-click to open the contextual menu. Select Edit Style | Create Empty to open the Create Style Resource modal window.

9. In the *Name* property field, type **MyTextBlockStyle** and make sure that This Document is selected. Click OK.

10. In the Properties window, expand the Brush property group, click the *Foreground* property, and, in the color picker, choose whatever color you like.

11. Take a look at the XAML View, every operation executed in the Properties window is being recorded as a *Setter* of the style object.

 Note It is possible to set the Setters of a Style object through the XAML View by directly typing the corresponding XAML code, or by using the visual tools exposed by the Properties window in Visual Studio 2012.

12. In the Properties window, expand the *Text* property and set the *FontSize* property to *48px*. This property is located next to the drop-down list box containing the name of the font.

13. Expand Show Advanced Properties in the Text section.

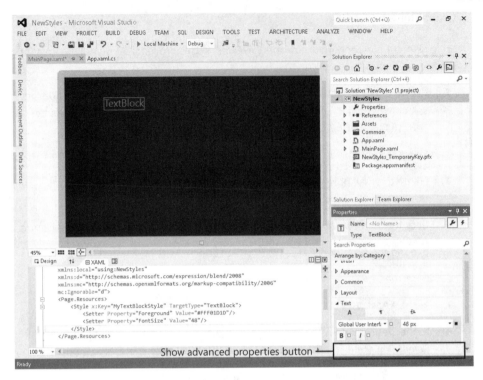

14. Set the *FontWeight* property to *Light*.

15. Click the Document Outline tab.

16. Click Return Scope To [Page], located at the left by the style name (MyTextBlockStyle).

17. Click the Toolbox tab.

18. Expand the Common XAML Controls section.

19. Click the *TextBlock* control and drag it within the form, and then move it below the previously added control.

20. Click the *TextBlock* control you just added and right-click to open the contextual menu. Select Edit Style | Apply Resource and then select the new MyTextBlockStyle style that you just created.

21. On the Debug menu, click Start Debugging. The result will look similar to the last graphic of the previous procedure.

Create a new template

The *ControlTemplate* of a control defines the appearance of the control. In this procedure, you will create a new template from scratch.

1. Create a new Application project. To do that, open Visual Studio 2012 and, from the File menu, select New Project. Choose Windows Store from the list of installed templates, and then choose Blank App (XAML) from the list of available projects.

2. Select version 4.5 as the .NET Framework version for your new project.

   Name the new project **NewTemplate**, and then choose a location on your file system and a solution name. When you're finished, click OK.

3. Click the Toolbox tab that appears on the left-hand side of the form in the Design View window, expand the Common XAML Controls section, click the *Button* control, and drag it within the form.

4. In the Properties window, expand the Layout property group and set the *Width* property to *400* and the *Height* property to *400*.

5. In the Design View, drag the *Button* control to roughly the center of the page, right-click the button to open the contextual menu, and select Edit Template | Create Empty to open the Create ControlTemplate Resource modal window.

6. In the *Name* property field, type **MyButtonControlTemplate** and make sure that This Document is selected. Click OK.

   Visual Studio 2012 will enter the editing mode of the *ControlTemplate* of the button.

   A *ControlTemplate* is a fragment of XAML code capable of representing the structure of a user interface control.

7. Click the Document Outline tab.

> **Note** If you want to keep the Document Outline always visible, click Auto Hide, positioned to the right of the title bar.

   Notice the default structure of a *ControlTemplate*—Visual Studio 2012 has inserted a *Grid* control as the root element of the template.

8. Click the Toolbox tab, expand the All XAML Control section, click the *Ellipse* control, and drag it inside the *Grid* control.

9. In the Design View, click the *Ellipse* control and right-click to open the contextual menu. Select Reset Layout | All. The *Ellipse* control will fill the whole parent element.

10. In the Properties window, expand the *Brush* property group, click the *Fill* property, and then click the Local button positioned to the right of the rectangle showing the preview.

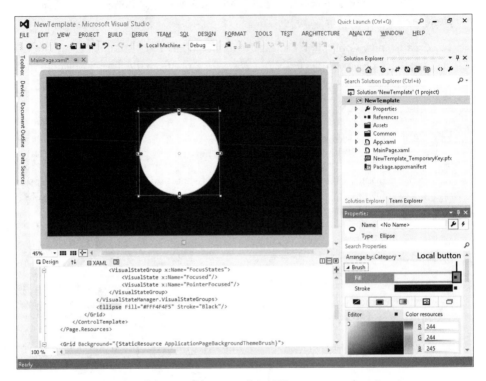

11. In the contextual menu of the Local button of the *Fill* property, select Reset.

Make sure that the background of the *Ellipse* control is set to transparent.

12. In the Properties window, click Stroke and in the color picker, choose white (#FFFFFFFF).

13. Expand the *Appearance* property and set the *StrokeThickness* property to *10*.

 Note The *StrokeThickness* property represents the width of the object outline.

14. Click the Toolbox tab, expand the All XAML Controls section, and click the *TextBlock* control and drag it within the form, inside the *Grid* control.

15. In the Properties window, expand the *Layout* property group.

16. In the contextual menu of the Local button of the *Margin* property, select Reset.

17. In the Properties window, set both *HorizontalAlignment* and *VerticalAlignment* to *Center.*

Observe how the *TextBlock* control is being centered within the parent *Grid* control.

18. Expand the *Miscellaneous* property group, click the Default button next to the *Style* property and from the contextual menu, select Local Resources | PageHeaderTextStyle.

19. Expand the *Layout* property group (if not already expanded) and set both the right and bottom margins to *0.*

20. Expand the *Common* property group, click the Local button next to the *Text* property and from the contextual menu, select Template Binding | Content.

With this operation, you have bound the *Content* property of the button, which is going to use this template with the *Text* property of the *TextBlock* control.

21. Click the Document Outline tab and click Return Scope to [Page], which is located next to the name of the template (MyButtonControlTemplate).

22. In the Design View, click the *Button* control.

In the Properties window, expand the *Common* property group and, in the *Content* property, type **Save**.

23. Click the Toolbox tab, expand the Common XAML Controls section, and click the *Button* control and drag it within the form, side by side with the previously added control.

In the Properties window, expand the *Layout* property group and set both the *Width* and the *Height* properties to *400.*

Expand the *Common* property group and, in the *Content* property, type **Cancel.**

24. In the Design View, click the *Button* control you just added and right-click to open the contextual menu. Select Edit Template | Apply Resource, and then choose the new MyButtonControlTemplate template that you just created.

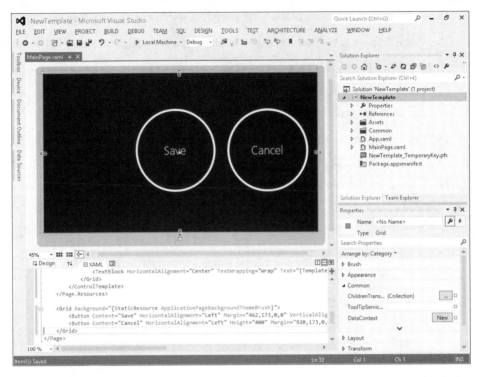

25. On the Debug menu, click Start Debugging. The application will look similar to the designer surface shown in the previous graphic.

If the right side of the Cancel button is cut off, return to Visual Studio 2012 and move the two buttons to the left side of the screen.

Use a predefined template

The *ControlTemplate* of a control defines the appearance of the control. In this procedure, you will reuse a *ControlTemplate* element included in the Visual Studio 2012 project template.

1. Create a new Application project. To do that, open Visual Studio 2012 and, from the File menu, select New Project. Choose Windows Store from the list of installed templates, and then choose Blank App (XAML) from the list of available projects.

2. Select version 4.5 as the .NET Framework version for your new project.

3. Name the new project **UsingTemplate**, and then choose a location on your file system and a solution name. When you're finished, click OK.

4. Click the Toolbox tab that appears on the left-hand side of the form in the Design View window.

5. Expand the Common XAML Controls section.

6. Click the *Button* control and drag it within the form.

7. In the Properties window, expand the *Layout* property group, and set both the *Width* and the *Height* properties to *400*.

8. In the Design View, drag the *Button* control to roughly the center of the page.

9. In the Design View, click the *Button* control and right-click to open the contextual menu. Select Edit Template | Apply Resource | TextButtonStyle.

This *ControlTemplate* will make the button very similar to a *TextBlock* visually without affecting its behavior. The ability to manage the common events of the *Button* class, such as the *Click* event, will not be affected.

Customize a predefined template

The *ControlTemplate* of a control defines the appearance of the control. In this procedure, you will customize a *ControlTemplate* element included in the Visual Studio 2012 project template.

1. Create a new Application project. To do that, open Visual Studio 2012 and, from the File menu, select New Project. Choose Windows Store from the list of installed templates, and then choose Blank App (XAML) from the list of available projects.

2. Select version 4.5 as the .NET Framework version for your new project.

3. Name the new project **CustomTemplate**, and then choose a location on your file system and a solution name. When you're finished, click OK.

4. Click the Toolbox tab that appears on the left-hand side of the form in the Design View window.

5. Expand the Common XAML Controls section.

6. Click the *Button* control and drag it within the form.

7. In the Properties window, expand the *Layout* property group, and set both the *Width* and the *Height* properties to *400*.

8. In the Design View, drag the *Button* control to roughly the center of the page.

9. In the Design View, click the *Button* control and right-click to open the contextual menu Select Edit Template | Apply Resource | TextButtonStyle.

10. In the Design View, click the *Button* control again and right-click to open the contextual menu. Select Edit Template | Edit Current.

11. Click the Document Outline tab.

12. In the Document Outline tab, expand the *Template* node (if not already expanded), expand the *Grid* node, and finally, click the *Text* node.

Thanks to this operation, you have selected the *TextBlock* control inside the template.

Note You can select a control of the *ControlTemplate* by clicking it in the Design View.

13. In the Properties window, expand the *Brush* property group and click the Default button next to the *Foreground* property. Select Template Binding | Foreground.

14. Expand the *Layout* property group, click the Default button next to the *Margin* property, select Template Binding, and then click Padding.

 Note The *Padding* property represents the distance between the child elements of a control.

15. In the Document Outline tab, click Return Scope To [Page] next to the template name (Text-ButtonStyle).

16. In the Design View, click the *Button* control.

17. In the Properties window, expand the *Brush* property group, and choose whatever color you like for the *Foreground* property.

18. Expand the *Text* property and set the *FontSize* property to *72px*.

19. Click Show Advanced Properties and set the *FontWeight* property to *Light*.

20. Expand the *Layout* property group, click Show Advanced Properties, and set both the left and top padding to *80*.

Summary

In this chapter, you have learned how to use Visual Studio 2012 to create an application by using visual tools, how to define the layout of a Windows 8 application through the *Canvas*, *Grid*, *StackPanel*, and *ScrollViewer* panels, and finally, how to customize the appearance of a visual control through the *Style* and *ControlTemplate* objects.

Quick reference

To	Do this
Add a *Grid* control to the layout	Click the Toolbox tab, expand the All XAML Controls, click the *Grid* control, and drag it within the form.
Add a *StackPanel* control to the layout	Click the Toolbox tab, expand the All XAML Controls, click the *StackPanel* control, and drag it within the form.
Add a *Canvas* control to the layout	Click the Toolbox tab, expand the All XAML Controls, click the *Canvas* control, and drag it within the form.
Use a predefined style	In the Design View, click the desired control, right-click and select Edit Style	Apply Resource, and select the style.
Use a predefined template	In the Design View, click the desired control, right-click and select Edit Template	Apply Resource, and select the template.

CHAPTER 8

Asynchronous patterns

After completing this chapter, you will be able to

- Write code using the asynchronous pattern in WinRT.

- Use the *async* and *await* keywords in C#.

- Choose the right synchronization context in your code.

The preceding chapters showed how to write a Windows Store app, and you have already seen and written asynchronous code related to the Windows Runtime (WinRT) methods and events. This chapter explains how asynchronous calls work in WinRT and how to write your own asynchronous code correctly in application and library code. By reading this chapter, you will learn how to leverage the new asynchronous patterns available in .NET 4.5 and Windows Store applications.

await and async keywords for asynchronous patterns

In previous versions of Windows and .NET, many application programming interfaces (APIs) were exposed mainly through synchronous methods; rarely were asynchronous methods available. Thus, when you needed to implement asynchronous code, even while invoking methods available only synchronously, you had to write asynchronous wrappers and choose the right pattern at your own risk.

For example, to read the content of a text file in a string variable, you could have written this code in a traditional windows application in .NET.

```
void Operation()
{
    string content;
    using (StreamReader sr = new StreamReader("document.txt"))
    {
        content = sr.ReadToEnd();
    }
    DisplayContent(content);
}
```

Because the *ReadToEnd* call is synchronous, if the time required to access the file took a long time, and the code was embedded in an event connected to, for example, the click of a button or a menu item selection, the user interface of the entire application would have been frozen for the full duration required to read the content from the Document.txt file.

To avoid this issue, the code would ideally read the file in an asynchronous way in the background, returning control immediately to the application that handles the user interface, and avoiding problems. To do that, the method attached to the user interface event has to return as soon as possible. Performing an operation in an asynchronous manner means that the caller of a function does not need to wait for its completion before continuing, but will obtain the result of the completed operation later, after that operation has finished executing.

Because the function *ReadToEnd* did not expose an asynchronous pattern, to prevent the interface from freezing it was necessary to wrap the *ReadToEnd* call in a separate task that executed in a separate thread. This was the pattern required in .NET 4.0, which resulted in code similar to the following code:

```
void Operation()
{
    Task.Factory.StartNew(
        () =>
        {
            using (StreamReader sr = new StreamReader("document.txt"))
            {
                return sr.ReadToEnd();
            }
        }
    ).ContinueWith(
        (t) => DisplayContent(t.Result)
    );
}
```

However, .NET 4.5 libraries offer a simpler syntax for creating a *Task* object for traditional Windows applications. Each function that may result in a long response time offers an asynchronous version, which returns a *Task<T>* object. In .NET 4.5 the same code can be written as follows:

```
void Operation()
{
    StreamReader sr = new StreamReader(@"document.txt");
    Task<string> readTask = sr.ReadToEndAsync();
    readTask.ContinueWith((t) => DisplayContent(t.Result));
}
```

Note The code of the previous asynchronous example in .NET 4.5 is not functionally identical to the synchronous code. In fact, the *using* statement disappeared and the side effect is that the Document.txt file will be kept open much longer than required. To avoid that, you should write the following code:

```
void Operation()
{
    StreamReader sr = new StreamReader(@"document.txt");
    Task<string> readTask = sr.ReadToEndAsync();
    readTask.ContinueWith(
        (t) =>
        {
            sr.Close();
            return t.Result;
        }
    ).ContinueWith(
        (t) => DisplayContent(t.Result)
    );
}
```

This code is *still* not identical to the initial version, because if an exception occurs it doesn't immediately close the file—that happens when the *sr* instance of the *StreamReader* class is collected by the garbage collector. For these reasons, it is important to use the asynchronous pattern based on the *await* keyword that you will see shortly.

To simplify the code and handle the *using* statement correctly (which was not included in the previous example), you can use the new *async* and *await* keywords available in C# 5.0. The *await* keyword executes the block of code that follows as a subsequent method call in a separate task, which is executed in a way similar to the *ContinueWith* call you have seen before. Because the method containing an *await* statement no longer executes all the lines of code before returning to the caller, it has to return a *Task*, which will have a completed result as soon as all the lines of the original method are executed. For this reason, it is marked with the *async* statement—transforming a *void* method into a method returning a *Task* object, whereas the *async* statement applied to a method returning a string would result in a method returning a *Task<string>*.

```
static async void Asynchronous2_Ok()
{
    string content;
    using (StreamReader sr = new StreamReader(@"document.txt"))
    {
        content = await sr.ReadToEndAsync();
    }
    DisplayContent(content);
}
```

The importance of *await* and *async* statements becomes evident when you realize that WinRT APIs offer only asynchronous versions of the API for each method that might have a response time higher than 50 milliseconds. In practice, any API performing an I/O operation either in an explicit or implicit way will result in this category, because the response time of an I/O operation is not always predictable.

In this procedure, you will use *async* and *await* statements to perform asynchronous operations that call the WinRT API to let a user select a file from a document library and then display its content.

1. Create a new Application project. To do that, open Visual Studio 2012, and from the File menu, select New Project (the sequence can be File | New | Project for full-featured versions of Visual Studio). Choose Visual C# in the Templates tree and then Windows Store from the list of installed templates, and then choose Blank App (XAML) project type from the list of available projects.

2. Select version 4.5 as the Microsoft .NET Framework target version for your new project. (This step is not necessary in the Visual Studio Express edition.)

3. Name the new project **DisplayFile**, and then choose a location on your file system without changing the default solution name. When you have finished, click OK.

   As you saw in Chapter 3, "My first Windows 8 app," the Windows Store Application template provides a default page (MainPage.xaml), an application entry point in the *App* class (App.xaml.cs), a default application description and a declaration in the Package.appxmanifest file, as well as four default images representing logos and a splash screen.

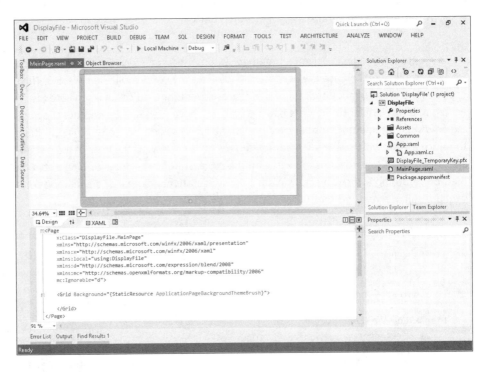

4. Scroll down the MainPage.xaml source code and insert a *TextBox* control and a *Button* control inside a *StackPanel* control, as illustrated in the bold lines of the following code excerpt:

```xml
<Page
    x:Class="DisplayFile.MainPage"
    xmlns="http://schemas.microsoft.com/winfx/2006/xaml/presentation"
    xmlns:x="http://schemas.microsoft.com/winfx/2006/xaml"
    xmlns:local="using:DisplayFile"
    xmlns:d="http://schemas.microsoft.com/expression/blend/2008"
    xmlns:mc="http://schemas.openxmlformats.org/markup-compatibility/2006"
    mc:Ignorable="d">

    <Grid Background="{StaticResource ApplicationPageBackgroundThemeBrush}">
        <StackPanel>
            <Button Click="ChooseFile_Click" Content="Choose File" />
            <TextBlock x:Name="Result" Height="600" />
        </StackPanel>
    </Grid>
</Page>
```

The *TextBlock* control will be filled with the content of the file selected by the user through the *FileOpenPicker* picker; the button will simply fire the code to start the picker, read the file in a string, and put it in the *TextBlock*.

5. Open MainPage.xaml.cs and add the method *ChooseFile_Click*, which implements the event handler for the button. You can also double-click the button in the Integrated Development Environment IDE designer. Add the *async* keyword to the method because it will call asynchronous methods using the .NET 4.5 pattern you saw earlier.

The following code represents the complete method definition.

```csharp
private async void ChooseFile_Click(object sender, RoutedEventArgs e)
{
}
```

6. Add the following code to the method body to open the File Picker, retrieve the selected file, and display its content in the *TextBlock*.

```csharp
var picker = new Windows.Storage.Pickers.FileOpenPicker();
picker.FileTypeFilter.Add("*");
var file = await picker.PickSingleFileAsync();
string content = await Windows.Storage.FileIO.ReadTextAsync(file);
this.Result.Text = content;
```

The first three lines of code create an instance of the *FileOpenPicker* class, as you saw in Chapter 6, "Windows Runtime APIs." In this case, the *PickSingleFileAsync* method is used in order to select just one file. This call is marked as *async*, so the remaining part of the method will be executed after the user selects a file, but *ChooseFile_Click* immediately returns control to its caller, which is the Windows message pump, so any other user interaction with this application will be handled correctly.

The value returned by *PickSingleFileAsync* is of type *Task<Windows.Storage.StorageFile>*, but because the *await* keyword was used, it can be used as a *Windows.Storage.StorageFile* type within a method marked with the *async* keyword. All the code required to get the value from the *Result* property of a *Task* instance and to create a new *Task* every time a new asynchronous call is performed is automatically created by the compiler thanks to the *await* and *async* keywords.

When a user has chosen a file, the code continues, reading the file content by calling the static method named *Windows.Storage.FileIO.ReadTextAsync*, which internally handles the required opening and closing of the file, removing the need to make the call within a *using* statement.

The complete code for MainPage.xaml.cs should look like the following:

```
using System;
using System.Threading.Tasks;
using Windows.System.Threading;
using Windows.UI.Xaml;
using Windows.UI.Xaml.Controls;

namespace DisplayFile
{
    public sealed partial class MainPage : Page
    {
        public MainPage()
        {
            this.InitializeComponent();
        }

        private async void ChooseFile_Click(object sender, RoutedEventArgs e)
        {
            var picker = new Windows.Storage.Pickers.FileOpenPicker();
            picker.FileTypeFilter.Add("*");
            var file = await picker.PickSingleFileAsync();
            string content = await Windows.Storage.FileIO.ReadTextAsync(file);
            this.Result.Text = content;
        }
    }
}
```

7. Run the application, choose a text file from your Documents folder and you will see its content on the screen. The following graphic shows the user interface for the main page of the application after we read a sample text document containing three lines.

Writing asynchronous methods

As you have seen in the previous section, handling an event in an asynchronous way is very simple. You just have to do two things: include the *async* keyword in the declaration of the method attached to the event, and inside the method body, write one or more *await* keywords corresponding to each call to other methods made through asynchronous patterns.

It is important to understand that the method for an event is always called in a synchronous way and does not release control to the message pump until the first call with *await* is executed. Thus, you have to evaluate whether you are executing code that could require a significant amount of time to be executed or not. You could consider that such a condition exists for any operation that might require more than 50 milliseconds to be completed, adopting the same metric used for WinRT APIs.

For example, suppose you need to make a calculation that could require a few seconds, such as the following *LongCalculation* method that simulates a long calculation by looping for the number of seconds specified in the parameter:

```
public static void LongCalculation(int seconds)
{
    DateTime exitTime = DateTime.Now.AddSeconds(seconds);
    while (DateTime.Now < exitTime) ;
}
```

If you call this method before any *await* call in an *async* method handling an event, the application will become unresponsive until code execution reaches the first *await* call. For example, consider what would happen if you call *LongCalculation* in the first line of the *ChooseFile_Click* method of the previous example, resulting in the following version of code:

```
private async void ChooseFile_Click(object sender, RoutedEventArgs e)
{
    LongCalculation(5);
    var picker = new Windows.Storage.Pickers.FileOpenPicker();
    picker.FileTypeFilter.Add("*");
    var file = await picker.PickSingleFileAsync();
    string content = await Windows.Storage.FileIO.ReadTextAsync(file);
    this.Result.Text = content;
}
```

By running this code, you will see that when you click the Choose File button, the application will become unresponsive for five seconds (the value passed as parameter to *LongCalculation*). The user interface to choose the file will display only after that calculation completes. This is because the call to *ChooseFile_Click* is synchronous until execution encounters the first *await*, so it returns control to the message pump after calling the *PickSingleFileAsync* method.

To avoid such problems, you should write the *LongCalculation* method using the asynchronous pattern, so that you can call it with the *await* keyword in the *ChooseFile_Click* method. However, if you just add just the *async* keyword in the *LongCalculation* definition, as shown here:

```
public static async void LongCalculation(int seconds)
```

You get the following error when you try to call the *LongCalculation* method with an *await* keyword:

```
'DisplayFile.MainPage.LongCalculationAsync(int)' does not return a Task and cannot be awaited.
Consider changing it to return Task.
```

What you should understand from this is that the *async* keyword does not really make a method asynchronous—*async* is just a keyword that enables (and forces) the use of *await* within the method. In order to be called with *await*, a method must implement the following asynchronous pattern:

- If the method is void, the asynchronous method must return a *Task*.

- If the method returns a type *T*, the asynchronous method must return a *Task<T>*.

In other words, the three following methods:

```
public static void Sample1();
public static int Sample2();
public static string Sample3();
```

have the following corresponding asynchronous signatures:

```
public static async Task Sample1();
public static async Task<int> Sample2();
public static async Task<string> Sample3();
```

A simple way to transform a CPU-intensive function into an asynchronous one is to change its signature according to the previous pattern and to embed its body within a *Task* action, as in the following example:

```
public static async Task LongCalculationAsync(int seconds)
{
    await Task.Factory.StartNew( () =>
    {
        DateTime exitTime = DateTime.Now.AddSeconds(seconds);
        while (DateTime.Now < exitTime) ;
    });
}
```

> **Note** The reason why an event method (such as the previous *ChooseFile_Click* one) does not need to return a *Task* is because it is not called through *await*; instead, it's called using a *fire-and-forget approach*. In other words, there is no code waiting for the end of the asynchronous part of the event method.

However, remember that creating a new *Task* might execute code in a different thread, introducing a possible race condition caused by executing code in parallel threads. You will see how to synchronize execution of your code in the proper context later in this chapter. In general, if your code has slow response times because it is calling other APIs or libraries, always favor calling existing asynchronous versions of the methods of a library by using the *await* call, and only create new *Task* objects when you cannot rely on existing asynchronous methods.

Implementing asynchronous methods

In this procedure, you will implement an asynchronous method to avoid having the user interface become unresponsive while your code is executing a long-running operation.

1. Open the MainPage.xaml source code and add a *ProgressBar* control inside the existing *Stack-Panel* control, as illustrated in the bold line of the following code excerpt:

```
<Page
    x:Class="DisplayFile.MainPage"
    xmlns="http://schemas.microsoft.com/winfx/2006/xaml/presentation"
    xmlns:x="http://schemas.microsoft.com/winfx/2006/xaml"
    xmlns:local="using:DisplayFile"
    xmlns:d="http://schemas.microsoft.com/expression/blend/2008"
    xmlns:mc="http://schemas.openxmlformats.org/markup-compatibility/2006"
    mc:Ignorable="d">

    <Grid Background="{StaticResource ApplicationPageBackgroundThemeBrush}">
        <StackPanel>
            <Button Click="ChooseFile_Click" Content="Choose File" />
            <ProgressBar x:Name="Progress" HorizontalAlignment="Left"
                         Height="10" Width="1024"/>
            <TextBlock x:Name="Result" Height="600" />
        </StackPanel>
    </Grid>
</Page>
```

The *ProgressBar* control will be updated through the code you add in the next step.

2. Open the MainPage.xaml.cs file and add the method *InitializeProgressBar*, which implements continuous update of the progress bar. This will be an indicator of the fact that the message pump is running and the application is responsive. If the message pump is blocked, the progress bar update will freeze for as long as the application is in an unresponsive state.

   The following code is the complete method definition:

```
private void InitializeProgressBar()
{
    var ui = System.Threading.SynchronizationContext.Current;
    ThreadPoolTimer.CreatePeriodicTimer((timer) =>
    {
        ui.Post((a) =>
        {
            this.Progress.Value = (this.Progress.Value >= 100)
                ? 0 : this.Progress.Value + 1;
        }, null);
    }, new TimeSpan(0, 0, 0, 0, 100));
}
```

3. Change the *MainPage* constructor to add the call to the *InitializeProgressBar* method after the call to *InitializeComponent*. The following code is the complete method definition:

```
public MainPage()
{
    this.InitializeComponent();
    InitializeProgressBar();
}
```

4. Add the following method to the MainPage.xaml.cs file:

```
public static void LongCalculation(int seconds)
{
    DateTime exitTime = DateTime.Now.AddSeconds(seconds);
    while (DateTime.Now < exitTime) ;
}
```

5. Insert the call to *LongCalculation* as the first line of the *ChooseFile_Click* method.

```
private async void ChooseFile_Click(object sender, RoutedEventArgs e)
{
    LongCalculation(5);
    var picker = new Windows.Storage.Pickers.FileOpenPicker();
    picker.FileTypeFilter.Add("*");
    var file = await picker.PickSingleFileAsync();
    string content = await Windows.Storage.FileIO.ReadTextAsync(file);
    this.Result.Text = content;
}
```

6. Run the application and you will see that the progress bar continuously changes its state until you click the Choose File button, at which point the application will become unresponsive for five seconds and the progress bar will be frozen for those five seconds, resulting in a state similar to the following graphic.

7. After the five seconds elapses, you will see the user interface for selecting a file. At this point, you can close the application and apply the changes required to make an asynchronous call to *LongCalculation* discussed in the following steps.

8. Change the code in this way. First, rename the method to *LongCalculationAsync*, embed the code in a lambda expression passed to the *Task.Factory.StartNew* method, called by using the *await* keyword, and transform the method from void to *async Task*. Finally, put the *await* keyword before the *LongCalculationAsync* call. These changes are highlighted in bold in the following code:

```
using System;
using System.Threading.Tasks;
using Windows.System.Threading;
using Windows.UI.Xaml;
using Windows.UI.Xaml.Controls;
```

```
namespace DisplayFile
{
    public sealed partial class MainPage : Page
    {
        public MainPage()
        {
            this.InitializeComponent();
            InitializeProgressBar();
        }

        private void InitializeProgressBar()
        {
            var ui = System.Threading.SynchronizationContext.Current;
            ThreadPoolTimer.CreatePeriodicTimer((timer) =>
            {
                ui.Post((a) =>
                {
                    this.Progress.Value =
                        (this.Progress.Value >= 100) ? 0 : this.Progress.Value + 1;
                }, null);

            }, new TimeSpan(0, 0, 0, 0, 100));
        }

        private async void ChooseFile_Click(object sender, RoutedEventArgs e)
        {
            await LongCalculationAsync(5);
            var picker = new Windows.Storage.Pickers.FileOpenPicker();
            picker.FileTypeFilter.Add("*");
            var file = await picker.PickSingleFileAsync();
            string content = await Windows.Storage.FileIO.ReadTextAsync(file);
            this.Result.Text = content;
        }

        public static async Task LongCalculationAsync(int seconds)
        {
            await Task.Factory.StartNew( () =>
            {
                DateTime exitTime = DateTime.Now.AddSeconds(seconds);
                while (DateTime.Now < exitTime) ;
            } );
        }
    }
}
```

9. Run the application again. This time, after you click the Choose File button, the progress bar will continue to update during the five seconds you must wait before the file selection user interface appears. This is because the message pump is not blocked and the application is still responsive even though it's executing a long operation before asking the user to select a file.

Wait for an event asynchronously

In the previous section, you saw how to call a long-running operation without blocking the responsiveness of the user interface of your application. However, this long operation was still called in a synchronous way in respect to the operation the user wanted to perform (pick a file). As you saw in the previous procedure, the file picker user interface displayed five seconds after the initial click. What do you have to do to perform such a long-running operation while still letting the user complete the file picker operation, without having to wait? To do that, you have to execute the operation in an asynchronous way without using the *await* keyword; instead directly manipulate the *Task* object returned by the asynchronous call you make.

In practice, if you save the result of an asynchronous call into a *Task* object, you can write an *await* statement targeting such an object in order to stop the code flow of a method until the corresponding asynchronous call has been terminated. In practice, if you write the following the code, the *InputData* call is made after the *LongCalculationAsync* completes, meaning the only reason to use *await* is to avoid the user interface becoming unresponsive.

```
await LongCalculationAsync(5);
InputData();
DisplayData();
```

However, suppose you move the await statement after the *InputData* call and before the line calling *DisplayData*, as shown in the following code.

```
Task longCalculation = LongCalculationAsync(5);
InputData();
await longCalculation;
DisplayData();
```

Now, the *LongCalculationAsync* call will be executed at the same time as *InputData*, and the *DisplayData* method will be called only after both *LongCalculationAsync* and *InputData* have completed.

Implementing asynchronous calls

In this procedure, you will implement an asynchronous call to an asynchronous method in order to execute parallel actions in your user interface without having to wait for a background action to complete.

1. Open the MainPage.xaml.cs file and locate the following call to *LongCalculationAsync* in the *ChooseFile_Click* method.

   ```
   await LongCalculationAsync(5);
   ```

2. Remove the *await* keyword from that call, change the parameter from *5* to *40*, and save the result returned from the call in a variable of type *Task*, so that the line becomes the following.

   ```
   Task longTask = LongCalculationAsync(40);
   ```

3. In the *ChooseFile_Click* method you want to wait for *longTask* completion—after the file read operation but before displaying the content of the selected file in the textbox. To achieve such a wait, you use the *await* keyword, without using a call to one of the wait methods of the *Task* class (such as *WaitOne*), which might cause application deadlock. The resulting *ChooseFile_Click* method code should look like the following (changes made to the previous example are highlighted in bold).

```
private async void ChooseFile_Click(object sender, RoutedEventArgs e)
{
    Task longTask = LongCalculationAsync(40);
    var picker = new Windows.Storage.Pickers.FileOpenPicker();
    picker.FileTypeFilter.Add("*");
    var file = await picker.PickSingleFileAsync();
    string content = await Windows.Storage.FileIO.ReadTextAsync(file);
    await longTask;
    this.Result.Text = content;
}
```

4. Run the application, click the Choose File button, and select a file. If you perform the file selection within 40 seconds and click Open within 40 seconds, you will wait before seeing the file content on screen. This is because the content will be displayed only after at least 40 seconds from the click of the Choose File button, waiting for the completion of the *LongCalculationAsync* call.

Handling exceptions in asynchronous code

If an exception occurs during an asynchronous call, it can be difficult to catch the exception properly because of the different threads involved in regular *Task* objects. However, the asynchronous pattern in WinRT and the *await* and *async* keywords automatically generate the wrapping code required to handle such exceptions in a simple way. You can continue writing your code with a sequential approach, without worrying about the need to place *try/catch* statements in the right place, because the compiler automatically generates the required code, such as in the following code example:

```
try
{
    var picker = new Windows.Storage.Pickers.FileOpenPicker();
    picker.FileTypeFilter.Add("*");
    var file = await picker.PickSingleFileAsync();
    string content = await Windows.Storage.FileIO.ReadTextAsync(file);
    this.Result.Text = content;
}
catch( Exception ex )
{
    // TODO - write exception handling code here
}
```

If an exception is thrown in an asynchronous call, it is propagated through the call chain even if different threads are involved. For example, if the *PickSingleFileAsync* returned a null value because the user canceled the operation, the following *ReadTextAsync* call would throw an exception because the first parameter would be null. To describe what happens internally, the *ReadTextAsync* call starts a new *Task* object and any exception thrown there is saved in the *Task* object and propagated to the caller of a waiting function. This would usually require several lines of code, but thanks to the *await* keyword the resulting code is almost the same as the code you would write for sequential calls.

What is important to know is that exceptions corresponding to the *await* call are thrown in your own code. Therefore, if you call an asynchronous method, save its result in a *Task* object, and then execute the *await* later in your code, all the lines you write between the asynchronous code and the *await* statement are executed regardless of whether the asynchronous call throws an exception. For example, consider the following code:

```
try
{
    var file = await ReadFileAsync();
    Task<string> processResult = ProcessFileAsync(file);
    DisplayInfo();
    string result = await processResult;
}
catch( Exception ex )
{
    // TODO - write exception handling code here
}
```

The *DisplayInfo* method is always called and completed regardless of whether an exception is thrown during the asynchronous execution of the *ProcessFileAsync* call.

 Note You must be careful when you separate the *await* statement from the asynchronous call—save the task in a variable, such as the *processResult* variable in the previous example. Every time you do that, you need to be aware that an exception thrown in the asynchronous method might be hidden by subsequent exceptions thrown in methods that are executed before the *await* keyword.

Handling exceptions thrown in asynchronous calls

In this procedure, you will handle exceptions thrown in an asynchronous call.

1. Open the MainPage.xaml.cs file, locate the *ChooseFile_Click* method, and then embed its code within a *try/catch* statement. Pass 5 as the parameter to the *LongCalculationAsync* call. The resulting code of the *ChooseFile_Click* method should look like the following (changes made to the previous example are highlighted in bold):

```
private async void ChooseFile_Click(object sender, RoutedEventArgs e)
{
    try
    {
        Task longTask = LongCalculationAsync(5);
        var picker = new Windows.Storage.Pickers.FileOpenPicker();
        picker.FileTypeFilter.Add("*");
```

```
        var file = await picker.PickSingleFileAsync();
        string content = await Windows.Storage.FileIO.ReadTextAsync(file);
        await longTask;
        this.Result.Text = content;
    }
    catch( Exception ex )
    {
        this.Result.Text = ex.Message;
    }
}
```

2. Locate the *LongCalculationAsync* method definition and add a line that throws an exception after the loop simulating a long calculation. The resulting code of the *LongCalculationAsync* method should be like the following (changes made to the previous example are highlighted in bold):

```
public static async Task LongCalculationAsync(int seconds)
{
    await Task.Factory.StartNew( () =>
    {
        DateTime exitTime = DateTime.Now.AddSeconds(seconds);
        while (DateTime.Now < exitTime) ;
    } );
    throw new Exception("Long Calculation Error");
}
```

3. Run the application, click the Choose File button, wait at least five seconds, and then select a file name. You will see that, instead of displaying the file content, the following message will be displayed:

```
Long Calculation Error
```

This is because, after five seconds, the *LongCalculationAsync* call completed its asynchronous execution by throwing an exception, which does not stop the *PickSingleFileAsync* and *ReadTextAsync* execution. In fact, the exception thrown by *LongCalculationAsync* has been saved in the corresponding *Task* and breaks the *ChooseFile_Click* execution only when the corresponding *await* statement is executed, which is the following line:

```
await longTask;
```

Thus, you can easily handle exceptions thrown by asynchronous calls—but you need to consider that if you separate *await* from asynchronous calls, an exception does not stop the code until the corresponding *await* executes.

Cancel asynchronous operations

When an asynchronous operation needs to be canceled, you need to communicate the cancellation request to code that might be executing in another thread. You can do this using a simple Boolean flag and having the part of the method called asynchronously poll the flag and exit from the running function when it finds that flag active. However, because a method can call other methods that in turn could run other asynchronous operations, you need a standard pattern that can transfer a cancellation request to inner asynchronous methods, so that a request for cancellation can propagate to inner asynchronous method calls and keep the latency between a cancel request and the execution break as short as possible.

The internal asynchronous interfaces used by WinRT are mapped to the standard Task Based Asynchronous pattern, which uses .NET classes such as *CancellationToken* and *CancellationTokenSource* to provide a way to cancel an asynchronous operation, propagating the request to any asynchronous call depth as needed. The basic idea is that you pass a *CancellationToken* object that contains the request for the cancellation, so that if an asynchronous method has to call another method in an asynchronous way, the same token is used and the cancellation automatically propagates through the call chain.

Because the standard asynchronous methods provided by .NET return an *IAsyncInfo* interface, in order to simplify the wrapping in a *Task* class containing the desired *CancellationToken* it is necessary to call the *AsTask* method passing the *CancellationToken* instance as a parameter. For example, if you want to provide a *CancellationToken* to the *PickSingleFileAsync* method, you have to convert this line:

```
var file = await picker.PickSingleFileAsync();
```

into the following:

```
var file = await picker.PickSingleFileAsync().AsTask(cancelPickSingleFile.Token);
```

where the *cancelPickSingleFile* instance has been declared in this way:

```
CancellationTokenSource cancelPickSingleFile = new CancellationTokenSource();
```

The *cancelPickSingleFile* can be used to cancel the asynchronous operation to which the token is assigned. The *CancellationTokenSource* class offers a *Cancel* method to forward the request for cancelling operation to the related asynchronous call.

Cancel operation in asynchronous calls

In this procedure, you will add an automatic cancellation of the file pick operation if the user does not make a selection within 30 seconds after clicking the Choose File button.

1. Open the MainPage.xaml.cs file and add the following method:

    ```
    private static async void SetTimeoutOperation(int seconds, CancellationTokenSource cts)
    {
        await Task.Delay(seconds * 1000);
        cts.Cancel();
    }
    ```

2. Locate the *ChooseFile_Click* method, remove the call to *LongCalculationAsync* and its related *await* statement. Then add the declaration of a *CancellationTokenSource* that is passed as a parameter to the *AsTask* call over the *PickSingleFileAsync* result. The resulting code of the *ChooseFile_Click* method should look like the following (changes made to the previous example are highlighted in bold):

```
private async void ChooseFile_Click(object sender, RoutedEventArgs e)
{
    try
    {
        var picker = new Windows.Storage.Pickers.FileOpenPicker();
        picker.FileTypeFilter.Add("*");

        CancellationTokenSource cancelPickSingleFile = new CancellationTokenSource();
        SetTimeoutOperation(30, cancelPickSingleFile);

        var file = await picker.PickSingleFileAsync().AsTask(cancelPickSingleFile.Token);
        string content = await Windows.Storage.FileIO.ReadTextAsync(file);
        this.Result.Text = content;
    }
    catch (Exception ex)
    {
        this.Result.Text = ex.Message;
    }
}
```

3. Run the application, click the Choose File button, and then wait until the user interface for picking a file disappears and the initial window appears again. It will display the following message:

```
A task was cancelled
```

The reason is that in order to cancel the asynchronous operation, a *TaskCanceledException* exception is thrown and it propagates to the *catch* statement in the *ChooseFile_Click* method. The exception emerges in the *ChooseFile_Click* method corresponding to the *await* call to the *PickSingleFileAsync*. This way, the following lines in the same *try* block (the call to *ReadTextAsync* and the assignment to the Result textbox) do not execute because control is transferred directly to the *catch* statement when the exception occurs.

You can cancel asynchronous operations made by WinRT classes by passing a *Cancellation-Token* to the *Task* obtained with *AsTask* method from a WinRT asynchronous call. The best way to generate and interact with a *CancellationToken* is to create a *CancellationTokenSource*, which is a class offering methods to request the cancellation of an operation bind to the corresponding *CancellationToken* instance.

Track operation progress

During the progress of an asynchronous operation, you might need to display the progress state. WinRT asynchronous calls can be wrapped in a *Task* object that offers the *IProgress<T>* interface that standardizes communicating state for an asynchronous operation in the Task Based Asynchronous pattern.

```
public interface IProgress<in T>
{
    void Report( T Value );
}
```

By providing an object implementing *IProgress* to an asynchronous operation, it is possible to receive notifications about the state of the operation itself. All WinRT functions that return an *IAsyncActionWithProgress<TProgress>* object can be attached to code that displays the progress of the operation by using the *AsTask* syntax.

```
IProgress<TProgress> progress = ...;
await SomeMethodAsync().AsTask(progress);
```

The easiest way to obtain an object implementing the *IProgress<T>* interface is to create an instance of the *Progress<T>* class. For example, if you have a function that provides progress information through an *int* type, you have to pass a lambda function as parameter to the *Progress<int>* constructor that receives an integer as a parameter, such as in the following code:

```
IProgress<int> p = new Progress<int>( (value) =>
{
    // Code that displays progress
    // The value parameter is of type int
} );
```

The data type used in the progress interface depends on the asynchronous operation; you should refer to the WinRT documentation to determine the appropriate type for a specific method.

Track progress in asynchronous operation

In this procedure, you will add a method that simulates executing some work and reports the progress of the ongoing operation through the *IProgress<T>* interface.

1. Open the MainPage.xaml source code and add a *Button* control after the Choose File button, embedding the two buttons in a horizontal *StackPanel*. Next, add a *ProgressBar* named **ProgressSomework** after the *TextBlock* control, as illustrated in the bold lines of the following code excerpt:

```
<Page
    x:Class="DisplayFile.MainPage"
    xmlns="http://schemas.microsoft.com/winfx/2006/xaml/presentation"
    xmlns:x="http://schemas.microsoft.com/winfx/2006/xaml"
    xmlns:local="using:DisplayFile"
```

```
    xmlns:d="http://schemas.microsoft.com/expression/blend/2008"
    xmlns:mc="http://schemas.openxmlformats.org/markup-compatibility/2006"
    mc:Ignorable="d">

    <Grid Background="{StaticResource ApplicationPageBackgroundThemeBrush}">
        <StackPanel>
            <StackPanel Orientation="Horizontal">
                <Button Click="ChooseFile_Click" Content="Choose File" />
                <Button Click="Start_Click" Content="Run Work" />
            </StackPanel>
            <ProgressBar x:Name="Progress"
                        HorizontalAlignment="Left" Height="10" Width="1024"/>
            <TextBlock x:Name="Result" />
            <ProgressBar x:Name="ProgressSomework"
                        HorizontalAlignment="Left" Height="10" Width="1024"/>
        </StackPanel>
    </Grid>
</Page>
```

The button displaying Run Work will call the *Start_Click* method, while the ProgressSomework progress bar will display the state of the ongoing operation.

2. Open the MainPage.xaml.cs file and add the method *Start_Click*, which implements the event handler for the Run Work button. You can also double-click the button in the IDE designer. Add the *async* keyword to the method because it will use the *await* statement.

The code here represents the method definition:

```
private async void Start_Click(object sender, RoutedEventArgs e)
{
}
```

3. Add the following code to the method to display that the loop is running and then finished, calling the asynchronous *DoSomeWorkAsync* method passing an object implementing *IProgress<int>*. In order to do that, create an instance of *Progress<int>* and pass a lambda expression that updates the value of the ProgressSomework progress bar according to the number received as parameter:

```
this.Result.Text = "Start running...";
await DoSomeWorkAsync(
    new Progress<int>( (value) =>
    {
        this.ProgressSomework.Value = value;
    } ));
this.Result.Text = "Loop finished";
```

The code in the lambda expression will be executed every time a progress notification will be sent from the asynchronous operation to the *Progress* instance. In this case, we will update the value of the progress bar named ProgressSomework every time a notification is received.

4. Add the method *DoSomeworkAsync,* which implements a dummy loop notifying progress after a short pause of 20 milliseconds for each iteration. The code here represents the complete method definition:

```
private async Task DoSomeWorkAsync(IProgress<int> progress) {
    for (int i = 0; i <= 100; i++) {
        if (progress != null) {
            progress.Report(i);
        }
        await Task.Delay(20);
    }
}
```

The call to the *Report* method in the progress object will execute the lambda expression passed as parameter to the *Progress<int>* constructor called in the previous step.

The complete code for MainPage.xaml.cs should look like the following listing:

```
using System;
using System.Threading;
using System.Threading.Tasks;
using Windows.System.Threading;
using Windows.UI.Xaml;
using Windows.UI.Xaml.Controls;

namespace DisplayFile
{
    public sealed partial class MainPage : Page
    {
        public MainPage()
        {
            this.InitializeComponent();
            InitializeProgressBar();
        }

        private void InitializeProgressBar()
        {
            var ui = System.Threading.SynchronizationContext.Current;
            ThreadPoolTimer.CreatePeriodicTimer((timer) =>
            {
                ui.Post((a) =>
                {
                    this.Progress.Value = (this.Progress.Value >= 100)
                                    ? 0 : this.Progress.Value + 1;
                }, null);
            }, new TimeSpan(0, 0, 0, 0, 100));
        }

        private static async void SetTimeoutOperation(int seconds,
                    CancellationTokenSource cts)
        {
            await Task.Delay(seconds * 1000);
            cts.Cancel();
        }
```

```csharp
        private async void ChooseFile_Click(object sender, RoutedEventArgs e)
        {
            try
            {
                var picker = new Windows.Storage.Pickers.FileOpenPicker();
                picker.FileTypeFilter.Add("*");

                CancellationTokenSource cancelPickSingleFile =
                        new CancellationTokenSource();
                SetTimeoutOperation(5, cancelPickSingleFile);

                var file = await picker.PickSingleFileAsync().
                        AsTask(cancelPickSingleFile.Token);
                string content = await Windows.Storage.FileIO.ReadTextAsync(file);
                this.Result.Text = content;
            }
            catch (Exception ex)
            {
                this.Result.Text = ex.Message;
            }
        }

        private async void Start_Click(object sender, RoutedEventArgs e)
        {
            this.Result.Text = "Start running...";
            // Use Progress<T> instance for Progress info (same as WinRT/.NET Calls)
            await DoSomeWork(
                new Progress<int>((value) =>
                {
                    this.ProgressSomework.Value = value;
                } ));
            this.Result.Text = "Loop finished";
        }

        private async Task DoSomeWorkAsync(IProgress<int> progress)
        {
            for (int i = 0; i <= 100; i++)
            {
                if (progress != null)
                {
                    progress.Report(i);
                }
                await Task.Delay(20);
            }
        }

        public async Task LongCalculationAsync(int seconds)
        {
            await Task.Factory.StartNew(() =>
            {
                DateTime exitTime = DateTime.Now.AddSeconds(seconds);
                while (DateTime.Now < exitTime) ;
            } );
        }

    }
}
```

5. Run the application and you will see that the first progress bar continuously changes its state. Then click Run Work. You will see that a "Start running..." message is displayed and the progress bar below this message starts updating, rising from 0 to 100 percent in about two seconds. After that, a "Loop finished" message will replace the "Start running..." message displayed initially. The resulting state should be similar to the following graphic.

The progress action is always executed in a safe execution context, allowing you to safely up-date the user interface. If you are used to asynchronous programming in .NET, you know that this type of synchronization with an object handling the user interface could be cumbersome in previous versions of .NET, but thanks to the Task Based Asynchronous pattern the code required to execute the code in a proper way is heavily reduced and simplified.

Synchronization with multiple asynchronous calls

When you need to make multiple asynchronous calls active at the same time, there are useful func-tions that can help in writing the code to wait for the end of the first call or to wait for all the pending calls.

For example, consider the following code:

```
await Operation1Async();
await Operation2Async();
await Operation3Async();
```

The total time required to execute the previous three lines of code is equal to the sum of the times required to execute each of the three functions. However, because the three operations are independent, it could be better to use the *Task.WhenAll* function to execute all three functions at the same time. This provides a best case, so that the time required to execute the *Task.WhenAll* method corresponds to the time required for the longest operation. The previous code can be written in this way:

```
var t1 = Operation1Async();
var t2 = Operation2Async();
var t3 = Operation3Async();
await Task.WhenAll( t1, t2, t3 );
```

It is also possible to avoid creating all the variables by putting the asynchronous calls directly in *Task.WhenAll* parameters.

```
await Task.WhenAll(
        Operation1Async(),
        Operation2Async(),
        Operation3Async() );
```

Please note that for WinRT asynchronous calls it could be necessary to call the *AsTask()* method in order to obtain a valid *Task* object for *Task.WhenAll* or *Task.WaitAny*, which you will see shortly. Thus, if *OperationXAsync* were a WinRT function, the previous code would be the following.

```
await Task.WhenAll(
        Operation1Async().AsTask(),
        Operation2Async().AsTask(),
        Operation3Async().AsTask() );
```

In a similar way, it is possible to wait only for the first task to be completed in a list of tasks, by using the *Task.WhenAny function*, which returns when the first call in the list has completed. In the following code, the *firstCompleted* variable will be assigned to the first completed task, which will correspond to *t1*, *t2* or *t3*, depending on which call completed first.

```
var t1 = Operation1Async();
var t2 = Operation2Async();
var t3 = Operation3Async();
Task firstCompleted = await Task.WhenAny( t1, t2, t3 );
```

It is important to note that *Task.WhenAll* and *Task.WhenAny* should be used instead of *WaitHandle*, *WaitAny*, and *WaitHandle.WaitAll* methods, even when you have *WaitHandle* objects available. The reason is that the *WaitHandle* static methods ignore the need of using the proper synchronization context, which will be explained in the next section, and might block the current thread, resulting in a deadlock situation when such code is mixed with *await* statements.

Wait for multiple asynchronous calls executed in parallel

In this procedure, you will wait for the completion of all the asynchronous calls executed at the same time.

1. Open the MainPage.xaml source code, and add a *Button* control after the Run Work one within the same horizontal *StackPanel*, as illustrated in the bold line of the following code excerpt:

```
<Page
    x:Class="DisplayFile.MainPage"
    xmlns="http://schemas.microsoft.com/winfx/2006/xaml/presentation"
    xmlns:x="http://schemas.microsoft.com/winfx/2006/xaml"
    xmlns:local="using:DisplayFile"
    xmlns:d="http://schemas.microsoft.com/expression/blend/2008"
    xmlns:mc="http://schemas.openxmlformats.org/markup-compatibility/2006"
    mc:Ignorable="d">

    <Grid Background="{StaticResource ApplicationPageBackgroundThemeBrush}">
        <StackPanel>
            <StackPanel Orientation="Horizontal">
                <Button Click="ChooseFile_Click" Content="Choose File" />
                <Button Click="Start_Click" Content="Run Work" />
                <Button Click="WhenAll_Click" Content="WhenAll" />
            </StackPanel>
            <ProgressBar x:Name="Progress"
                        HorizontalAlignment="Left" Height="10" Width="1024"/>
            <TextBlock x:Name="Result" />
            <ProgressBar x:Name="ProgressSomework"
                        HorizontalAlignment="Left" Height="10" Width="1024"/>
        </StackPanel>
    </Grid>
</Page>
```

The button displaying WhenAll will call the *WhenAll_Click* method.

2. Also in the MainPage.xaml.cs file, add the following methods, which simulate three operations having different response times (1, 2, and 3 seconds, respectively):

```
private async Task Operation1Async() {
    await Task.Delay(1000);
}

private async Task Operation2Async() {
    await Task.Delay(2000);
}

private async Task Operation3Async() {
    await Task.Delay(3000);
}
```

3. Add the method *WhenAll_Click*, which implements the event handler for the WhenAll button. You can double-click the button in the IDE (Integrated Development Environment) designer to create the method stub. Add the *async* keyword to the method because it will use the *await* statement.

   The following code shows the full method definition:

   ```
   private async void WhenAll_Click(object sender, RoutedEventArgs e)
   {
   }
   ```

4. Add the following code to the method *WhenAll_Click* to execute the three asynchronous operation at the same time, waiting for all to complete and then displaying the elapsed time:

   ```
   this.Result.Text = "WhenAll starting ...";
   DateTime start = DateTime.Now;
   await Task.WhenAll(
               Operation1Async(),
               Operation2Async(),
               Operation3Async());
   this.Result.Text = String.Format(
       "WhenAll completed in {0} seconds",
       (DateTime.Now - start).Seconds );
   ```

5. Run the application, click the WhenAll button, and then wait until the following message is displayed:

   ```
   WhenAll completed in 3 seconds
   ```

   The total time required for executing the three operations is three seconds, whereas it would have been six seconds if the three functions were executed sequentially (by using three distinct *await* statements).

Choose SynchronizationContext in libraries

The default behavior of the *await* statement is to capture the current *SynchronizationContext* and use it to synchronize the execution of the completion code (the code following the *await* statement) by using that context. This is the reason why it is not necessary to write synchronization code when manipulating user interface objects in asynchronous methods using the *async* and *await* keywords. However, although this behavior is very good in code that interacts directly with the user interface, it might not be such a good idea for a library that might be called by code that does not have to interact with the user interface.

The following statement:

```
await task;
```

will continue execution after task completion in the same execution context of the *await* call. In other words, if you have this method:

```
private async Task DoSomeworkAsync()
{
    await OperationAsync();
    OtherActivity();
}
```

the *OtherActivity* method will be called within the synchronization context of the initial *DoSomework-Async* method, while part of the *OperationAsync* call might be executed in a different synchronization context, for example in a newly created thread.

When you write code at the application level, this is usually the expected behavior. However, when you are writing a library, this behavior might not be optimal, for performance reasons. For example, if the *DoSomeworkAsync* method is called from a service that does not have a user interface, or the *OtherActivity* method does not have to interact with the user interface in any way, the default behavior that forces synchronization performs the operation more slowly than necessary. You can avoid such slowdowns by executing the *OtherActivity* method in a different thread than the one in which *DoSomeworkAsync* was initially called. By calling the *ConfigureAwait* method it is possible to change this behavior, asking for a called operation to execute the following code in the same thread used by the task that completed this activity. The *ConfigureAwait* method must be called as a method of the *Task* that should continue in the same thread, ignoring the existing *SynchronizationContext* when *await* has been called. The changes applied to the previous code are highlighted in the following example:

```
private async Task DoSomeworkAsync()
{
    await OperationAsync().ConfigureAwait( false );
    OtherActivity();
}
```

Summary

In this chapter, you have learned how to use asynchronous patterns in WinRT. The most important keywords are *await* and *async*, which automatically generate much of the required code to handle asynchronous calls and synchronization, reducing the number of threads required, and minimizing the need for synchronization with the user interface. You implemented an event in an asynchronous way, handled exceptions with asynchronous code, and cancelled pending asynchronous operations. You also displayed the progress of an asynchronous operation and optimized synchronization with multiple operations executed in parallel. Finally, you have seen how to correctly handle synchronization in code written for general purpose libraries.

Quick reference

To	Do This
Call asynchronous methods	Use the *await* keyword to make asynchronous calls within methods marked with the *async* keyword.
Handle exceptions thrown in asynchronous code	Use standard *try/catch* statements around code calling asynchronous methods using await keyword.
Cancel an asynchronous operation	Pass a *CancellationToken* to the asynchronous operation and call the *Cancel* method on the *CancellationTokenSource*.
Track the progress of asynchronous operation	Implement a *IProgress<T>* interface by creating an instance of *Progress<T>* passing the code that update the progress state.
Write asynchronous code in libraries (DLLs)	Consider using *Task.ConfigureAwait(false)* to optimize performance and avoid possible deadlocks caused by callers that are unaware of *SynchronizationContext* used by the library.

CHAPTER 9

Rethinking the UI for Windows 8 apps

After completing this chapter, you will be able to:

- Use controls that are specific to Windows 8 apps

- Design flexible layouts

- Use Tiles and Toasts

In Chapter 7, "Enhance the user experience," you analyzed some common XAML controls—controls that you can also find in other presentation technologies, such as Windows Presentation Foundation (WPF), Microsoft Silverlight, and Windows Phone. In this chapter, you will become acquainted with objects of the XAML platform specific to Windows 8, and you will see how to define appropriate application layouts for each Windows 8 UI view state, including portrait, landscape, snapped, fill, and full-screen views. The last part of the chapter is dedicated to Tiles and Toasts, which are important ways to communicate with your application's users directly from the Windows Start screen. This chapter is dedicated to the user interface and the user experience, so we want to focus your attention on specific features and the use of specific controls.

Use Windows 8 UI-specific controls

This section discusses how to use some of the user interface controls that are specific to Windows 8 apps, such as *AppBar*, *WebView*, *ListView*, *GridView*, *FlipView*, and *SemanticZoom*.

Use the *Application Bar* control

The Application Bar, typically known as the App Bar, is a container for custom commands and for options specific to the user's current context. You can create up to two *App Bar* controls for a Windows Store app: usually the bottom App Bar is used to manage tasks related to the current context, while typically the top App Bar presents navigation aids to the user. In this procedure, you will add an *App Bar* control to a Windows Store app.

1. Create a new Application project. To do that, open Visual Studio 2012, and from the File menu, select New Project (the sequence can be File | New | Project for full-featured versions of Visual Studio). Choose Visual C# in the Templates tree and then Windows Store from the list of installed templates. Finally, choose the Blank App (XAML) project type from the list of available projects. Select version 4.5 as the .NET Framework target version for your new project (this step is not necessary in the Visual Studio Express edition).

2. Name the new project **AppBar**, and then choose a location on your file system without changing the default solution name. When you're finished, click OK.

   As you saw in Chapter 3, "My first Windows 8 app," the Windows Store Application template provides a default page (MainPage.xaml), an application entry point to the *App* class (App.xaml.cs), a default application descriptionand a declaration in the Package.appxmanifest, as well as four default images representing logos and a splash screen.

3. In the Solution Explorer window, expand the Common directory and double-click the Standard-Style.xaml file. Uncomment the following styles: *HomeAppBarButtonStyle*, *RefreshAppBarButton-Style*, and *SaveAppBarButtonStyle*. To uncomment, simply cut the entire style definition of the style and paste it above the green code area.

> **Note** See Chapter 7 for more details about the *Style* object.

4. On the File menu, select Save All.

5. In Solution Explorer, double-click MainPage.xaml to open the designer.

6. Click the Document Outline tab. If you can't see the Document Outline tab, select View | Other Windows | Document Outline.

> **Note** To keep the Document Outline always visible, click the Auto Hide button in the right-hand side of the title bar.

7. Expand the *Page* node, if it's not already expanded. Click the *BottomAppBar* node, and then right-click it to open the context menu.

8. Select Pin Active Container.

   By doing this, you have transformed the *BottomAppBar* node into the active container; this way, any object you drag from or draw using the Toolbox tab will become a child of that container. Note that the *BottomAppBar* node is boxed in yellow, which represents it as the active container.

9. Click the Toolbox tab. Expand the All XAML Controls section. Double-click the *AppBar* control.

   The *AppBar* control represents an application toolbar for displaying buttons and other controls.

10. Click the Document Outline tab. Expand the *BottomAppBar* node, if it is not already expanded.

11. Expand the child nodes of the *BottomAppBar* node; you will see that Visual Studio 2012 has created an *AppBar* control, which in turn contains a *Grid* element. The latter is divided into two columns of the same width, and each column contains a *StackPanel* control.

> **Note** See Chapter 7 for more details about the *Grid* and *StackPanel* controls.

12. In the Document Outline tab, click the first *StackPanel* control to select it. Right-click the first *StackPanel* to open the context menu.

13. Select Pin Active Container.

14. Click the Toolbox tab. Expand the Common XAML Controls section. Double-click the *Button* control.

Note that the *Button* control you just created has become a child of the first *StackPanel* control (the control you just selected as the active container).

Repeat this step two more times, until you have created three *Button* controls inside the *StackPanel* control.

15. In Design View, click the first *Button* control and right-click to open the context menu. From that menu, select Edit Template | Apply Resource | *HomeAppBarButtonStyle*.

16. In the Properties window, expand the Common section.

In the context menu for the Local button of the *Content* property, select the Reset option.

17. In Design View, click the second *Button* control and right-click to open its context menu. From the menu, select Edit Template | Apply Resource | *RefreshAppBarButtonStyle*.

18. In the Properties window, expand the Common section.

In the context menu for the Local button of the *Content* property, select Reset.

19. In the Design View, click the third *Button* control and right-click to open the context menu. From the menu, select Edit Template | Apply Resource | *SaveAppBarButtonStyle*.

20. In the Properties window, expand the Common section.

In the context menu of the Local button of the *Content* property, select Reset.

21. On the Debug menu, click Start Debugging.

Right-click to display the application bar, making it possible to interact with the buttons created earlier.

Note The controls of the platform have been designed to support different types of input natively; therefore it is possible to show the application bar through digital pen, mouse, keyboard, and touch gestures (in the latter case using a swipe gesture from bottom to top).

22. Return to Visual Studio 2012 by pressing ALT+TAB, and on the Debug menu, click Stop Debugging.

5. In the Solution Explorer, double-click MainPage.xaml. In the Document Outline tab, select the *[Page]* node.

In the Properties window, expand the Common section and click New, beside the *DataContext* property.

6. In the Select Object dialog, select the *DataSource* class of your ListView project and click OK.

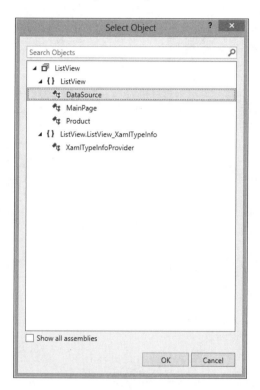

7. In the XAML View, take a look at the code produced by the former operation:

```
<Page.DataContext>
    <local:DataSource/>
</Page.DataContext>
```

Because the *DataContext* property of a control represents the data associated with that control, it is important to understand that such data are visible and usable, not only by the control that you set the *DataContext* property on (in this case, the page), but also by its logical descendant elements (in this case, all the child controls of the *Page* element will be able to see and use the custom object *DataSource*).

8. Click the Toolbox tab. Expand the Common XAML Controls section.

Click the *ListView* control and drag it within the form.

9. In the Design View, right-click the *ListView* control to open the context menu, and then select Reset Layout and click All—the *ListView* control will fill the whole parent element.

10. In the Properties window, expand the *Common* property. Click the Default button next to the *ItemsSource* property.

The *ItemsSource* property represents a collection of objects that will be used to generate the elements of a *ListView*.

11. From the context menu, select Create Data Binding to open the Create Data Binding For [List-View].ItemsSource modal window.

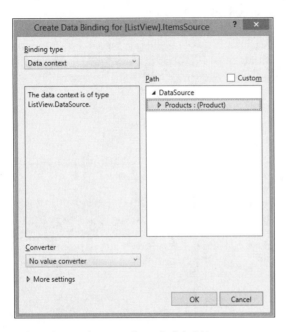

Select the Products node and click OK.

By doing this, you have bound the *ItemsSource* property of the *ListView* control to the *Products* property of the *DataSource* custom object.

12. Take a look at the *ListView* control in the Design View: you will see a series of strings with the text *ListView.Product*. Because the class currently in binding does not derive from *Windows. UI.Xaml.UIElement*, the XAML platform is forced to use the *ToString* method of the *Product* class for the rendering. In the following steps, you will customize the rendering of the *Product* object in binding by using *DataTemplate* elements.

13. In the Design View, right-click the *ListView* control to open the context menu. To open the Create DataTemplate Resource modal window, select Edit Additional Templates | Edit Generated Items (ItemTemplate) | Create empty.

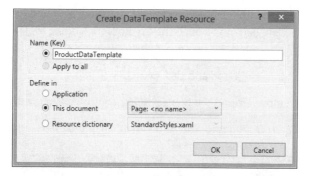

14. In the Name textbox, type **ProductDataTemplate**. In the Define In Radio button, make sure This Document is selected. Click OK.

Visual Studio 2012 will enter the editing mode of the DataTemplate.

A DataTemplate is a fragment of XAML code capable of representing the visual structure of an arbitrary data object.

15. Click the Document Outline tab.

Notice the default structure of a DataTemplate: Visual Studio 2012 has inserted a *Grid* control as the root element of the template.

16. Click the *[Grid]* node. In the Properties window, expand the *Layout* property and set the *Width* property to *400*, the *Height* property to *100*, the *Left Margin* property to *10*, and the *Top Margin* property to *10*.

17. Click the Toolbox tab. Expand the Common XAML Controls section. Double-click the *TextBlock* control.

18. In the Design View, right-click the *TextBlock* control to open the context menu, and then select Edit Style | Apply Resource | *SubheaderTextStyle*.

19. In the Properties window, expand the Common section. Click Local (next to the *Text* property) and select Create Data Binding to open the Create Data Binding for [TextBlock].Text modal window.

20. In the Path tree view, select the *Description* node and click OK.

The *Description* property of the *Product* custom object is now bound with the *Text* property of the *TextBlock* visual object.

21. Click the Toolbox tab. Expand the Common XAML Controls section and double-click the *Text-Block* control.

22. In the Design View, drag the new *TextBlock* control under the already existing *TextBlock* control.

Click the *TextBlock* control and right-click to open the context menu. Select Edit Style | Apply Resource | *CaptionTextStyle*.

23. In the Properties window, expand the Common section, click the Local button next to the *Text* property, and select Create Data Binding to open the Create Data Binding for [TextBlock].Text modal window.

24. In the Path tree view, select the *Price* node and click OK.

In the Design View, you can move around the two *TextBlock* controls as you wish.

25. On the Debug menu, click Start Debugging. The result is shown in the following graphic.

26. Return to Visual Studio 2012 and, on the Debug menu, click Stop Debugging.

Use the *GridView* control

The purpose of the *GridView* control is to represent a collection of data items within grid visualization. In this procedure, you will bind a list of custom objects to a *GridView* control.

1. Create a new Application project. To do that, open Visual Studio 2012 and from the File menu select New Project. Choose Windows Store from the list of installed templates, and then choose Blank App (XAML) from the list of available projects. Select version 4.5 as the .NET Framework version for your new project.

2. Name the new project **GridView**, then choose a location on your file system and a solution name. When you're finished, click OK.

3. In the Solution Explorer, right-click the project name node (in this case *GridView*) to open the context menu. Select Add | Existing Item.

   Select the Chapter 09 Demo Files directory, click the directory named Code, open the Grid-View directory, select the DataSource.cs file, and click Add.

4. Drag the Photos folder included in the Chapter 09 Demo Files directory into Visual Studio 2012. Point the cursor on the project name and then release the mouse button.

   Visual Studio 2012 will create a directory called Photos in the project's root (at the same level of the Assets and Common folders) containing some .jpg files.

   If you want to use your own personal photos, it is enough to name them as the demo files (01.jpg, 02.jpg, and so on). On the Build menu, click Build Solution.

5. In the Solution Explorer, double-click MainPage.xaml. In the Document Outline tab, select the [Page] page.

6. In the Properties window, expand the Common section, and then click New beside the *Data-Context* property.

   In the Select Object dialog window, select the *DataSource* class of your *GridView* project and click OK.

7. Click the Toolbox tab. Expand the Common XAML Controls section. Click the *GridView* control and drag it within the form.

8. In the Design View, right-click the *GridView* control to open the context menu. Select Reset Layout and click All—the *GridView* control will fill the whole parent element.

9. In the Properties window, expand the Common section. Click Default next to the *ItemsSource* property.

   The *ItemsSource* property consists of a collection of objects that will be used to generate the elements of the *GridView*.

10. To open the Create Data Binding for [GridView].ItemsSource modal window, select Create Data Binding from the context menu.

11. Select the *Products* node and click OK.

    The *ItemsSource* property of the *ListView* control is now bound to the *Products* property of the *DataSource* custom object.

12. In the Design View, right-click the *GridView* control to open the context menu. To open the Create DataTemplate Resource modal window. Select Edit Additional Templates | Edit Gener-ated Items (ItemTemplate) | Create Empty.

13. In the Name textbox, type **ProductDataTemplate.** In Define In, select This Document, and then click OK.

    Visual Studio 2012 will enter the editing mode of the *DataTemplate*.

14. Click the Document Outline tab. Click the *[Grid]* node.

15. In the Properties window, expand the *Layout* property and set the *Width* property to *300*, the *Height* property to *300*, and the *Left Margin* property to *10*.

16. Click the Toolbox tab. Expand the Common XAML Controls section. Double-click the *Image* control.

17. In the Document Outline View, select the *[Image]* node and right-click to open the context menu. Select Reset Layout and click All. The *Image* control will fill the whole parent element.

18. In the Properties window, expand the Common section. Click the Local button next to the *Source* property. To open the Create Data Binding for [Image].Source modal window, select Create Data Binding.

19. In the Path tree view, select the *Photo* node and click OK.

The *Photo* property of the *Product* custom object is now bound with the *Source* property of the *Image* visual object.

20. Click the Toolbox tab. Expand the Common XAML Controls section. Double-click the *TextBlock* control.

21. In the Design View, drag the new *TextBlock* control under the *Image* control.

Select the *TextBlock* control and right-click. From the menu, select Edit Style | Apply Resource | *SubheaderTextStyle*.

22. In the Properties window, expand the Common section. Click the Local button next to the *Text* property. To open the Create Data Binding for [TextBlock].Text modal window, select Create Data Binding.

23. In the Path tree view, select the *Description* node and click OK.

24. In the Design View, you can move the *TextBlock* control as you prefer.

On the Debug menu, click Start Debugging. The result is shown in the following graphic.

25. Return to Visual Studio 2012 and, on the Debug menu, click Stop Debugging.

Use the *FlipView* control

A *FlipView* control allows visualizing a collection of data items, one item at a time. In this procedure, you will learn how to bind a list of a custom entity to a *FlipView* control.

1. Create a new Application project. To do that, open Visual Studio 2012 and from the File menu select New Project. Choose Windows Store from the list of installed templates, and then choose Blank App (XAML) from the list of available projects. Select version 4.5 as the .NET Framework version for your new project.

2. Name the new project **FlipView**, and then choose a location on your file system and a solution name. When you're finished, click OK.

3. In the Solution Explorer, right-click the project name node (in this case *FlipView*) to open the context menu. Select Add | Existing Item.

   Select the Chapter 09 Demo Files directory. Click the Code directory, open the FlipView directory, and select DataSource.cs. Click Add.

4. Drag the Photos folder included in the Chapter 09 Demo Files into Visual Studio 2012, and then point the cursor on the project name.

   Visual Studio 2012 will create a directory called Photos in the project's root (at the same level of the Assets and Common folders) containing some .jpg files.

   On the Build menu, click Build Solution.

5. In the Solution Explorer, double-click MainPage.xaml. In the Document Outline tab, select the *[Page]* node.

   In the Properties window, expand the Common section. Click the New button beside the *DataContext* property.

6. In the Select Object dialog, select the *DataSource* class of your FlipView project and click OK.

7. Click the Toolbox tab. Expand the Common XAML Controls section. Select the *FlipView* control and drag it within the form.

8. In the Document Outline tab, select the *[FlipView]* node and right-click to open the context menu. Select Reset Layout and click All—the *FlipView* control will fill the whole parent element.

9. In the Properties window, expand the Common section. Click the Default button next to the *ItemsSource* property.

   The *ItemsSource* property represents a collection of objects that will be used to generate the elements of *FlipView*.

10. To open the Create Data Binding for [FlipView].ItemsSource modal window, select Create Data Binding. Select the *Products* node and click OK.

    The *ItemsSource* property of the *FlipView* control is now bound to the *Products* property of the *DataSource* custom object.

11. In the Design View, select the *FlipView* control and right-click to open the context menu. To open the Create DataTemplate Resource modal window, select Edit Additional Templates | Edit Generated Items (ItemTemplate) | Create Empty.

12. In the Name textbox, type **ProductDataTemplate.** In Define In, select This Document. Click OK.

Visual Studio 2012 will enter the editing mode of the *DataTemplate*.

13. Click the Document Outline tab. Click the *[Grid]* node.

14. In the Properties window, expand the Layout section (in case it's not expanded already) and make sure that the *Width* property is set to Auto. If it is not, click Set To Auto next to the *Width* property.

15. Click the Toolbox tab. Expand the Common XAML Controls section. Double-click the *Image* control.

16. In the Document Outline View, select the *[Image]* node and right-click to open the context menu. Select Reset Layout and click All—the *Image* control will fill the whole parent element.

17. In the Properties window, expand the Common section. To open the Create Data Binding for [Image].Source modal window, click the Local button next to the *Source* property and select Create Data Binding.

18. In the Path tree view, select the *Photo* node and click OK.

The *Photo* property of the *Product* custom object is now bound with the *Source* property of the *Image* visual object.

Set the *Stretch* property to *UniformToFill*.

19. Click the Toolbox tab. Expand the Common XAML Controls section. Double-click the *TextBlock* control.

20. In the Design View, drag the new *TextBlock* control on top of the *Image* control.

Select the *TextBlock* control and right-click to open the context menu. Select Edit Style | Apply Resource | *SubheaderTextStyle*.

21. In the Properties window, expand the Common section. To open the Create Data Binding for [TextBlock].Text modal window, click the Local button next to the *Text* property, and select Create Data Binding.

22. In the Path tree view, select the *Description* node and click OK.

In the Design View, you can move the *TextBlock* control as you prefer.

23. On the Debug menu, click Start Debugging. Click the arrow on the right side of the display.

Statue 1

24. Click the arrows to navigate among the different elements of the collection.

 Note The controls of the platform have been designed to support different types of input natively; therefore it is possible to navigate among the different elements using a digital pen, mouse, keyboard, and touch gestures (in the latter case using a swipe gesture from left to right or vice versa).

25. Return to Visual Studio 2012. On the Debug menu, click Stop Debugging.

Use the *SemanticZoom* control

Semantic zoom is a touch-optimized technique used by Windows 8 apps for presenting and navigating large sets of related data or content within a single view (such as a photo album, app list, or address book).

The page that displays all the Windows 8 applications installed on your machine offers an example of semantic zoom. The default view is displayed as "zoomed in," that is, it presents a complete list of applications; with a simple gesture of pinch and stretch or by scrolling the mouse wheel while pressing Ctrl, you can activate the "zoomed out" view that, in this case, will display a series of tiles with the initials of the existing applications.

The *SemanticZoom* control can be used to add the semantic zoom concept into a Windows 8 app. In this procedure, you will learn how to bind a *SemanticZoom* control to a list of custom data objects.

1. Create a new Application project. To do that, open Visual Studio 2012 and from the File menu select New Project. Choose Windows Store from the list of installed templates, and then choose Blank App (XAML) from the list of available projects. Select version 4.5 as the .NET Framework version for your new project.

2. Name the new project **SemanticZoom**, and then choose a location on your file system and a solution name. When you're finished, click OK.

3. In the Solution Explorer, click the project name node (in this case, *SemanticZoom*) and right-click to open the context menu. Select Add | Existing Item.

4. Select the directory named Chapter 09 Demo Files. Click the Code directory, open the SemanticZoom directory, and select DataSource.cs. Click Add.

5. Drag the Photos folder included in the Chapter 09 Demo Files directory into Visual Studio 2012, and point the cursor on the project name.

    Visual Studio 2012 will create a directory called Photos in the project's root (at the same level of the Assets and Common folders) containing some .jpg files.

6. On the Build menu, click Build Solution.

7. In the Solution Explorer, double-click MainPage.xaml.

8. Click the Toolbox tab.

9. Expand the Common XAML Controls section.

10. Click the *SemanticZoom* control and drag it within the form.

11. In the Document Outline tab, select the *[SemanticZoom]* node and right-click the mouse button to open the context menu. Select Reset Layout and click All. The *SemanticZoom* control will fill the whole parent element.

12. In the XAML view, take a look at the XAML code of the *SemanticZoom* control.

```
<SemanticZoom>
        <SemanticZoom.ZoomedInView>
                <GridView
                        ScrollViewer.IsHorizontalScrollChainingEnabled="False"
                        ScrollViewer.IsVerticalScrollChainingEnabled="False"/>
        </SemanticZoom.ZoomedInView>
        <SemanticZoom.ZoomedOutView>
                <GridView
                        ScrollViewer.IsHorizontalScrollChainingEnabled="False"
                        ScrollViewer.IsVerticalScrollChainingEnabled="False"/>
        </SemanticZoom.ZoomedOutView>
</SemanticZoom>
```

The *SemanticZoom* control exposes two properties, *ZoomedInView* and *ZoomedOutView*, which represent as many views of the same set of information.

13. Replace the whole source code of the MainPage.xaml.cs page with the following code:

```
<Page
    x:Class="SemanticZoom.MainPage"
    xmlns="http://schemas.microsoft.com/winfx/2006/xaml/presentation"
    xmlns:x="http://schemas.microsoft.com/winfx/2006/xaml"
    xmlns:local="using:SemanticZoom"
    xmlns:d="http://schemas.microsoft.com/expression/blend/2008"
    xmlns:mc="http://schemas.openxmlformats.org/markup-compatibility/2006"
    mc:Ignorable="d">
    <Page.Resources>
        <CollectionViewSource x:Name="Data" IsSourceGrouped="True" />
    </Page.Resources>
    <Grid Background="{StaticResource ApplicationPageBackgroundThemeBrush}">
        <SemanticZoom>
            <SemanticZoom.ZoomedInView>
                <GridView ItemsSource="{Binding Source={StaticResource Data}}"
                        SelectionMode="None">
                    <GridView.ItemTemplate>
                        <DataTemplate>
                            <Grid Width="300" Height="300">
                                <Image Source="{Binding Photo}"/>
                                <TextBlock HorizontalAlignment="Left" TextWrapping="Wrap"
                                        Text="{Binding Description}" VerticalAlignment="Top"
                                        Margin="0,256,0,0"
                                        Style="{StaticResource SubheaderTextStyle}"/>
                            </Grid>
                        </DataTemplate>
                    </GridView.ItemTemplate>
                </GridView>
            </SemanticZoom.ZoomedInView>
            <SemanticZoom.ZoomedOutView>
                <GridView
                    ItemsSource="{Binding CollectionGroups, Source={StaticResource Data}}" >
                    <GridView.ItemTemplate>
                        <DataTemplate>
                            <Border Background="#FF26A0DA" Width="230" Height="230">
                                <TextBlock Text="{Binding Group.Key}" FontSize="30"
                                        VerticalAlignment="Bottom" Margin="10,0,0,10" />
                            </Border>
                        </DataTemplate>
                    </GridView.ItemTemplate>
                </GridView>
            </SemanticZoom.ZoomedOutView>
        </SemanticZoom>
    </Grid>
</Page>
```

In this example, you used a *GridView* control for both views, but you could have used a *ListView* control instead. Both the *GridView* controls leverage the same concepts illustrated in the "Use the *GridView* Control" procedure: the *ItemsSource* property binds the collection and the *ItemTemplate* property defines the visual representation of the single item in binding. For the *GridView* control nested within the *ZoomedInView* property, you have reused the code presented in the previous procedure to define the *ItemTemplate* property.

For the *ZoomedInView* property, the *ItemsSource* property of the *GridView* has been bound to the complete data collection. While in the case of the *ZoomedOutView* property, the *Items-Source* will use the *CollectionGroups* property for the same dataset to show the initials in the photo captions.

14. In the Solution Explorer, double-click MainPage.xaml.cs.

15. Replace the following code:

```
protected override void OnNavigatedTo(NavigationEventArgs e)
{
}
```

With this one:

```
protected override void OnNavigatedTo(NavigationEventArgs e)
{
    Data.Source = new DataSource().Groups;
}
```

16. On the Debug menu, click Start Debugging. The result is shown in the following graphic.

17. Hold the Ctrl key down while scrolling to switch between the two views offered by the *SemanticZoom* control. You can also click the minus (-) icon that appears in the lower-right corner to obtain the overview display. Clicking the display area zooms the display again.

 Note The controls of the platform have been designed to support different types of input natively; therefore it is possible to navigate between the two views using a digital pen, mouse, keyboard, and touch gestures (in the latter case using a pinch and stretch gesture).

18. Return to Visual Studio 2012. On the Debug menu, click Stop Debugging.

Designing flexible layouts

The way that the content of your user interface adapts to how the app is manipulated by a user is call a *view*. View state refers to the three ways a user can choose to display your Windows 8 app: full screen, snap, and fill. The first—full—screen is the default state for all apps. When a user drags another window onto the screen, he has the option of having it become the current running app, snapping the new app to the side, or running it filled. Users can rotate and flip their devices, so ensure that your app can handle both landscape and portrait orientations.

Designing flexible layouts

1. Create a new Application project. To do that, open Visual Studio 2012 and from the File menu select New Project. Choose Windows Store from the list of installed templates, and then choose Blank App (XAML) from the list of available projects. Select version 4.5 as the .NET Framework version for your new project.

2. Name the new project **ViewState**, and then choose a location on your file system and a solution name. When you're finished, click OK.

3. In the Solution Explorer, click the project name node (*ViewState*, in this case) and right-click to open the context menu. Select Add | Existing Item.

4. Select the directory named Chapter 09 Demo Files, click the Code directory, open the ViewState directory, and select DataSource.cs. Click Add.

5. Drag the Photos folder included in the Chapter 09 Demo Files directory into Visual Studio 2012, and point the cursor on the project name.

   Visual Studio 2012 will create a directory called Photos in the project's root (at the same level of the Assets and Common folders) containing some .jpg files.

   On the Build menu, click Build Solution.

6. In the Solution Explorer, double-click MainPage.xaml. Replace the whole source code with the following:

```
<Page
    x:Class="ViewState.MainPage"
    xmlns="http://schemas.microsoft.com/winfx/2006/xaml/presentation"
    xmlns:x="http://schemas.microsoft.com/winfx/2006/xaml"
    xmlns:local="using:ViewState"
    xmlns:d="http://schemas.microsoft.com/expression/blend/2008"
    xmlns:mc="http://schemas.openxmlformats.org/markup-compatibility/2006"
    mc:Ignorable="d">
    <Page.Resources>
        <DataTemplate x:Key="ProductGridDataTemplate">
            <Grid Width="300" Height="300">
                <Image Source="{Binding Photo}"/>
                <TextBlock HorizontalAlignment="Left" TextWrapping="Wrap"
                    Text="{Binding Description}" VerticalAlignment="Top"
                    Margin="0,256,0,0" Style="{StaticResource SubheaderTextStyle}"/>
            </Grid>
        </DataTemplate>
        <DataTemplate x:Key="ProductListDataTemplate">
            <Grid Width="400" Height="100">
                <TextBlock HorizontalAlignment="Left" TextWrapping="Wrap"
                    Text="{Binding Description}" VerticalAlignment="Top"
                    Style="{StaticResource SubheaderTextStyle}"/>
                <TextBlock HorizontalAlignment="Left" TextWrapping="Wrap"
                    Text="{Binding Price}" VerticalAlignment="Top"
                    Margin="0,47,0,0" Style="{StaticResource CaptionTextStyle}"/>
```

```
                </Grid>
            </DataTemplate>
        </Page.Resources>
        <Page.DataContext>
            <local:DataSource/>
        </Page.DataContext>

        <Grid Background="{StaticResource ApplicationPageBackgroundThemeBrush}">
            <GridView x:Name="GridViewControl" ItemsSource="{Binding Products}"
                ItemTemplate="{StaticResource ProductGridDataTemplate}"/>
            <ListView x:Name="ListViewControl" ItemsSource="{Binding Products}"
                ItemTemplate="{StaticResource ProductListDataTemplate}" Visibility="Collapsed"/>

            <VisualStateManager.VisualStateGroups>
                <VisualStateGroup x:Name="ApplicationViewStates">
                    <VisualState x:Name="FullScreenLandscape"/>
                    <VisualState x:Name="FullScreenPortrait" />
                    <VisualState x:Name="Filled"/>
                    <VisualState x:Name="Snapped" />
                </VisualStateGroup>
            </VisualStateManager.VisualStateGroups>
        </Grid>

    </Page>
```

In this listing, you can see two *DataTemplate* items already used in the former procedures "Use the *ListView* Control" and "Use the *GridView* Control." Inside the main *Grid* control, there is a *GridView* control, which will be used in both the full-screen and filled views (you will soon understand the difference between the two views) and a *ListView* control that will be displayed in the snapped view.

The *VisualStateManager* object manages states and the transitions between states for controls.

7. In the Solution Explorer, double-click MainPage.xaml.cs. Replace the whole source code with the following:

```
using System;
using System.Collections.Generic;
using System.IO;
using System.Linq;
using Windows.Foundation;
using Windows.Foundation.Collections;
using Windows.UI.Xaml;
using Windows.UI.Xaml.Controls;
using Windows.UI.Xaml.Controls.Primitives;
using Windows.UI.Xaml.Data;
using Windows.UI.Xaml.Input;
using Windows.UI.Xaml.Media;
using Windows.UI.Xaml.Navigation;
```

```
namespace ViewState
{
    public sealed partial class MainPage : Page
    {
        public MainPage()
        {
            this.InitializeComponent();
            Window.Current.SizeChanged += OnSizeChanged;
        }

        public void OnSizeChanged(object sender,
            Windows.UI.Core.WindowSizeChangedEventArgs args)
        {
            switch (Windows.UI.ViewManagement.ApplicationView.Value)
            {
                case Windows.UI.ViewManagement.ApplicationViewState.FullScreenLandscape:
                    VisualStateManager.GoToState(this, "FullScreenLandscape", false);
                    break;
                case Windows.UI.ViewManagement.ApplicationViewState.FullScreenPortrait:
                    VisualStateManager.GoToState(this, "FullScreenPortrait", false);
                    break;
                case Windows.UI.ViewManagement.ApplicationViewState.Snapped:
                    VisualStateManager.GoToState(this, "Snapped", false);
                    break;
                case Windows.UI.ViewManagement.ApplicationViewState.Filled:
                    VisualStateManager.GoToState(this, "Filled", false);
                    break;
                default:
                    break;
            }
        }
    }
}
```

In the *Window.Current.SizeChanged* event handler, the *GoToState* method of the *VisualState-Manager* is called to set the page state. The state will have the same name for the *Value* property of the *Windows.UI.ViewManagement.ApplicationView* object.

The next step consists of defining a "shape" for each state of the page.

8. In the Solution Explorer, double-click MainPage.xaml. Click the Device tab.

> **Note** If you want to keep the Device always visible, click the Auto Hide button positioned to the right of the title bar.

9. In the *View* property, click Snapped.

The snapped state is one of the possible application view states. Snapping an app resizes the app to 320 pixels wide, which allows it to share the screen with another app.

Visual Studio 2012 will display the area available for that state in the Design View.

10. In the *Visual State* property, select Enable State Recording.

Visual Studio 2012 will enter into recording mode, marked by a red border around the Design View. Any control property that is set through the Properties window will be recorded within the state (in this case, into the snapped state).

11. In the Document Outline tab, click the *ListViewControl* node.

In the Properties window, expand the *Appearance* property and set the *Visibility* property to Visible.

12. In the Document Outline tab, click the *GridViewControl* node.

In the Properties window, expand the *Appearance* property and set the *Visibility* property to Collapsed.

13. In the Device tab, click Portrait in the *View* property.

Visual Studio 2012 will display the change in the orientation in the Design View.

14. In the *Visual State* property, select Enable State Recording.

15. In the Document Outline tab, click the *GridViewControl* node.

In the Properties window, expand the *Layout* property and set the *Margin top* property to *80*.

16. In the Device tab, click Landscape in the *View* property.

17. In the Visual Studio 2012 toolbar, click the drop-down list by the Local Machine button to open the menu. Select the Simulator. Click the green play icon labeled Simulator.

Visual Studio 2012 will start the Windows 8 Simulator and then will run the application. In the Simulator, click Rotate clockwise (90 degrees).

The simulator shows the application in portrait view; note that the margins of the *GridView* control are different from the landscape view.

18. In the simulator, click Change Resolution and select the first entry: "10.6 1024 x 768."

Note that the scrollbar is visible, which allows the use of the entire content.

 Note Always be sure to try different resolutions and different orientations for your application.

19. In the Simulator, click Rotate Counterclockwise (90 degrees) to switch back to the original landscape position.

In the Simulator, click Change Resolution and select the second entry: "10.6 1366 x 768."

Click the Windows button of the Simulator to go back to the Windows 8 Start screen.

20. Launch the Weather App.

21. Place the cursor in the top-left corner of the Simulator to open the thumbnail of the previous active application, that is, your application.

Drag the thumbnail to the center of the Simulator and, once the snapped area is defined, release the mouse button.

Your application is currently in the snapped state and the *GridView* control has stepped aside to leave its place to the *ListView* control—more suitable for the current state.

22. Move the delimiter of the snapped area to the right and release the mouse button at around two-thirds of the overall screen size (of the Simulator).

The application is now in the filled state. In this example, you did not customize the user interface of this state. However, now you understand how to use the Visual State Manager to perform this task.

23. Return to Visual Studio 2012. On the Debug menu, click Stop Debugging.

To shut down the Windows 8 Simulator, go to the Windows 8 desktop, right-click the Simulator icon in the Windows 8 taskbar, and select Close.

Using tiles and toasts

In this section, you will learn how to modify an application tile to display the application logo in the Windows 8 Start screen from the application manifest, and then how you can modify it from code to create a Live Tile.

A tile represents the application in the Start screen, so it has to be both graphically good-looking and interesting for the user. In fact, the Start screen can be very full of tiles and your application can be confused or simply very difficult to reach if you do not carefully create your tile.

A tile can be considered an application icon. In fact, it represents the application in the ocean of apps that a user can see in her Start screen. In previous versions of Windows, the Start menu helped the user to organize the applications in groups and subgroups. Think for a moment about the Microsoft Office suite: it is composed of 10 different applications but they are grouped together in the Microsoft Office menu item. In Windows 8, every application is listed in the Start screen using its tile: the user can keep applications together by creating group of tiles, but she cannot create a tile representing a group of applications.

A user can also look for applications using Windows+Q or activating the Search charm; in this case, applications are listed using the application logo and application name, not their tile.

Figure 9-1 shows some application tiles.

FIGURE 9-1 Windows 8 Start screen with square and rectangular tiles grouped by the user.

As you can see, there are some applications in the section on the left of the Start screen. Some of them have a wide tile (Learn with the Animals, Learn with the Fruits, and Learn with the Colors), some of them a square tile (Internet Explorer, Learn with the Food, DevLeap, and so on), and one of them (Weather) is wide and presents the temperature of Florence. The latter is a live tile that will be explained in the following procedures.

In Chapter 3, you changed the default tile logo for your first application simply by copying some .png files on the Assets directory of the project. In the following procedures, you will learn how to define the square and the wide tile images, how to change default tile behavior, and then how to change the tile from code.

Define the appearance on the Start screen

The information that Windows 8 uses to deploy an application to the system is defined in the application manifest. This file defines the images that will represent the application tiles, the colors of the UI elements in the Start screen (and in the Windows Store), and some properties that are useful to change the default behavior.

In this procedure, you will learn how to change the static definition for tiles.

1. Create a new Application project. To do that, open Visual Studio 2012, and from the File menu, select New Project. Choose Windows Store from the list of installed templates, and then choose Blank App (XAML) from the list of available projects. Select version 4.5 as the target .NET Framework version for your new project.

2. Name the new project **Tile_Toast**, and then choose a location on your file system, as well as a solution name. When you're finished, click OK.

3. Copy the .png files found in the Chapter 09 Demo Files in the Logos folder to the Assets folder of the project. The files have the default names so you do not need to modify their names in the Package.appxmanifest.

4. Open the manifest designer by double-clicking package.appxmanifest in the Solution Explorer.

   Change the Wide Logo definition to point to the LogoWide.png file in the Asset folder by clicking the button with the ellipses or typing **Assets\LogoWide.png** in the related textbox.

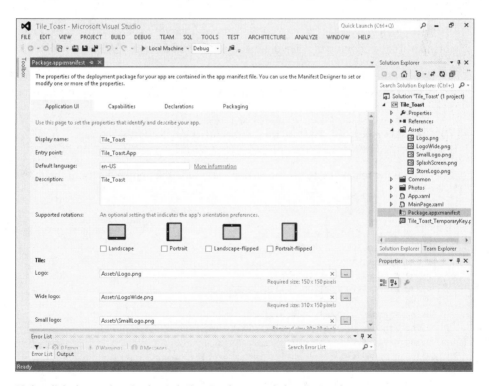

5. Right-click the project in the Solution Explorer and choose Deploy.

6. Go to the Start screen, move to the right until you find the new application. Right-click the application and select Larger from the App Bar. Windows will use the wide logo to represent the application tile.

7. Right-click the application again, and select Smaller from the lower toolbar. The tile will return squared.

Define a live tile

As you saw in the previous figure for the Weather App, an application can modify its tile to present information to the user. In fact, tiles are considered an external view of the application that can present useful information to the user without needing to open the application itself.

The native weather application, for instance, after you configure it to display the forecast for a particular city, presents the most important information in the tile as the temperature, the city, and the image of the current weather. A game application can present the latest score or the record or both to the user in the tile.

The application you will implement in this procedure is very similar to the one you implemented in Chapter 3, with the addition of a live tile that displays the name of the person selected by the user.

1. Modify the MainPage.xaml file of the application you implemented in the previous procedure to present a list of names. Use the following code to replace the existing *Grid* control.

```
<Grid Background="{StaticResource ApplicationPageBackgroundThemeBrush}">
  <ListView x:Name="list" DisplayMemberPath="FullName" />
</Grid>
```

2. Modify the related code behind to build and bind the people list using the following code:

```
using System;
using System.Collections.Generic;
using System.IO;
using System.Linq;
using Windows.Foundation;
using Windows.Foundation.Collections;
using Windows.UI.Xaml;
using Windows.UI.Xaml.Controls;
using Windows.UI.Xaml.Controls.Primitives;
using Windows.UI.Xaml.Data;
using Windows.UI.Xaml.Input;
using Windows.UI.Xaml.Media;
using Windows.UI.Xaml.Navigation;


namespace Tile_Toast
{
    /// <summary>
    /// An empty page that can be used on its own or navigated to within a Frame.
```

```
/// </summary>
public sealed partial class MainPage : Page
{
    public MainPage()
    {
        this.InitializeComponent();

        list.ItemsSource = this.GetPeople();
    }

    public List<Person> GetPeople()
    {
        return new List<Person>()
        {
            new Person() { FullName = "Roberto Brunetti" },
            new Person() { FullName = "Paolo Pialorsi" },
            new Person() { FullName = "Marco Russo" },
            new Person() { FullName = "Luca Regnicoli" },
            new Person() { FullName = "Vanni Boncinelli" },
            new Person() { FullName = "Guido Zambarda" },
            new Person() { FullName = "Jessica Faustinelli" },
            new Person() { FullName = "Katia Egiziano" }
        };
    }
}

public class Person
{
    public string FullName { get; set; }
}

}
```

3. Press F5 to test the application. It will present the list of names. Verify that you can select a name. You will use the *SelectionChanged* event handler to modify the application tile displaying the name of the person selected.

4. Go to the MainPage.xaml page and add a *SelectionChanged* event to the *ListView* control, as shown in bold in the following code:

```
<ListView x:Name="list" DisplayMemberPath="FullName"
          SelectionChanged="list_SelectionChanged" />
```

5. Add the event handler in the code behind for this event.

```
private void list_SelectionChanged(object sender, SelectionChangedEventArgs e)
{
    var person = list.SelectedItem as Person;
}
```

This line of code takes the item selected in the *ListView* control and assigns it to the local variable named *person*. You will use it in the next steps to create the live tile.

A tile is represented internally by an XML fragment that contains its definition. Windows 8 presents different templates to create many different visual tiles. For instance, there is a simple text-based template that can be used to display a single line of text in the tile, or a more sophisticated one that is suitable to display three lines of text and an image in the tile.

6. Create an .xml fragment as a string in the *SelectionChanged* event by using the following code right after the first line:

```
string tileXmlString = "<tile>"
    + "<visual>"
    + "<binding template='TileWideText03'>"
    + "<text id='1'>" + person.FullName + "</text>"
    + "</binding>"
    + "<binding template='TileSquareText04'>"
    + "<text id='1'>" + person.FullName + "</text>"
    + "</binding>"
    + "</visual>"
    + "</tile>";
```

The code is very simple. The visual element of the tile uses the template TileWideText03 (the third template for a wide tile) to display the full name of the selected person in the first line of text. It also defines the text for the square tile to display the same name using a different template. As is now apparent, the two tiles can display completely different things. For instance, the wide tile can display the photo of the person and the square one can display only the name.

7. Add the following four lines of code after the string definition to create the XML representation of the string. Then create a new tile definition to update the current tile.

```
var tileXml = new Windows.Data.Xml.Dom.XmlDocument();
tileXml.LoadXml(tileXmlString);

var tile = new Windows.UI.Notifications.TileNotification(tileXml);

Windows.UI.Notifications.TileUpdateManager.CreateTileUpdaterForApplication()
    .Update(tile);
```

8. Run the code by pressing F5.

9. Select Paolo Pialorsi from the list.

10. Click the Start button to go to the Windows 8 Start screen, and scroll until you find the tile that presents "Paolo Pialorsi."

11. Right-click to open the lower toolbar and select Smaller to reveal the square tile that will present the same text.

12. Right-click to open the lower toolbar and select Turn Live Tile Off. As you can see, the application will display the default square tile with the DevLeap logo.

13. Right-click another time to open the lower toolbar again and select Turn Live Tile On. As you can see, the application will display the name you selected again.

With some practice you will learn how the different tile templates work, how to change the tile foreground and background color, and how to add images (stored in the package or downloaded directly from the web) to the tile to achieve the sorts of results shown by the applications in the previous image. At the time of this writing, the complete reference for the Tile Template type is available at *http://msdn.microsoft.com/library/windows/apps/windows.ui.notifications.tiletemplatetype.*

For instance, this code creates a tile with text and an image using the simplest template for this kind of tile.

```
string tileXmlString = "<tile>"
                + "<visual>"
                + "<binding template='TileWideImageAndText01'>"
                + "<text id='1'>Tile with image</text>"
                + "<image id='1' src='ms-appx:///dir/x.png' alt='Red image'/>"
                + "</binding>"
                + "</visual>"
                + "</tile>";
```

You can also create a secondary tile for an application to display different kinds of information and to provide a "callback" to the application passing a parameter of your choice. For example, a weather application can create a secondary tile for a different city the user chooses in the application. This way, the Start screen presents two different tiles for the same application—one displaying the information for the main city and the other for the secondary city. When the code creates the secondary tile, it can pass an argument that will be received during the application launch so that the code can present the forecast of the secondary city directly instead of on the main page.

The application can also request the system to display a badge on the application tile with some predefined glyphs and/or a number. For instance, you can enable multiselection (SelectionMode="Multiple") on the *ListView* control you used in the previous examples and provide the code to display the number of selected people in the badge by using the following code.

```
string badgeXmlString = "<badge value='" + list.SelectedItems.Count + "'/>";

var badgeXml= new Windows.Data.Xml.Dom.XmlDocument();
badgeXml.LoadXml(badgeXmlString);

var badge = new Windows.UI.Notifications.BadgeNotification(badgeXml);
Windows.UI.Notifications.BadgeUpdateManager.CreateBadgeUpdaterForApplication()
    .Update(badge);
```

As a sample, Microsoft provides a library that facilitates the use of the template that hides all the XML details and provides some simple classes to create tiles and badges. You can find the library in the "App tiles and badges sample" of the Windows 8 samples. You can download it from MSDN in the Windows 8 Dev Center at *http://code.msdn.microsoft.com/windowsapps/*.

With this library, the code to create the tile can be as easy as this:

```
var tileContent = TileContentFactory.CreateTileWideText03();
tileContent.TextHeadingWrap.Text = person.Fullname;
```

Create and schedule a toast

An application can provide alerts to the user using Toasts. A toast can be simple text or an image or a combination of the two. In this procedure, you will create a simple toast to remind the user to change the selected person. Let's consider the simple application you wrote in the previous section, a shift workers' application that manages the shift change. When the user selects the current worker, the application can remind the user to change the worker every, let's say, 10 seconds (likely and luckily to be more in real applications).

1. Add the following lines at the end of the *SelectionChanged* event handler you created in the previous section.

```
toastXmlString = "<toast>"
                + "<visual version='1'>"
                + "<binding template='ToastText01'>"
                + "<text id='1'>" + person.FullName + " is tired!</text>"
```

```
                    + "</binding>"
                    + "</visual>"
                    + "</toast>";
var toastXml = new Windows.Data.Xml.Dom.XmlDocument();
toastXml.LoadXml(toastXmlString);

var toastNotification =
    new Windows.UI.Notifications.ScheduledToastNotification(toastXml,
        DateTime.Now.AddSeconds(10));

var toastNotifier = Windows.UI.Notifications.ToastNotificationManager.
    CreateToastNotifier();
toastNotifier.AddToSchedule(toastNotification);
```

The first line of code builds the toast string definition and the two subsequent lines transform it into an XML document. Then the code creates a notification for the toast in 10 seconds and the last two lines of code ask the *ToastNotificationManager* class to add the notification to the system toast schedule.

2. Before you run the sample, you have to define the application as toast capable. To do that, open the Package.appxmanifest and set Toast Capable (in the Notification section) to Yes using the drop-down list.

3. Run the sample, select a name, click the Start button to leave the application, and go to the Start screen.

You can also use local images (provided with the package) or images coming from the web, change the default sound to reflect the toast type, create a long duration toast, and receive an event in the application when the user clicks the toast. You can even change the snooze interval and maximum snooze count to tailor the toast for your needs.

Microsoft provides a sample library for manipulating toasts. To be more precise, the library is the same one cited before for tiles, and it lets you code against toasts, tiles, badges, and related features.

A toast can be sent from the cloud using the Windows Notification Service (WNS). The application can ask the service for a unique channel that a remote service can use to send toasts to the Windows 8 box from anywhere.

For information on the service, use "Windows Notification Service" as keywords in the MSDN Developer Center to find documentation and samples.

Summary

In this chapter, you have learned how to use the advanced controls of the XAML platform for a Windows 8 application (*Application Bar*, *WebView*, *ListView*, *GridView*, *FlipView*, and *SemanticZoom*), as well as how to customize their appearance by using *DataTemplate* objects. You have also learned how to use the *VisualStateManager* element and the *Window.Current.SizeChanged* event to support different view states, including portrait, landscape, snapped, fill, and full screen.

Additionally, you now know how to enhance the user experience using tiles, live tiles, badges, and toasts.

Quick reference

To	Do this
Add a *ListView* control to the layout	Click the Toolbox tab, expand the All XAML Controls, click the *ListView* control, and drag it within the form.
Add a *GridView* control to the layout	Click the Toolbox tab, expand the All XAML Controls, click the *GridView* control, and drag it within the form.
Add a *WebView* control to the layout	Click the Toolbox tab, expand the All XAML Controls, click the *WebView* control, and drag it within the form.
Handle different view states and orientations	Use the *VisualStateManger* element and the Window.*Current.SizeChanged* event handler.
Run your Windows 8 app in the Windows Simulator	In the Visual Studio 2012 toolbar, click the drop-down list by the Local Machine button to open the menu and select the Simulator. Click the green play icon labeled Simulator.
Create a tile	To create a tile, use one of the provided templates for passing the .xml definition to the WinRT classes.
Create a toast	To create a toast, use one of the provided templates for passing the .xml definition to the WinRT classes.

CHAPTER 10

Architecting a Windows 8 app

After completing this chapter, you will be able to

- Understand the general architecture of an application.

- Define the architecture of a Windows 8 app.

- Consume a remote service from a Windows 8 app.

This chapter provides some useful information about the architecture of software solutions, with particular focus on those solutions that include a Windows 8 app as one of the available presentation layers.

Application architecture in general

Any software solution, even the smallest one, should be implemented starting with the overall architecture definition. In fact, every single time you develop a software solution you should take care of how to organize code and logical partitioning in order to satisfy function, usability, maintainability, and performance requirements.

In recent decades, the software development world has moved toward what are called *N-tier solutions*, which are solutions defined to satisfy maintainability, scalability, security, and the capability to consume remote services in a secure, safe, and fast manner.

A multitier solution is a software project that usually targets many concurrent users. It is divided into *n* layers—generally at least two or three layers. Applications that use a two-tier scenario are also referred to as client-server software. One layer is the back-end server infrastructure, which is generally made up of a database persistence layer. The other layer, the client, includes all the required code to connect to the back-end database and display the user interface. Generally, in two-tier scenarios the business logic and domain knowledge required for the solution is implemented within the client software. Sometimes such solutions also include database logic, such as intelligent stored procedures, triggers, and so on.

Software is scalable when its performance remains constant and independent, regardless of the number of users. Scalable software is not necessarily fast—it simply has a fixed performance score regardless of the number of customers served, unless you expand the hardware infrastructure when the number of customers increases, without any changes to the code of the software. The very nature of a client-server solution prevents scalability—specifically, an increase in the number of users can have a huge impact on the back-end database layer.

Although client-server architecture is suitable for implementing solutions that will have a relatively small number of users, this book does not cover it in detail because, aside from its scalability limitations, you should not create a Windows 8 app that consumes a database directly. On the contrary, you should implement Windows 8 apps that consume remote services, which eventually can provide indirect access to data stored in a database.

Over the past several years, partly for scalability reasons, architectures with at least three tiers have become more common. Many modern software solutions are available on a network and the Internet, and serve a large (and unpredictable) number of concurrent users. Three-tier solutions have a data access layer, a business layer, and a presentation layer. The data access layer (DAL) represents the set of code and data structures used to implement information persistence. The business layer (BIZ) defines business logic, business workflows, and rules that drive the behavior of the application. The presentation layer, or user interface (UI) layer, delivers the information to users. The presentation layer, in particular, has become more complex, because it can (and often must) be implemented in many different ways—one for each kind of consumer and/or device (for example the web, a desktop PC with Microsoft Windows, a tablet, or a smartphone device). In general, DAL and BIZ are deployed on specific and dedicated application servers, whereas the UI can be deployed on both consumer devices (desktop PC, tablet, smartphone, and so on) or delivered to browsers from specific publishing application servers (web applications on front-end web servers).

Technologies such as Simple Object Access Protocol (SOAP) services, REST (Representational State Transfer), smart clients, smartphones, or workflow services have influenced many software architects to add other layers. The now-common definition of n-tier solution architecture is one in which n designates a value greater than or at least equal to three. In general, as you can see from Figure 10-1, these n layers are targeted to meet specific application requirements, such as security, workflow definition, management and governance, or communication.

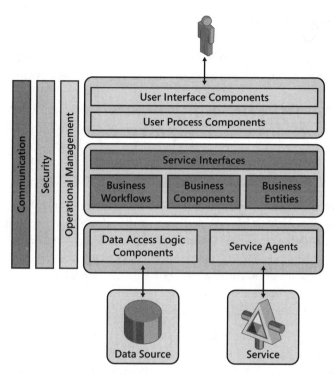

FIGURE 10-1 A schema of the architecture of an *n*-tier software solution.

The main reasons for dividing a software solution's architecture into layers are to improve maintainability, availability, security, and deployment.

Maintainability results from the ability to change and maintain small portions (for example, single layers) of an application without needing to touch the other layers. By working this way, you reduce maintenance time and can also more accurately assess the cost of a fix or a feature change because you can focus your attention only on the layers involved in the change. Client-server software is more costly to maintain because any code modifications must be deployed to each client. Well-defined multitier solutions are also available to users more often because critical or highly stressed layers can be deployed in a redundant infrastructure.

From a security perspective, a layered solution can make use of different security modules—each one tightly aligned with a particular software layer to make the solution stronger. Last but not least, multitier software is usually deployed with more ease because each layer can be configured and sized somewhat independently from other layers.

Architectures for Windows 8 apps

Generally speaking, from a Windows 8 app perspective, a two-tier architecture solution is not a good solution because you should not access databases directly from the app. There are many reasons that support this perspective. First of all, due to the .NET portable and restricted profile you learned about in Chapter 5, "Introduction to the Windows Runtime," you don't have the types of *System.Data.** namespaces available in a Windows 8 app. Thus, you simply cannot use a *SqlConnection* or an *OleDb-Command* to consume data. Of course, you could evaluate third-party solutions to work around these limitations and to consume databases directly from a Windows 8 app. However, you would implement a solution that goes against the suggested usability guidelines provided by Microsoft.

In fact, a Windows 8 app should be capable of working online (connected to the network) and eventually offline, leveraging some data caching features. Moreover, it should be capable of supporting a user while working on multiple devices (desktop PC, laptop, tablet, and so on), keeping the same configurations and contexts. In order to support this last scenario, Microsoft introduced the capability of sharing the user profile configuration and the user application data through the cloud and the Windows Live profile. The final goal of this approach should be to have a user with her own data, regardless of the device she uses, simply determined by her Windows Live ID.

Starting with these considerations, you can argue that a Windows 8 app that stores data locally on a single device is not a smart idea, because you would be able to consume that data only on that specific device. On the contrary, a Windows 8 app that consumes data from a remote site—through a SOAP or REST service—eventually published in the cloud (for example on Windows Azure) absolutely is a better option.

Nevertheless, there are areas in software development that require working with tons of data records, and that may need to have local data repositories for usability and performance reasons. Think about an app for a sales force, where a user needs to be able to insert customers' orders even if there is no network connectivity. You would probably need to have an offline copy of the products catalog, or a subset of it, as well as an offline copy of the customers that every single seller should meet during a specific work day. Moreover, it would probably be smart to keep a client-side copy of all those reference data that are useful for inserting a new customer or a new order, for example, and that you should not have to download from the network every single time. Think about the list of countries, states, products' categories, and so on. In order to give a suitable answer to all these needs, a Windows 8 app can leverage the local storage and a set of XML files consumed using the LINQ to XML API, which is available in the .NET profile for Windows 8 apps.

The security infrastructure is yet another topic that can be affected by the new development model introduced by Windows 8 apps. In fact, in a standard Windows application it could suffice to leverage Windows integrated security. On the contrary, a Windows 8 app installed on a mobile device could benefit from using a cross-platform authentication method, like Windows Live ID, Facebook, or something similar. In general, a Windows 8 app will probably need to support multiple authentication techniques and protocols. Thus, technologies like claims-based authentication, Open Authentication (OAuth), and identity federation are fundamental in such architectures.

In the following sections of this chapter, you will inspect all the layers of a distributed architecture that are fundamental and specific to a Windows 8 app. Moreover, for the sake of simplicity there will be many areas where software architecture layers will be discussed from a logical view point. Nevertheless, for the sake of brevity some merging of layers from a code and assembly fragmentation perspective will occur in the examples. However, in a real solution you will probably need to introduce more abstraction and code fragmentation.

Implementing the data layer

One of the fundamental layers of a distributed architecture is the data layer. In fact, even if generally speaking, the data layer can be really easy to implement and can be automated mainly using object relational mapping (ORM) technologies, nevertheless the efficiency, the scalability, and the versatility of software architectures depends on the data layer.

Since 2008, the official enterprise-level ORM in Microsoft .NET has been the ADO.NET Entity Framework. In .NET 4.5 and Microsoft Visual Studio 2012 you can leverage the Entity Framework 5, which is a mature and complete ORM framework.

The goal of an ORM in software architectures is to convert data, which are stored into an external and physical repository, into entities describing the domain model of the software from a business perspective. Moreover, an ORM provides all the facilities to query, manage, and transfer data back and forth from external repositories. Generally speaking, in modern software the external repository is a relational database management system (DBMS) like Microsoft SQL Server. Nevertheless, from the ORM viewpoint the external repository could be anything else.

In this section, you will create a data layer based on Entity Framework 5 that is useful to model the *Customer* domain model entity that, for the sake of simplicity, will be consumed from the generally well-known and famous Northwind sample database.

Implementing a data layer in C# with Entity Framework 5

In this procedure, you will create a data layer using C# and Entity Framework 5. Later, this data layer will be published by a Windows Communication Foundation (WCF) service layer and will be consumed by a sample Windows 8 app implemented using CLR and C#. Later in the chapter, the same data layer will be published through an Open Data Protocol (OData) service.

1. Download the Northwind sample database from the Microsoft website (*http://www.microsoft. com/download/details.aspx?id=23654)* and install it. Double-click the SQL script under the folder SQL Server 2000 Sample Databases. The script will open in Visual Studio 2012. From there, you can execute it against your local SQL Server database, which eventually could be SQL Server Express, in case you installed it during the installation of Visual Studio 2012.

2. Create a new Application project. To do that, open Visual Studio 2012, and from the File menu, select New Project. Choose Other Project Types and then Visual Studio Solutions. Choose Blank Solution as the target template.

3. Select version 4.5 as the Microsoft .NET Framework target version for your new project.

4. Name the new solution **NorthwindSolution**, and then choose a location on your file system. When you have finished, click OK.

5. Add a new Project to the solution you have just created. Right-click the solution item in the Solution Explorer and select Add | New Project. Choose Windows from the list of installed templates in the Visual C# group, and then select Class Library. Keep version 4.5 as the Microsoft .NET Framework target version.

6. Name the class library project **NorthwindSolution.DataLayer**, and then choose a location on your file system. When you have finished, click OK.

7. Delete Class1.cs, which was created in the project automatically.

8. Right-click the class library project in the Solution Explorer and select Add | New Item. In the Add New Item window, select the ADO.NET Entity Data Model item template. Give the new file the name **NorthwindModel.edmx**.

9. You will be prompted with a wizard. In the first step, Choose Model Contents, select Generate From Database. Click Next.

10. In the second step, Choose Your Data Connection, add a New Connection, configure a connection to the Northwind database in your target SQL Server instance, and click Next.

11. In the third step, Choose Your Database Objects and Settings, expand the *Tables* node. Under dbo, select Customers and any other data table you want to map to an entity. In order to complete the exercises for this chapter, it will suffice to map the Customers table. Select Pluralize or Singularize Generated Object Names. Click Finish.

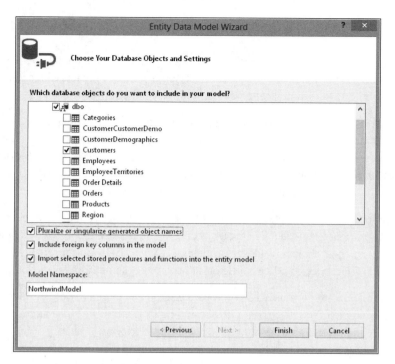

If Visual Studio 2012 prompts you with a Security Warning, trust it, and click OK.

The wizard you have just followed creates an .EDMX file, as well as a set of .TT (Text Template) code-generation files, and a bunch of .CS files with auto-generated code. The whole result of this procedure is a class library with the definition of a *NorthwindEntities* class, providing an entry point to access a collection of *Customers* defined with an auto-generated *Customer* type.

Explaining the Entity Framework and the inner workings of its engine is beyond the scope of this book. Nevertheless, in case you need more information, you should read *Programming Microsoft LINQ in Microsoft .NET Framework 4* (Microsoft Press) by Paolo Pialorsi and Marco Russo.

Implementing the communication layer using a SOAP service

Without a shadow of a doubt, the communication layer is one of the fundamental layers of a distributed architecture. Any Windows 8 app that consumes external data or interacts with external services needs to be based on a solid communication infrastructure.

Communication is based on various technologies and protocols. For example, you can use SOAP services transferred across HTTP channels, or you can leverage REST services transmitting either POX (Plain Old XML) messages, or RSS (Rich Site Summary, often also called Really Simple Syndication), or JSON (JavaScript Object Notation) serialized objects. You may also like to use the OData service (*www.odata.org*), which is going to become an OASIS international open standard.

Depending on the development platform, any of the previously mentioned protocols and technologies can be appropriate. For example, if you are developing a website or a Windows 8 app built with HTML5/WinJS, the best choices would be probably REST with JSON object serialization, or POX/RSS. Meanwhile, a SOAP service could be a little bit difficult to consume from JavaScript.

On the contrary, if you are developing a Windows 8 app built with CLR (C# or VB), then SOAP or OData provide the best solutions. Even using REST could be okay—but the SOAP and OData are simpler to define and easier to share across multiple devices and platforms.

Implementing a SOAP service to consume from C#

In this procedure, you will create a SOAP service based on WCF and publish the data layer defined previously that provides a list of customers to consume.

1. Open the NorthwindSolution you created in the previous exercise, when you implemented the data layer with Entity Framework 5.

2. Right-click the solution item in the Solution Explorer and select Add | New Project. Choose Windows from the list of installed templates in the Visual C# group, and select Class Library. Keep version 4.5 as the Microsoft .NET Framework target version.

3. Name the class library project **NorthwindSolution.Contracts**, and then choose a location on your file system. When you have finished, click OK.

4. In the Solution Explorer, right-click the class library project item you just created and select Add Reference. In the Assemblies group of the references, select the following assemblies: *System.ServiceModel* and *System.Runtime.Serialization*.

5. In the Solution Explorer, right-click the class library project item you just created and select Add Reference. In the Solution group of the references, select the NorthwindSolution.Data-Layer project.

6. Remove Class1.cs and add a new interface definition item. In order to add the new interface definition, right-click the class library project in the Solution Explorer and select Add | New Item. In the Add New Item window, select the Interface code template. Name the new file **ICustomersService.cs**.

7. Replace the interface code with the following code:

```
using NorthwindSolution.DataLayer;
using System;
using System.Collections.Generic;
using System.Linq;
using System.ServiceModel;
using System.Text;
using System.Threading.Tasks;

namespace NorthwindSolution.Contracts {
    [ServiceContract(Namespace = "http://services.devleap.com/Northwind/Customers")]
    public interface ICustomersService {
        [OperationContract(Action =
        "http://services.devleap.com/Northwind/Customers/GetCustomer")]
        Customer GetCustomer(String customerId);

        [OperationContract(Action =
        "http://services.devleap.com/Northwind/Customers/ListCustomers")]
        List<Customer> ListCustomers();
    }
}
```

In the previous procedure about leveraging Entity Framework 5 in the Data Layer, you defined the *Customer* type.

The *ServiceContract* and *OperationContract* attributes declare that the interface defines a new service interface, whereas the methods are the operations of the service interface.

In case you are not familiar with WCF, you can read the book *Learning WCF*, written by Michele Leroux Bustamante and published by O'Reilly Media.

8. Now add a new class library project to the solution like you did in steps 2 through 5. Name this new project **NorthwindSolution.Services**.

9. In the Solution Explorer, right-click the class library project item you just created and select Add Reference. In the Solution group of references, add the NorthwindSolution.Contracts project.

10. In the Solution Explorer, right-click the NorthwindSolution.Services project item you just created and select Manage NuGet Packages.

11. In the next window, select EntityFramework (version 5.0.0) under the group NuGet Official Package Source in the Online group. Click Install and then click Close.

12. In the Solution Explorer, right-click Class1.cs, defined in the project you've just created, and select Rename. Provide the new name **CustomersService.cs**. When prompted by Visual Studio, confirm that you also want to rename the class. Open CustomersService.cs and replace its code with the following:

```
using NorthwindSolution.DataLayer;
using NorthwindSolution.Contracts;
using System;
using System.Collections.Generic;
using System.Linq;
using System.Text;
using System.Threading.Tasks;

namespace NorthwindSolution.Services {
    public class CustomersService : ICustomersService {

        public Customer GetCustomer(string customerId) {
            NorthwindEntities nw = new NorthwindEntities();
            return (nw.Customers.FirstOrDefault(c => c.CustomerID == customerId));
        }

        public List<Customer> ListCustomers() {
            NorthwindEntities nw = new NorthwindEntities();
            return (nw.Customers.ToList());
        }
    }
}
```

Again, the *Customer* type is the same one you defined in the previous procedure about leveraging Entity Framework 5 in the Data Layer. As you can see, the service implementation simply invokes the data layer in the back end.

Notice that in a real solution you will probably have a business layer in the middle, between the data layer and the service definition, in order to infer custom business logic, security, validation, and other aspects needed in modern software architectures. For the sake of simplicity, in this example there is a short circuit between the service implementation and the underlying data layer.

13. Right-click the solution item in the Solution Explorer and select Add | New Web Project. Choose ASP.NET Empty Web Site from the list of installed templates in Visual C# group. Keep version 4.5 as the Microsoft .NET Framework target version.

14. Name the website project **NorthwindSolution.WebHost**, and then choose a location on your file system. When you have finished, click OK. If Visual Studio 2012 asks you if you want to create the target folder, select Yes.

15. In the Solution Explorer, right-click the website project item you just created and select Add Reference. In the Assemblies group of references, select the following assemblies: *System. ServiceModel* and *System.Runtime.Serialization*.

16. In the Solution Explorer, right-click the website project item you just created and select Add Reference. In the Solution group of references, select *NorthwindSolution.DataLayer*, *NorthwindSolution.Contracts*, and *NorthwindSolution.Services*.

17. In the Solution Explorer, right-click the website project item you just created and select Manage NuGet Packages. In the next window, select EntityFramework (version 5.0.0) under the group NuGet Official Package Source in the Online group set. Click Install | Close.

18. Right-click the website project in the Solution Explorer and select Add | Add New Item. In the Add New Item window, select the WCF Service code template. Give the new file the name **CustomersService.svc**.

19. Remove the files created under the App_Code folder of the website project, and keep only CustomersService.svc.

It is better to keep contracts, implementations, and endpoints separated into different assemblies, rather than mixing all of them into a unique website project. Thus, the exercise asks you to remove the code auto-generated by Visual Studio 2012 and to create a well-layered and organized solution.

20. Double-click on CustomersService.svc to open the file and replace its code with the following:

```
<%@ ServiceHost Language="C#" Debug="true" Service="NorthwindSolution.Services.
CustomersService" %>
```

The *CodeBehind* attribute has been removed, because the code of the service in this exercise is not behind the .svc file but it is compiled in the *NorthwindSolution.Services* assembly. The value of the *Service* attribute has been changed, providing the full name of the *CustomersService* class created in step 12.

21. Rebuild the entire solution (Ctrl+Shift+B) and then right-click CustomersService.svc in the Solution Explorer. Select View In Browser. You will see, in your default browser, the welcome page of the WCF service you've just created.

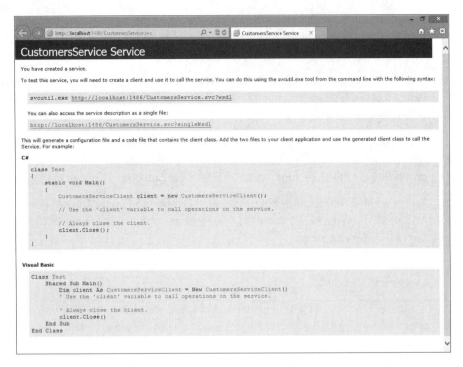

Later in this chapter you will consume this service from a Windows 8 app.

Implementing the communication layer using an OData service

In this section, you will learn how to implement a simple OData service—functionally equivalent to the SOAP service you created in the previous procedure. You should consider that an OData service still uses WCF in its infrastructure, and simply leverages a specific set of communication contracts and behaviors.

Implementing an OData service to consume from C#

In this procedure, you will create an OData service for publishing the previously defined data layer.

1. Open the NorthwindSolution you created in the previous procedure, when you implemented the data layer with Entity Framework 5.

2. Right-click the website project NorthwindSolution.WebHost in the Solution Explorer and select Add | Add New Item. In the Add New Item window, select the WCF Data Service code template. Name the new file **CustomersDataService.svc**.

3. Under the App_Code folder of the website project, open CustomersDataService.cs and replace the class declaration with the following line of code:

```
public class CustomersDataService : DataService<NorthwindSolution.DataLayer.
NorthwindEntities>
```

The *DataService<T>* base class that the *CustomerDataService* type inherits from is part of the .NET Framework and provides all the basic infrastructure to publish an OData service based on a generic type *T*—which has to be a class publishing one or more collections of entities implementing a specific interface named IQueryable. The *NorthwindEntities* class created while defining the data layer adheres to these requirements and can be used to publish the collection of entities of type *Customer* directly.

4. Replace the whole source code of the *CustomerDataService* class with the following code:

```
public class CustomersDataService : DataService<NorthwindSolution.DataLayer.
NorthwindEntities> {
    public static void InitializeService(DataServiceConfiguration config) {
        config.SetEntitySetAccessRule("Customers", EntitySetRights.AllRead);
        config.DataServiceBehavior.MaxProtocolVersion = DataServiceProtocolVersion.V3;
    }
}
```

The first line of code inside the *InitializeService* method declares that the *Customer* entity provided by the NorthwindEntities model will be read-only accessible by everybody. In Table 10-1, you can see all of the available values for the *EntitySetRights* enumeration. The second line of code, still in the *InitializeService* method, defines that the OData service will be capable of talking with external consumers using version 1, 2, or 3 of the protocol.

TABLE 10-1 The list of permissions available for configuring entity set rights

Value	Description
None	Denies all rights to access data.
ReadSingle	Authorization to read single data items.
ReadMultiple	Authorization to read sets of data.
AllRead	Authorization to read data.
WriteAppend	Authorization to create new data items in data sets.
WriteReplace	Authorization to replace data.
WriteDelete	Authorization to delete data items from data sets.
WriteMerge	Authorization to merge data.
AllWrite	Authorization to write data.
All	Authorization to create, read, update, and delete data.

5. Open the web.config file of the website project and configure the connection string to the SQL Server database under the cover of the NorthwindEntities model. You can copy the connection string configuration from the App.config file available in the NorthwindSolution. DataLayer project. Copy the following code from the App.config file and paste it in the web. config file.

```
<connectionStrings>
    <add name="NorthwindEntities" connectionString="metadata=res://*/NorthwindModel.
        csdl|res://*/NorthwindModel.ssdl|res://*/NorthwindModel.msl;provider=System.
        Data.SqlClient;provider connection string=&quot;data source=.;initial
```

```
              catalog=Northwind;integrated security=True;MultipleActiveResultSets=True;
              App=EntityFramework&quot;" providerName="System.Data.EntityClient" />
    </connectionStrings>
```

6. Rebuild the entire solution (Ctrl+Shift+B) and then right-click CustomersDataService.svc in
the Solution Explorer. Select View In Browser. As in the previous procedure, in your default
browser you will see the welcome page of the OData service you've just created. In this case,
the welcome page will be an XML document declaring the entities published by the service.
The XML document will look like the following code excerpt:

```
<?xml version="1.0" encoding="utf-8"?>
<service xml:base="http://localhost:1486/CustomersDataService.svc/"
     xmlns="http://www.w3.org/2007/app" xmlns:atom="http://www.w3.org/2005/Atom">
  <workspace>
    <atom:title>Default</atom:title>
    <collection href="Customers">
      <atom:title>Customers</atom:title>
    </collection>
  </workspace>
</service>
```

7. Try to navigate to the service URL—*http://localhost:1486/CustomersDataService.svc/*—by
adding Customers at the end of the URL. The URL to navigate in our example would be *http://
localhost:1486/CustomersDataService.svc/Customers*. As you can see, the result looks like an
RSS feed.

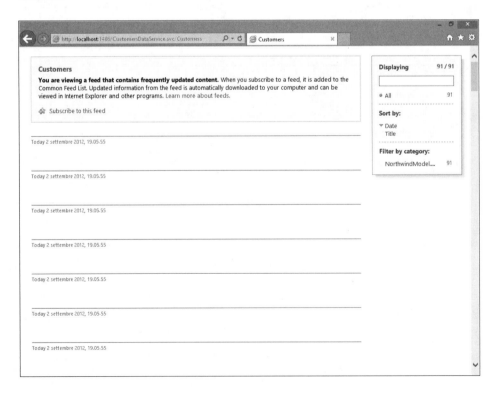

8. In order to have a look at the XML under the covers, you can change the default configuration of Internet Explorer. Select Tools | Internet Options. Select the Content tab of the Internet Options window. Click Settings under Feed And Web Slices. Deselect Turn On Feed Reading View when you are prompted.

Click OK, and click OK again. Now, go back in the web browser and request the page at the previously determined URL.

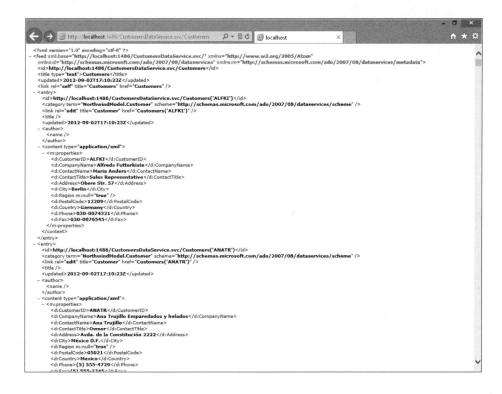

As you can see, the result is an RSS feed with an entry item for each customer entity in the collection of *Customers* published by the OData service. In case you want to access a specific customer instance, you can use a direct access URL providing the CustomerID as a selection key in the URL. In the XML shown in the browser, you can see that every entry element has an *id child* element that contains a URL. Copy the URL of any *Customer* entry into the address bar of the browser and you will see XML that defines the single customer instance. The result should be something like the following code.

```xml
<?xml version="1.0" encoding="utf-8" ?>
<entry xml:base="http://localhost:1486/CustomersDataService.svc/" xmlns="http://www.w3.org/2005/
Atom" xmlns:d="http://schemas.microsoft.com/ado/2007/08/dataservices" xmlns:m="http://schemas.
microsoft.com/ado/2007/08/dataservices/metadata">
  <id>http://localhost:1486/CustomersDataService.svc/Customers('ALFKI')</id>
  <category  term="NorthwindModel.Customer"
      scheme="http://schemas.microsoft.com/ado/2007/08/dataservices/scheme" />
  <link  rel="edit" title="Customer" href="Customers('ALFKI')" />
  <title  />
  <updated>2012-09-02T17:20:50Z</updated>
  <author>
    <name  />
  </author>
  <content type="application/xml">
  <m:properties>
    <d:CustomerID>ALFKI</d:CustomerID>
    <d:CompanyName>Alfreds Futterkiste</d:CompanyName>
    <d:ContactName>Maria Anders</d:ContactName>
    <d:ContactTitle>Sales Representative</d:ContactTitle>
    <d:Address>Obere Str. 57</d:Address>
    <d:City>Berlin</d:City>
    <d:Region  m:null="true" />
    <d:PostalCode>12209</d:PostalCode>
    <d:Country>Germany</d:Country>
    <d:Phone>030-0074321</d:Phone>
    <d:Fax>030-0076545</d:Fax>
  </m:properties>
  </content>
</entry>
```

Under the *m:properties* element, you can see the list of data properties of the current customer. Later in this chapter, you will consume this data from a Windows 8 app.

Consuming data from a Windows 8 app

Now you are ready to consume the already implemented services from a Windows 8 app. First of all, you need to create the app by completing the following procedure.

Implementing a Windows 8 app to consume the SOAP service

1. Open the NorthwindSolution you created in the previous procedure, when you implemented the data layer with Entity Framework 5.

2. Right-click the solution item in the Solution Explorer and select Add | New Project. Choose Windows Store from the list of installed templates in the Visual C# group, and then select Grid App (XAML). Keep version 4.5 as the Microsoft .NET Framework target version.

3. Name the class library project **NorthwindSolution.SOAPClientApp**, and then choose a location on your file system. When you have finished, click OK.

4. In the Solution Explorer, right-click the NorthwindSolution.SOAPClientApp project item you just created and select Add Service Reference. In the Add Service Reference window, insert the URL of the CustomersService.svc service file you created in the procedure "Implementing a SOAP Service to Consume from C#." In this case, the URL is *http://localhost:1486/CustomersService.svc*. Click Go. You will see the definition of the *CustomersService*. In the lower side of the window, provide a value of *CustomersServiceReference* for the *Namespace* property and click OK.

5. Double-click the package.appxmanifest file of the new app. Select the Packaging tab and provide a suitable value for the *Package Name* property. For example, you might use the value NorthwindSoapApp.

6. Right-click the NorthwindSolution.SOAPClientApp project and select Debug | Start New Instance. The app will start and you will see a grid of fake items, arranged into multiple fake groups. Close the app by pressing ALT+F4 or stopping the debugger in Visual Studio 2012.

7. Expand the DataModel folder of the NorthwindSolution.SOAPClientApp project and rename the SampleDataSource.cs file with the name **NorthwindDataSource.cs.** Now rename the *SampleDataSource* type with name **NorthwindDataSource,** both in code and text. To complete that task, right-click the class name and select Refactor | Rename. Provide the new name and select Search In Strings. At the preview window, click Apply.

   This code file contains all the client-side logic to manage the data model behind the scenes of a Windows 8 app. The *SampleDataSource* class represents the entry point for the data source. The *SampleDataCommon* type is the base class for every data item. The *SampleDataItem* type defines a single data item. Lastly, the *SampleDataGroup* type declares the groups of items.

8. Using the same approach as step 7, rename the *SampleDataItem* type with **CustomerDataItem**; the *SampleDataCommon* type with **NorthwindDataCommon**; and the *SampleDataGroup* type with **CustomersDataGroup**.

9. Insert the following code, just after the default constructor of the *NorthwindDataSource* type.

```
private String[] shadowedFaces = new String[] {
    "shadow-black-face",
    "shadow-blue-face",
    "shadow-orange-face",
    "shadow-red-face",
};

private async void populateDataSource() {
    CustomersServiceReference.CustomersServiceClient nw =
        new CustomersServiceReference.CustomersServiceClient();

    var customers = await nw.ListCustomersAsync();
```

```
    String fakeCustomerContent = "Lorem ipsum dolor sit amet, consectetur adipiscing
elit. Vivamus tempor scelerisque lorem in vehicula. Aliquam tincidunt, lacus ut sagittis
tristique, turpis massa volutpat augue, eu rutrum ligula ante a ante";
    String previousCountry = String.Empty;
    CustomersDataGroup group = null;

    // Create a random number generator
    Random rnd = new Random(DateTime.Now.Second);

    foreach (var c in customers.OrderBy(c => c.Country)) {
        // Check if I need to create a new group
        if (previousCountry != c.Country) {

            // Add the previous group
            if (group != null) this.AllGroups.Add(group);

            // Create the new group
            group = new CustomersDataGroup(c.Country,
                c.Country,
                String.Format("Customers from: {0}", c.Country),
                "Assets/LightGray.png",
                String.Empty);
        }

        // Add the current customer to the current group
        group.Items.Add(new CustomerDataItem(c.CustomerID,
            c.ContactName,
            c.CompanyName,
            String.Format("Assets/{0}.png", shadowedFaces[rnd.Next() % 4]),
            String.Format("{0} {1} working at {2}", c.ContactTitle,
                c.ContactName, c.CompanyName),
            fakeCustomerContent,
            group));

        // Set the previous country
        previousCountry = c.Country;
    }
}
```

This new code will download the list of customers asynchronously from the external SOAP service and will put them into a collection of *CustomerDataItem*, grouped by country, where groups will be based on the *CustomersDataGroup* type. In order to better understand the asynchronous behavior, you can read Chapter 8, "Asynchronous patterns."

10. Replace the default constructor code of the *NorthwindDataSource* type with the following code.

```
public NorthwindDataSource() {
    populateDataSource();
}
```

11. Add the following files, available in the book code samples under the Ch10 folder, into the Assets folder of the Windows 8 app project: shadow-black-face.png, shadow-blue-face.png, shadow-orange-face.png, shadow-red-face.png.

12. Rebuild the entire solution (Ctrl+Shift+B) and then execute the app.

Now you can play with your new Windows 8 app, navigating back and forward through the countries and customers, consuming data from the SOAP external service.

Moreover, you can also create a similar app to consume the OData service. In order to consume an OData service from a Windows 8 app, you need to download and install the "OData Client Tools for Windows Store Apps" from *http://msdn.microsoft.com/jj658961*.

Implementing a Windows 8 app to consume the OData service

1. Open the NorthwindSolution you created in the previous procedure, when you implemented the data layer with Entity Framework 5.

2. Right-click the solution item in the Solution Explorer and select Add | New Project. Choose Windows Store from the list of installed templates in Visual C# group, and then select Grid App (XAML). Keep version 4.5 as the Microsoft .NET Framework target version.

3. Name the class library project NorthwindSolution.ODataClientApp, and then choose a location on your file system. When you have finished, click OK.

4. In the Solution Explorer, right-click the *NorthwindSolution.ODataClientApp* project you just created and select Add Service Reference. In the Add Service Reference window, insert the URL of the CustomersDataService.svc service file you created in the exercise "Implementing an OData Service to Consume from C#." In this case, the URL is *http://localhost:1486/Customers-DataService.svc*. Click Go. You will see the definition of the *CustomersDataService*. In the lower side of the window, provide a value of **CustomersDataServiceReference** for the *Namespace* property and click OK. Note that the previously mentioned installation of the "OData Client Tools for Windows Store Apps" is mandatory in order to complete this step.

5. Double-click the package.appxmanifest file of the app project. Select the Packaging tab and provide a suitable value for the *Package Name* property. For example, you might use the value NorthwindODataApp.

6. Right-click the NorthwindSolution.ODataClientApp project and select Debug | Start New Instance. The app will start and you will see a grid of fake items, arranged into multiple fake groups. Close the app by pressing ALT+F4 or stopping the debugger in Visual Studio 2012.

7. Expand the DataModel folder of the NorthwindSolution.ODataClientApp project and rename the SampleDataSource.cs file with the name **NorthwindDataSource.cs**. Now rename the *SampleDataSource* type with name **NorthwindDataSource**, both in code and text. To complete that task, right-click the class name and select Refactor | Rename. Provide the new name and select Search In Strings. At the preview window click Apply.

This code file contains all the client-side logic to manage the data model behind the scenes of the Windows 8 app. The *SampleDataSource* class represents the entry point for the data source. The *SampleDataCommon* type is the base class for every data item. The *SampleData-Item* type defines a single data item. Lastly, the *SampleDataGroup* type declares the groups of items.

8. Using the same approach as step 7, rename the *SampleDataItem* type with **CustomerData-Item**; the *SampleDataCommon* type with **NorthwindDataCommon**; and the *SampleData-Group* type with **CustomersDataGroup**.

9. Insert the following code, just after the default constructor of the *NorthwindDataSource* type.

```
private String[] shadowedFaces = new String[] {
    "shadow-black-face",
    "shadow-blue-face",
    "shadow-orange-face",
    "shadow-red-face",
};

private DataServiceCollection<Customer> customers = null;

private void populateDataSource() {
    CustomersDataServiceReference.NorthwindEntities nw =
        new CustomersDataServiceReference.NorthwindEntities(
            new Uri("http://localhost:1486/CustomersDataService.svc/"));

    customers = new DataServiceCollection<Customer>(nw);
```

```
            customers.LoadCompleted += customers_LoadCompleted;
            customers.LoadAsync(
                from c in nw.Customers
                orderby c.Country
                select c);
}

async void customers_LoadCompleted(object sender, LoadCompletedEventArgs e) {

    if (e.Error != null) {
        MessageDialog errorDialog = new MessageDialog(
            e.Error.Message, "An error occorred!");
        await errorDialog.ShowAsync();
    }

    String fakeCustomerContent = "Lorem ipsum dolor sit amet, consectetur adipiscing
elit. Vivamus tempor scelerisque lorem in vehicula. Aliquam tincidunt, lacus ut sagittis
tristique, turpis massa volutpat augue, eu rutrum ligula ante a ante";
    String previousCountry = String.Empty;
    CustomersDataGroup group = null;

    // Create a random number generator
    Random rnd = new Random(DateTime.Now.Second);

    foreach (Customer c in customers) {

        // Check if I need to create a new group
        if (previousCountry != c.Country) {
            // Add the previous group
            if (group != null) this.AllGroups.Add(group);

            // Create the new group
            group = new CustomersDataGroup(c.Country,
                c.Country,
                String.Format("Customers from: {0}", c.Country),
                "Assets/LightGray.png",
                String.Empty);
        }

        // Add the current customer to the current group
        group.Items.Add(new CustomerDataItem(c.CustomerID,
            c.ContactName,
            c.CompanyName,
            String.Format("Assets/{0}.png", shadowedFaces[rnd.Next() % 4]),
            String.Format("{0} {1} working at {2}", c.ContactTitle,
                c.ContactName, c.CompanyName),
            fakeCustomerContent,
            group));

        // Set the previous country
        previousCountry = c.Country;
    }
}
```

This new code will download the list of customers asynchronously from the external OData service. Take note of the variable of type *DataServiceCollection<T>*, which will hold the results of the query executed by the external OData service. Also notice the error handling in the *customers_LoadCompleted* method implementation. In case of any communication exception, the app will show a dialog with the error message that occurred through a *MessageDialog* type instance.

10. Replace the default constructor code of the *NorthwindDataSource* type with the following.

```
public NorthwindDataSource() {
    populateDataSource();
}
```

11. Add the following files, available in the book code samples under the Ch10 folder, into the Assets folder of the Windows 8 app project: shadow-black-face.png, shadow-blue-face.png, shadow-orange-face.png, shadow-red-face.png.

12. Rebuild the entire solution (Ctrl+Shift+B) and then execute the app. The result will be almost identical to the one shown in the previous graphic.

Implementing an app storage/cache

In the previous sections, you saw how to publish and consume data from a Windows 8 app. However, as already stated at the beginning of this chapter, there are many cases where you also need to manage temporary data and lookup and reference data. Also, many cases require working while offline with some kind of offline cache. For example, imagine that you want to cache the whole list of customers locally, in order to navigate through them even if offline. In a real solution, you should carefully consider caching such data because a list of customers could be very large and consume many resources. In a real solution, it might be best to cache only active customers, or customers in target for the current user. Nevertheless, and for the sake of simplicity, in this section you will cache the entire list of customers.

First, you need to understand the tools available to cache data locally in a Windows 8 app. The Windows Runtime (WinRT) provides a Windows.Storage WinMD library and a corresponding namespace, which contains a bunch of types for managing local, remote, and temporary storage. All these storage types work the same way and share the same behavior by implementing the same basic types. For example, in case you want to save a setting locally from a Windows 8 app, you can use a code excerpt like the following:

```
Windows.Storage.ApplicationData.Current
    .LocalSettings.Values["LastExecutionDateTime"] = DateTime.Now.ToString();
```

Under the cover, this simple line of code will save a variable locally with name LastExecutionDateTime and a value corresponding to the current DateTime.

However, in case you want to read the value you saved previously, you can use the following code excerpt:

```
Object lastExecutionDateTimeValue;
if (Windows.Storage.ApplicationData.Current
    .LocalSettings.Values.TryGetValue("LastExecutionDateTime",
        out lastExecutionDateTimeValue)) {
                String lastExecutionDateTime = lastExecutionDateTimeValue.ToString();
}
```

Notice that the name of each setting can be at most 255 characters in length. Each setting can be up to 8 KB in size, and each composite setting can be up to 64 KB in size.

Moreover, in case you want to save the same settings on remote storage, based on a roaming profile linked to the Windows LiveID account of the current user, you can replace the *LocalSettings* property of the current *ApplicationData* class with the *RoamingSettings* property. Again, in the following code excerpt you can see how to save a value into the roaming profile, for sharing across multiple machines based on the same Microsoft LiveID user account.

```
Windows.Storage.ApplicationData.Current
    .RoamingSettings.Values["LastExecutionDateTime"] = DateTime.Now.ToString();
```

In the following code excerpt, you can see how to retrieve its value from the roaming profile:

```
Object lastExecutionDateTimeValue;
if (Windows.Storage.ApplicationData.Current
    .RoamingSettings.Values.TryGetValue("LastExecutionDateTime",
        out lastExecutionDateTimeValue)) {
                String lastExecutionDateTime = lastExecutionDateTimeValue.ToString();
}
```

Also, when using a roaming profile, the same limitations in size and property naming do apply as those of the *LocalSettings* storage.

Due to the size limitations you have in saving values, you cannot rely on this feature to persist a large set of data. However, the *ApplicationData* class also provides access to a virtual file system, which is almost like the isolated storage you had prior to the Windows 8 apps era.

In fact, the *ApplicationData* class provides a *LocalFolder* property that gets the root folder of a local app data store. It also provides a *RoamingFolder* property, which corresponds to the root folder of a roaming app data store. In order to create a file in these folders, you simply need to leverage the available WinRT API. In fact, both the *LocalFolder* and the *RoamingFolder* are implementations of the *StorageFolder* type. Through this type, you can open, create, update, rename, or delete a file or a subfolder, with up to 32 nesting levels for folders.

For example, in the following code excerpt you can see the code behind the click event of a button, which creates an XML file with an empty element inside.

```
private async void WriteLocalStorageFile_Click(object sender, RoutedEventArgs e) {
    var file = await Windows.Storage.ApplicationData.Current
        .LocalFolder.CreateFileAsync("SampleFile.xml",
        Windows.Storage.CreationCollisionOption.ReplaceExisting);

    using (var stream = await file.OpenStreamForWriteAsync()) {
        XElement x = new XElement("EmptyLocalXmlFile");
```

```
        x.Save(stream);
        await stream.FlushAsync();
    }
}
```

In the following code example, you can see how to retrieve that file and how to read its content.

```
private async void ReadLocalStorageFile_Click(object sender, RoutedEventArgs e) {
    var file = await Windows.Storage.ApplicationData.Current
        .LocalFolder.GetFileAsync("SampleFile.xml");

    using (var stream = await file.OpenStreamForReadAsync()) {
        XElement x = XElement.Load(stream);
        OutputText.Text = x.ToString();
    }
}
```

Roaming storage has a storage quota of 100 KB for each app, as you can see by checking the *App licationData.RoamingStorageQuota* property. If your roaming data exceeds that quota, it won't roam until its size is less than the quota again. Also notice that roaming application data is not intended for simultaneous use by applications on more than one device at a time. In case of concurrency conflict, the system will always favor the value that was written last.

One last option you have is a *TemporaryFolder*, which is again available through the *Application-Data* class and behaves exactly like the *LocalFolder* and *RoamingFolder* properties, because it inherits from the same type (*StorageFolder*). However, the *TemporaryFolder* can be deleted at any time by the WinRT and should not be used to store critical data. Lastly, consider that the storage options available for a Windows 8 app are tied to the lifetime of the app. Therefore, if you remove an app, the local, roaming, and temporary data also will be removed. In case you want to keep contents and files out of any app lifetime, you should rely on user's libraries (Documents, Pictures, and so on) or Microsoft SkyDrive.

Caching data in a Windows 8 app

1. Open the NorthwindSolution you used in the previous exercises.

2. Open the NorthwindSolution.SOAPClientApp project and edit the code of the NorthwindDa-taSource.cs file, under the DataModel folder.

3. At the very top of the file, add the following, using statements:

    ```
    using Windows.Networking.Connectivity;
    using System.IO;
    using System.Runtime.Serialization;
    ```

4. Replace the first two lines of code in the *populateDataSource* method implementation with the following code:

```
private async void populateDataSource() {
    ObservableCollection<CustomersServiceReference.Customer> customers = null;

    ConnectionProfile internetProfile = NetworkInformation.
GetInternetConnectionProfile();


    // In case there is no internet connectivity
    if (internetProfile == null || internetProfile.GetNetworkConnectivityLevel() ==
NetworkConnectivityLevel.None) {

        // Load the customers from an XML file saved in the local app storage
        var customersXmlFile = await Windows.Storage.ApplicationData.Current
            .LocalFolder.GetFileAsync("Customers.xml");

        using (var stream = await customersXmlFile.OpenStreamForReadAsync()) {
            DataContractSerializer dcs = new DataContractSerializer(typeof(
                ObservableCollection<CustomersServiceReference.Customer>));

            customers = dcs.ReadObject(stream) as
                ObservableCollection<CustomersServiceReference.Customer>;
        }
    }
    else {

        // Otherwise load the customers from the remote SOAP service
        CustomersServiceReference.CustomersServiceClient nw =
            new CustomersServiceReference.CustomersServiceClient();

        customers = await nw.ListCustomersAsync();

        // Save the customers into an XML file
        var customersXmlFile = await Windows.Storage.ApplicationData.Current
            .LocalFolder.CreateFileAsync("Customers.xml",
                Windows.Storage.CreationCollisionOption.ReplaceExisting);

        using (var stream = await customersXmlFile.OpenStreamForWriteAsync()) {
            DataContractSerializer dcs = new DataContractSerializer(typeof(
                ObservableCollection<CustomersServiceReference.Customer>));
            dcs.WriteObject(stream, customers);
        }
    }

    // Code omitted for the sake of brevity ...

}
```

As you can see, the code checks if there is an Internet connection and if it is active by using the *NetworkInformation* type. If there is connectivity, the code will invoke the remote SOAP service. Otherwise, in case of no Internet connectivity, it will try to use an XML file saved in the local app storage. For the sake of simplicity, the code illustrated in this exercise does not handle any kind of exception and does not check if the file exists prior to accessing it.

5. Rebuild the entire solution (Ctrl+Shift+B) and then execute the project NorthwindSolution .SOAPClientApp—first with network connectivity enabled and then with network connectivity disabled. In order to check the behavior of the local app storage cache, insert a breakpoint at the very beginning of the *populateDataSource* method.

SOAP security infrastructure

One last fundamental layer to implement in a solid and reliable architecture is the security infrastructure. You should manage both authentication and authorization tasks through this layer. The authorization topic is out of the scope of this chapter, because the authorization infrastructure should be implemented on the service/server-side. However, authentication is a key topic for the app you are implementing. In fact, regardless of the authorization policies you will apply on the service-side, the user of your app will have to authenticate while using the app.

Let's start by considering the SOAP service. Depending on the target deployment and the target users of your Windows 8 app, you will have multiple authentication options. For example, if your app targets users of a Windows 8 domain, you could leverage the integrated Windows Authentication for free. You simply need to change the configuration of the binding for publishing the SOAP service.

From a WCF perspective, the binding is the set of transport, encoding, security, and infrastructural layers involved in the communication pipeline that receives or sends messages across the wire. By default, a WCF service published through an ASP.NET website over HTTP will use a binding called *basicHttpBinding*, which leverages a set of configurations compliant with the Web Services Interoperability Organization (WS-I) Basic Profile specification.

By default, the *basicHttpBinding* relies on transport-level security, which means HTTPS, to satisfy confidentiality and integrity requirements. Optionally, you can also leverage HTTP authentication (Basic, Digest, NTLM, Windows, and Certificate) at the transport level. Another available option, while working with *basicHttpBinding*, is to configure the *TransportWithMessageCredentials* configuration, which means using HTTPS for confidentiality and integrity together with a WS-Security authentication SOAP header for handling client's authentication. In that case, the authentication can be based on a set of usernames and passwords. Exploring all the available security configurations available on the service-side is out of the scope of this book. The most useful and the most frequently used authentication options, from a Windows 8 app perspective, will be covered here. For further details about all the available bindings and security options available while developing a WCF service, you can read the following article on MSDN: *http://msdn.microsoft.com/ms732362.aspx*.

From a service-side viewpoint, you could also leverage many other bindings—even those that are more secure and affordable and still HTTP-based like *wsHttpBinding*, *wsFederationHttpBinding*, and so on. Nevertheless, the WinRT client profile allows you to use only *basicHttpBinding* as the HTTP-based binding. As an alternative option, you can publish your service using the *netTcpBinding* binding over a custom WCF-specific TCP protocol. However, in that case you will need to open communication between your Windows 8 app and the service layer across TCP ports that are not guaranteed to be open on every network and through every firewall.

In order to configure the binding of the service to support authentication, you simply need to change the web.config of the website publishing the service. Also, eventually you will need to refresh the service reference on the consumer side, depending on the configuration changes you will make.

Enabling *basicHttpBinding* with *TransportWithMessageCredentials*

1. Open the NorthwindSolution you used in the previous procedures.

2. Open the NorthwindSolution.WebHost website project and edit the content of the web.config file by adding the following XML excerpt as a child of the *system.serviceModel* element.

```
<bindings>
  <basicHttpBinding>
    <binding>
      <security mode="TransportWithMessageCredential">
        <message clientCredentialType="UserName" />
      </security>
    </binding>
  </basicHttpBinding>
</bindings>
```

This custom configuration instructs WCF to enforce transport-level security (HTTPS) with the username and password transferred within a SOAP header, for the default binding based on *basicHttpBinding*.

3. Click the NorthwindSolution.WebHost website project and change the value of SSL Enabled to a value of *True* in the project property grid. In fact, you cannot publish a WCF service declaring that you want transport-level security unless you effectively publish it through HTTPS.

4. Right-click CustomersService.svc in the Solution Explorer and select View In Browser. You will see, in your default browser, the welcome page of the WCF service. By clicking the link to the WSDL file, you will see that the WSDL of the service is now more complex than before. The augmented complexity is derived from the presence of a bunch of new XML elements describing the WS-SecurityPolicy aspects.

Consuming the SOAP service with username and password authentication

1. Open the NorthwindSolution you used in the previous procedures.

2. Open the NorthwindSolution.SOAPClientApp project and right-click CustomersServiceReference, available under the Service References folder. Select Update Service Reference. Through this action, Visual Studio 2012 will reload the WSDL and will update the auto-generated code of the service consumer.

3. Open the DataModel folder of the NorthwindSolution.SOAPClientApp project and edit the NorthwindDataSource.cs file by adding the following lines of code in the *populateDataSource* method, just after the code that creates a new instance of the *CustomerServiceClient* class.

```
CustomersServiceReference.CustomersServiceClient nw =
    new CustomersServiceReference.CustomersServiceClient();

nw.ClientCredentials.UserName.UserName = "Paolo.Pialorsi";
nw.ClientCredentials.UserName.Password = "Pass@word1!";
```

As you can see, the code simply configures the username and the password that will be used by the SOAP client to authenticate against the service. In your testing environment, you will need to provide the username and the password of an existing user, defined either in the local development machine or in the active directory domain. Of course, in a real software solution, you should ask for the username and password through a specific user interface, instead of storing them in the code of the app.

4. Rebuild the entire solution (Ctrl+Shift+B) and then execute NorthwindSolution.SOAPClientApp. You will see an exception because the IIS Express that is used under the cover of the website project is using a self-issued SSL certificate—which is not trusted by your Windows 8 app. You also can experience the issue by using Internet Explorer to browse the URL of the service, using the SSL endpoint. By default, IIS Express uses the 44300 port to publish over SSL. In order to fix this issue, you will need to publish your service under IIS—using a trusted SSL certificate—or you can replace the self-issued certificate used by IIS Express with a trusted certificate. The final option you have is to trust the self-publisher used by IIS Express to emit the self-issued certificate.

5. Launch the Microsoft Management Console tool by pressing Windows+Q and typing **MMC** in the search box. Right-click the mmc.exe application that is returned by the search and select Run As Administrator. Click Yes at the security question. Under the File menu of the MMC console, select Add/Remove Snap-in. In the dialog box, select Certificates on the left and click Add. In the next step of the wizard, select Computer Account | Local Computer. Click Finish and then click OK.

6. Under the Personal Certificates folder, you will find a certificate named localhost. Double-click it. On the Certification Path tab, check that this is the certificate self-issued by IIS Express. Click OK.

7. Right-click the localhost certificate and select All Tasks | Export. In the wizard, select to not export the private key. Then, select to export a DER certificate file with .CER extension. In the last step, provide a filename for the exported file. Click Next and then Finish.

8. Select the Trusted Root Certification Authorities certificates folder. Right-click and select Import. Click Next and provide the filename and path you have just used for saving the localhost certificate. Choose to place the certificate in the Trusted Root Certification Authorities store. Click Next and then click Finish.

9. Use Internet Explorer to browse to the service URL published under the SSL. You will see that the service URL is trusted by the browser.

10. Place a breakpoint in the *ListCustomers* method of the service implementation, which is inside of the CustomersService.cs file in the *NorthwindSolution.Services* class library project. Restart your client app in debug mode, debugging the web host project. To debug the host project, in the Debug menu of Visual Studio 2012, use Attach To Process to attach the IISExpress.exe process. As soon as you invoke the service, the debugger will hit the breakpoint. By pressing SHIFT+F9 you will be able to inspect the contents of the *System.Threading.Thread.CurrentPrincipal* property. You will see that the *Identity.Name* property of *CurrentPrincipal* will assume a value equal to the username you provided for authentication.

Execute the next procedure in order to provide the current username and authentication method to the calling client app by using a fake customer with a *ContactName* equal to the *Identity.Name* of the calling *CurrentPrincipal*, and a *CompanyName* property with a value corresponding to the *AuthenticationType* used while securing the communication.

Validating and checking the customer authentication through the SOAP service

1. Open the code of the CustomersService.cs file, defined in the *NorthwindSolution.Services* class library project.

2. Replace the code of the *ListCustomers* method with the following code excerpt:

```
public List<Customer> ListCustomers() {
    NorthwindEntities nw = new NorthwindEntities();

    List<Customer> result = nw.Customers.ToList();
    if (System.Threading.Thread.CurrentPrincipal != null &&
        System.Threading.Thread.CurrentPrincipal.Identity != null) {
        result.Add(new Customer {
            Country = "A Fake Country",
            CustomerID = "FAKE",
            ContactName = System.Threading.Thread.CurrentPrincipal.Identity.Name,
            CompanyName = System.Threading.Thread.CurrentPrincipal.Identity.
                AuthenticationType,
        });
    }
    return (result);
}
```

The code highlighted in bold inserts a fake customer at the very top of the list of customers, ordered by country. The fake customer will hold some useful information, like the currently called username and the authentication method used to authenticate the caller.

3. Rebuild the entire solution (Ctrl+Shift+B), and then execute NorthwindSolution.SOAPClientApp. The following screenshot shows a new and fake customer at the very top of the customers list.

The username and password credentials provided by the client application can be validated, not only against a Windows directory service, but also by using a custom username and password validator. For example, you could use a custom database with a table of users and passwords, or you could even use the standard ASP.NET membership API and a classic ASPNETDB to authenticate users.

OData security infrastructure

In this last section, you will see how to enforce authentication while calling an OData service.

From a security viewpoint, an OData service is just another service channel published over HTTP/HTTPS, as is a SOAP channel. Thus, one option to secure an OData channel is to leverage the standard HTTP/HTTPS authentication techniques. For example, you could configure the web host application to use HTTP Windows Authentication. To do that in your development environment, you simply need to change the configuration of the web host application. Click the project in the Solution Explorer and change Windows Authentication from Disabled to Enabled in the project property grid. Furthermore, you also need to disable Anonymous Authentication, in order to force clients to provide credentials while consuming your services. Figure 10-2 shows a screenshot of the proper configuration for your service host.

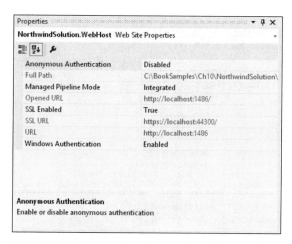

FIGURE 10-2 The property grid panel for configuring the IISExpress bindings of the current web service app.

From a Windows 8 app consumer perspective, you will only need to configure the *Credentials* property to a suitable set of credentials—which can be the current user credentials taken from the *CredentialCache* object of .NET, or a specific set of credentials defined using a dedicated instance of the *System.Net.NetworkCredential* type. In the following lines of code, you can see both the alternative options:

```
nw.Credentials = System.Net.CredentialCache.DefaultCredentials;

nw.Credentials = new System.Net.NetworkCredentials(
    "Paolo.Pialorsi", "Pass@word1!", "WIN8DEV1");
```

As shown in the previous examples, you will need to change the credentials and the machine or domain name with those in your own environment. Nevertheless, in the world of Windows 8 apps, you probably will not always have an Active Directory available for users' authentication. For instance, think about a Windows 8 app that you are offering to the world. It probably would be a better choice to allow users to authenticate using their LiveID, Facebook, or Twitter account. All these identity management systems provide support for the OAuth (Open Authentication—*www.oauth.net*) specification.

Windows 8 apps support authentication through OAuth, or any other web-based authentication technique, by leveraging the *WebAuthenticationBroker* class. This class renders a dialog box containing the web sign-in page of the authentication platform you choose to use.

Imagine that you have a Windows 8 app that you want to use for authenticating users with their Facebook account. The following code excerpt shows how to implement a click event of a button, which will prompt the users of your app for their Facebook account information.

```
private async void ShowLoginPage_Click(object sender, RoutedEventArgs e) {
    try {
        String FacebookURL = "https://www.facebook.com/dialog/oauth?client_id=" +
            FacebookClientID.Text + "&redirect_uri=" +
            Uri.EscapeUriString(FacebookCallbackUrl.Text) +
            "&scope=" + FacebookPermissions.Text +
            "&display=popup&response_type=token";
```

```
                System.Uri StartUri = new Uri(FacebookURL);
                System.Uri EndUri = new Uri(FacebookCallbackUrl.Text);

                WebAuthenticationResult WebAuthenticationResult =
                    await WebAuthenticationBroker.AuthenticateAsync(
                        WebAuthenticationOptions.None,
                        StartUri,
                        EndUri);

                if (WebAuthenticationResult.ResponseStatus == WebAuthenticationStatus.Success) {
                    OutputToken(WebAuthenticationResult.ResponseData.ToString());
                }
                else if (WebAuthenticationResult.ResponseStatus == WebAuthenticationStatus.ErrorHttp) {
                    OutputToken("HTTP Error returned by AuthenticateAsync() : " +
                    WebAuthenticationResult.ResponseErrorDetail.ToString());
                }
                else {
                    OutputToken("Error returned by AuthenticateAsync() : " +
                        WebAuthenticationResult.ResponseStatus.ToString());
                }
            }
            catch (Exception ex) {
                MessageDialog errorDialog = new MessageDialog(
                    e.Error.Message, "An error occorred!");
                await errorDialog.ShowAsync();
            }
        }
```

As you can see, the code creates a URL string (*FacebookURL* variable) corresponding to the OAuth authentication URL of Facebook. The URL requires having some query string parameters in it, that are used to declare the *ClientId* of the Facebook App that will be associated with your Windows 8 app, as well as the callback URL to route the customer back to after a valid authentication and the list of permissions required by the app.

You can find more details about the OAuth support provided by Facebook at *http://developers. facebook.com/docs/reference/dialogs/oauth/.* You can also create a *ClientID* and configure the callback URL by going to *https://developers.facebook.com/apps.* After authenticating with your Facebook account, create a new app integration. Note that the Facebook side of this story is out of the scope of this chapter.

Additionally, the code invokes the static method *AuthenticateAsync* of the *WebAuthentication-Broker* class to start the authentication process. In Figure 10-3, you can see the output that will be prompted for the user.

As soon as the user provides a valid set of credentials, the identity management system (Facebook, in our example) will prompt the user in order to ask for consent allowing the Windows 8 app to access his profile information. Depending on the type of integration you will need, you will have the capability to request various information like published posts, email, friends, or pictures.

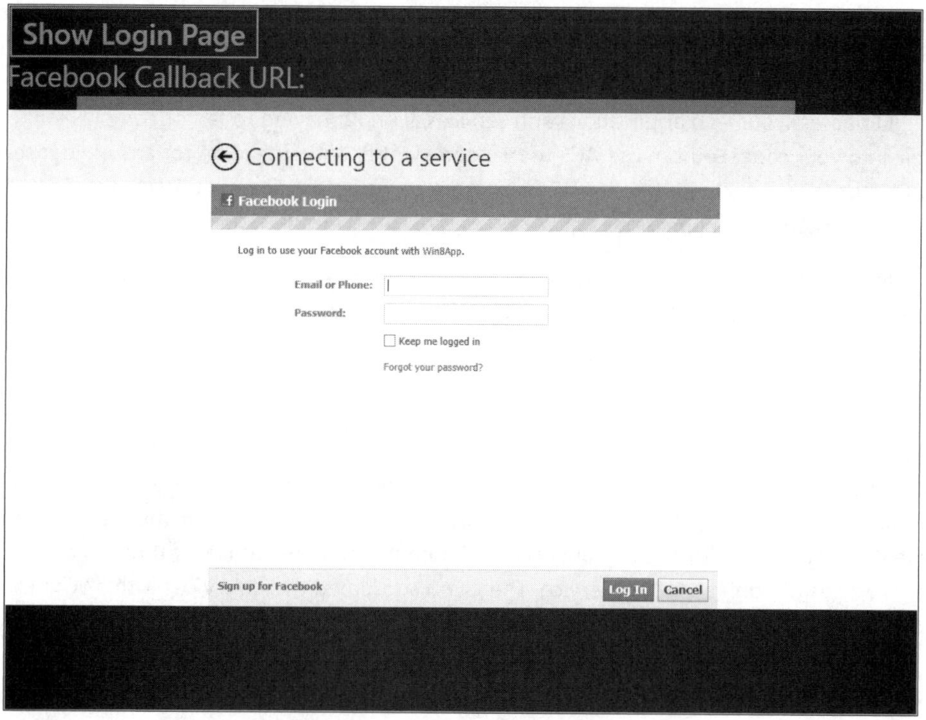

FIGURE 10-3 The login page of Facebook within the WebAuthenticationBroker.

The result of the authentication process will be a variable of type *WebAuthenticationResult* that contains the property *WebAuthenticationStatus*, which can assume one of the following values:

- **ErrorHttp**   An HTTP occurred.

- **Success**   The authentication process completed correctly.

- **UserCancel**   The user cancelled the authentication process.

In case of an exception, you will find details in the *ResponseErrorDetail* property of the *Web AuthenticationResult* instance. In case of a successful login, you will find the result in the *ResponseData* property.

In the case of Facebook authentication, you will get back a URL that is the callback URL you originally provided with an access token (*access_token*) parameter appended to the end of the URL, together with an expiration timeout (*expires_in*) for the token. You can see a sample of the resulting URL:

```
http://www.devleap.com/#access_token=AAADp1Ykd5hwBAM3r0VDE9ZC9wuj9BnUdvfBdHwxz84YZCx5X8mwOv8Xwfx
IJFUMv4ZAi3mls5ZARRbwpvQ67FyzrDSUcFwl5d7rnhQzpugZDZD&expires_in=6624
```

Within your code, you should extract the value of the *access_token* parameter and use it to talk with Facebook proprietary APIs, for example the Facebook Graph API. Nevertheless, exploring the Facebook APIs is out of the scope of this book.

Using the *WebAuthenticationBroker* class to authenticate against any other authentication platform, such as Microsoft Windows Azure Access Control Service (ACS), is within the scope of this chapter. In fact, ACS is a Windows Azure service that provides an easy way of authenticating users who need to access your web applications and services, without having to factor complex authentication logic into your code. You can use ACS to manage identity authentication for any of your services, either SOAP or OData. Furthermore, the ACS can redirect the authentication process to any external and largely adopted identity provider like Windows Live ID, Facebook, Google, and so on.

Because ACS supports OAuth 2.0, you can use it to authenticate access to your services—almost the same way you used it in the previous sample while authenticating against Facebook.

Summary

In this chapter, you learned the basic information about contemporary software architectures, and you saw how those apply to a Windows 8 app. Moreover, you saw how to implement a very basic data layer based on ADO.NET Entity Framework 5. You published the data layer through a SOAP service, as well as through an OData service. Then, you consumed these services with a Windows 8 app, which leverages local storage for local data caching. Lastly, you learned how to make secure calls to a service—whether it is SOAP based or OData based—using an OAuth authentication platform like Facebook or Microsoft Windows Azure ACS.

Quick reference

To	Do This
Consume data from a Windows 8 app	Create a service reference to a SOAP service or to an OData service.
Publish a dataset via OData	Create a web application and define a WCF Data Service item, for example, publishing a model created with ADO.NET Entity Framework 5.
Cache some local data in a Windows 8 app	Use the Windows.Storage namespace of WinRT leveraging the local app storage.
Sharing some settings/preferences across multiple devices for a single Windows Live ID account	Use the Windows.Storage namespace of WinRT leveraging the roaming app storage.
Authenticate against an external web-based sign-in platform like Facebook or ACS	Use the *WebAuthenticationBroker* class.

Index

Symbols

A

UI (user interface), *continued*

About the Authors

LUCA REGNICOLI is a consultant, trainer, and author who has specialized in user interface technologies for .NET applications since 2003. He developed the presentation tier of many enterprise applications in Windows Presentation Foundation, Silverlight, and Windows Phone. Luca is a co-founder of DevLeap, a company focused on providing high-value content and consulting services to professional developers. He is the author of a book in Italian language about ASP.NET. He is also a regular speaker at major conferences since 2001.

PAOLO PIALORSI is a consultant, trainer, and author who specializes in developing distributed applications architectures and Microsoft SharePoint enterprise solutions. He is the author of about 10 books, which include *Programming Microsoft LINQ in Microsoft .NET Framework 4* and *Microsoft SharePoint 2010 Developer Reference*. Paolo is a founder of DevLeap, a company focused on providing content and consulting to professional developers. He is also a popular speaker at industry conferences.

ROBERTO BRUNETTI is a consultant, trainer, and author with experience in enterprise applications since 1997. Roberto is a founder of DevLeap, together with Paolo Pialorsi, Marco Russo, and Luca Regnicoli, a company focused on providing high-value content and consulting services to professional developers. He is the author of a couple of books: one about ASP.NET, published in 2003, another about Windows Azure Beta, and the last one on Windows Azure published by Microsoft Press in 2011. He is also a regular speaker at major conferences since 1996 and he works closely with Microsoft in events and training courses.

What do you think of this book?

We want to hear from you!

To participate in a brief online survey, please visit:

microsoft.com/learning/booksurvey

Tell us how well this book meets your needs—what works effectively, and what we can do better. Your feedback will help us continually improve our books and learning resources for you.

Thank you in advance for your input!

 **Microsoft**

How To Download Your eBook

Thank you for purchasing this Microsoft Press® title. Your companion PDF eBook is ready to download from O'Reilly Media, official distributor of Microsoft Press titles.

To download your eBook, go to
http://go.microsoft.com/FWLink/?Linkid=224345
and follow the instructions.

Please note: You will be asked to create a free online account and enter the access code below.

Your access code:

QNLMDHL

Build Windows® 8 Apps with Microsoft® Visual
C#® and Visual Basic® Step by Step

Your PDF eBook allows you to:

- Search the full text
- Print
- Copy and paste

Best yet, you will be notified about free updates to your eBook.

If you ever lose your eBook file, you can download it again just by logging in to your account.

Need help? Please contact:
mspbooksupport@oreilly.com
or call 800-889-8969.